Quality of Life in Asia

Volume 10

This series, the first of its kind, examine both the objective and subjective dimensions of life quality in Asia, especially East Asia. It unravels and compares the contours, dynamics and patterns of building nations, offering innovative works that discuss basic and applied research, emphasizing inter- and multi-disciplinary approaches to the various domains of life quality. Thus, the series appeals to a variety of fields in humanities, social sciences and other professional disciplines. Asia is the largest, most populous continent on Earth, and it is home to the world's most dynamic region, East Asia. In the past three decades, East Asia has been the most successful region in the world in expanding its economies and integrating them into the global economy, offering lessons on how poor countries, even with limited natural resources, can achieve rapid economic development. Yet while scholars and policymakers have focused on why East Asia has prospered, little has been written on how its economic expansion has affected the quality of life of its citizens. The series publish several volumes a year, either single or multiple-authored monographs or collections of essays.

More information about this series at http://www.springer.com/series/8416

Takashi Inoguchi

Exit, Voice and Loyalty in Asia

Individual Choice under 32 Asian Societal Umbrellas

Springer

Takashi Inoguchi
J.F. Oberlin University
Tokyo
Japan

ISSN 2211-0550 ISSN 2211-0569 (electronic)
Quality of Life in Asia
ISBN 978-981-10-4722-0 ISBN 978-981-10-4724-4 (eBook)
DOI 10.1007/978-981-10-4724-4

Library of Congress Control Number: 2017938322

Printed on acid-free paper

This Springer imprint is published by Springer Nature
The registered company is Springer Nature Singapore Pte Ltd.
The registered company address is: 152 Beach Road, #21-01/04 Gateway East, Singapore 189721, Singapore

Acknowledgement

I would like to thank many organizations and many individuals who helped me to complete this book. First of all, the Ministry of Education, Culture, Sports, Science and Technology of Japan provided funding for conducting the AsiaBarometer Survey from 2005 through 2008. The Ministry awarded Grants-in-Aid for Scientific Research to the project director, Takashi Inoguchi at Chuo University (project identification number 170020022) for the 2005–2008 period. Also, the Ministry awarded Grants-in-Aid for Scientific Research to Takashi Inoguchi at the University of Niigata Prefecture (project number 21243010) for the 2009–2010 period. Business firms and the Ministry of Foreign Affairs of Japan funded the AsiaBarometer Survey in 2003 and 2004, respectively. The 32-country survey (nationally randomly sampled and executed with face-to-face interviewing) covering all the 29 societies in Asia and 3 societies adjacent to Asia, i.e., the United States, Russia, and Australia, were carried out by their fundings. Without their generous fundings, I could have neither executed the survey nor completed the book.

Since Asia had long been terra incognita for quality of life studies, the funders' courage and foresight, believing in the merit of basic research being the fountain of knowledge and truth, should be applauded. Second, the four universities I was affiliated with successively to carry out this project, i.e., the University of Tokyo, Chuo University, the University of Niigata Prefecture, and J.F. Oberlin University (Tokyo), offered the ideal environment where space and warmness were provided for the project. Third, inspiration and intellectual support came from all over the world. Jacques-René Rabier at Institut français d'opinion publique (IFOP) inspired me when I visited him in Paris in 1978. He insisted two things: clarity and familiarity to ordinary people in questions and persistence in asking the same set of questions. Second, those academics cooperatively working on survey-based research have been steadfastly encouraging: Jean Blondel (European University Institute), Richard Sinnot (University College Dublin) and Ian March (University of Sydney) working on democracy in Asia and Europe, Ijaz Shaffi Gilani (Pakistan Institute of Public Opinion Research) working on global sampling theory and practice, Miguel Basanez (Tufts University) on survey research in non-Western societies, Ronald Inglehart (University of Michigan) and Christian Welzel (Leuphana University) on World Values Survey and many splendid applications, Richard Rose (University of Strathclyde) on corruption, Doh Chull Shin (University of California, Irvine), Russell Dalton (University of California, Irvine), Ian McAlister (Australian National University), Christin Collet (International Christian University, Tokyo) on comparative survey research, Alex Michalos (University of Northern British Columbia), Daniel Shek (Hong Kong Polytechnic University), Doh Chull Shin, Soo Jiuan Tan (National University of Singapore), Siok Kuan Tambiah (National University of Singapore), Richard Estes (University of Pennsylvania), M. Joseph Sirgy (Virginia Polytechnic Institute and University), Wolfgang Glatzer (University of Hamburg) on quality of life studies. Fourth, analytic-cum-logistic support has been indispensable: Shigeto Sonoda (University of Tokyo), Shiro Harada (University of Tokyo), Hideaki Uenohara (University of Tokyo), Ken Anno (University of Tokyo), Lucien Hotta (University of Tokyo), and Seiji Fujii (University of Niigata Prefecture). Seiji Fujii has single-handedly shouldered logit regression analysis for this book. Fifth, in running the project, secretarial and logistic support was no less indispensable: Kimiko Goko and Fumie Shiraishi have offered miraculous help to the project. Last but not least, Kuniko Inoguchi, my wife and an academic-cum-senator, has given me unflinching moral support throughout all the phases of the project.

*Permission is granted by Iwanami shoten, the publisher, for Chap. 7 of this book. The original Japanese article entitled "Ridatsu, hatsugen, chusei (Exit, Voice and Loyalty)," Takashi Inoguchi, *Ajia no Kofuku* (Happiness in Asia), Tokyo: Iwanami shoten, pp. 53–83, has been moderately revised while translating Japanese to English.

Contents

Chapter 1
Introduction

The next four vignettes tell a story of individual choice. They show how individual choices vary and how government and individual choices can impact the outcome.

Tunisian police arrested a street vendor for selling fruits and vegetables without a government permit. Having lost his and his family's means to earning a livelihood, he committed suicide. A swirl of protests against the government gradually and steadily led to what is called the Arab Spring in North Africa and the Middle East on a very wide scale. His suicide is a protest voice opposing government policy. His voice resonated with many citizens in North Africa and the Middle East. It was individually an exit while collectively it was a voice against a regime.

A Japanese vendor in Shinjuku, Tokyo, who for many years operated without a permit, decided to close his "illegal" business. The *koban* (police box in the neighborhood) gave him a retirement gift. For many years, police allowed him to operate his stall, prodding him to change his spot from time to time as a fixed location made it an easy target for policy regulation. He sustained a livelihood for him and his family because of the decision of the local police from the *koban* to treat benignly his illegal vendor status. Individually he chose an exit option as he did not abide by the law. Yet in Japanese society, he was given a free pass of a sort to get around the situation (Imamura 2013).

A Russian farmer from Novosibirsk petitioned the President of the Russian Federation at the Kremlin in Moscow. In the Kremlin, a bureaucratic office receives these petitions and processes a large number of them on the president's behalf. The petitions are usually about a concrete and specific action that the president can benevolently resolved, if he so desires. A small number of petitioners, about 20 or so petitioners per year, decide to self-immolate outside the Kremlin gates. Despair led them to suicide. Individually it is an exit. Collectively it is an exit with callous inattention by the government (Nakamura 2005).

A Chinese peasant from Lufeng, Guandong, did not want the state to confiscate his land for infrastructure and factory development. He joined a group of citizens, criticizing the mayor for encouraging more infrastructure and industry development. A candidate of his liking won a relatively democratic rural election. Once the

T. Inoguchi, *Exit, Voice and Loyalty in Asia*,
Quality of Life in Asia 10, DOI 10.1007/978-981-10-4724-4_1

new mayor started his office, the party apparatus of the provincial and central governments decided to pacify and appease the mayor by ensuring that the direction of the mayor's policy wishes overlapped with the government's policy objectives. Wang Yang, the provincial party chief of Guandong province, who was known as a reformist and liberal, won over the new mayor so that policy goals could evolve together. It was individually and collectively a voice (Mori et al. 2012).[1]

As you see from the above, these snapshots of individual action range widely. The contexts and consequences of individual action differ immensely. To systematically capture the range of individual choice in a daily life context on a regional scale of Asia, I have organized the chapters as follows. Chapter 2 examines Albert Hirschmann's concept of exit, voice, and loyalty for an organization (1970) and applies it to the daily life decisions of individuals for a specific problem. The data comes from one of the questions posed in the *AsiaBarometer Survey* project (Inoguchi 2012). The survey, conducted annually from 2003 to 2008, covered a total of 29 Asian societies plus three adjacent societies. In the countries selected for each year's survey, approximately 1000 respondents in each society were interviewed face to face. The survey takes a bottom-up approach and focuses on collecting and analyzing social data of ordinary people. Chapter 3 explains the model specification used to explain the individual choice of exit, voice, and loyalty through a set of variable clusters. Chapter 4 makes an argument for why a focus on the individual in society or bottom-up approach is valuable to scholarship. Chapter 5 sets up the specific problem and the choices presented to the individual and how they can be analyzed through Hirschmann's three option framework of exit, voice, and loyalty. The responses are analyzed by region and by country. Factors that influence individual choice are also examined. Chapter 6 looks at logit regression analysis of the 29 Asian societies. Chapter 7 compares Asian and non-Asian societies in this exploration of choice and the quality of life factors that influence this choice. The chapter also acknowledges the challenges of both conducting cross-national surveys and interpreting these survey results. In the last chapter, discussion is made up the proneness of exit, voice, and loyalty in relation to the societal types drawn from factor analysis of daily life domains, aspects and styles, society by society (Inoguchi 2017). This discussion in one step foward beyond analysis of copy specific proneness to exit, voice and loyalty. Then condition is made. While further analysis relating to societal types may bring us one more step forward, largely country-specific analysis carried out in this book remain to be the basic foundation on which further analysis can be attempted.

---

[1]Mori Kazuko and Matsudo Yoko, eds., *Chinjo: Chugoku shakai no teihen kara* (Petition: From the Bottom of Chinese Society), Tokyo: Tohoshoten, 2012.

References

Imamura, Yuri. 2013. Takoyaki 42-nen [Octopus dumpling vendor for 42 years]. *Asashi Shinbun Evening Edition* April 25.

Inoguchi, Takashi. 2012. AsiaBarometer's achievements, underutilized areas of the survey materials, and future prospects, *Comparative Democratization Newsletter,* vol. 10, no. 3, 2, 13–15. Washington D.C.: The American Political Science Association.

Inoguchi, Takashi. forthcoming in 2017a. An Evidence-based typology of asian societies: what do societies look like from the bottom up instead of top down?. *Japanese Journal of Political Science* 8(1) pp. 216–234.

Mori, Kazuko, and Matsudo Yoko (eds.). 2012. *Chinjo: Chugoku shakai no teihen kara (Petition: From the Bottom of Chinese Society)*. Tokyo: Toho Shoten.

Nakamura, Itsuro. 2005. *Teisei minshushugi kokka Russia: Putin no jidai (Imperial Democratic State: An Era of Vladimir Putin)*, 236. Tokyo: Iwanami Shoten.

Chapter 2
Exit, Voice, and Loyalty

Albert Hirschmann formulates individual choices in an organization or in a society as consisting of exit, voice, and loyalty. The organization can be a business organization, a political party, a non-profit civic organization, or anything. Irrespective of the nature, aim, and scope of the organization, individuals face three choices: exit, voice, and loyalty. Hirschmann's interest lies in the relationship among the three as conditions on the organizational quality of life deteriorate. The individual can get out if they don't want to stay; they can raise their hand and register constructive criticism for the betterment of the organization; or they can remain quiet while others harshly critique the organization, thus waving the flag of loyalty. As loyalty becomes a rare commodity, power shifts to those solid and loyal organizational members.

My interest is in what factors lead an individual in an Asian society to choose one of the three options of exit, voice, and loyalty. The factors that I am interested in the relation to quality-of-life components under varying Asian societal umbrellas.

The question we pose to respondents in the *AsiaBarometer Survey* interview is:

You requested a government permit. You were told to wait some time patiently. What would you do? Choose one from among the following seven choices: (1) use connections; (2) nothing can be done; (3) wait and hope that things will go well; (4) write a letter; (5) act without a permit; (6) bribe an official; (7) don't know.

The style of the question needs attention. The question assumes the context in which respondents would choose one of the seven actions. Why not adopt more straightforward questions like: Did you bribe an official? Or did you act without a permit? The most important factor for not posing these types of questions is the predominance of authoritarian politics in many of the 29 surveyed Asian societies. Respondents may not be as forthcoming and may distort their responses as saying that one bribed officials or that one operated a business without a permit, even in the form of a response to an interview, for instance, would cause severe hesitation. In many authoritarian regimes, public opinion companies are often tied to the internal security agency, thus making respondents legitimately apprehensive to answer honestly. Therefore, the direct straightforward question as adopted by the

T. Inoguchi, *Exit, Voice and Loyalty in Asia*,
Quality of Life in Asia 10, DOI 10.1007/978-981-10-4724-4_2

Transparency International or some others when asking about bribes may not be appropriate in trying to attain responses not unnecessarily distorted.

The crux of the matter is whether the question posed elicits real honest responses. Here, the fundamental issue of getting responses through face-to-face interviews and getting verbal responses to an interviewee in survey research methodology comes up. My answer is that the survey research method has developed in societies where freedom of expression and democracy are reasonably solid. In an extremely authoritarian society where the phrase "open your mouth only to a dentist" is not a joke but has real meaning, survey methods require modification to suit the political reality. Nevertheless, polling has become such a popular practice in business, politics, and academic research for all kinds of society that it is difficult not to use it, even in an authoritarian political context. If that is the case, the wording of a question may as well be made to suit both free and unfree societies. And that is the choice we made in wording the question. Even when considering these restraints, responses can still be "distorted" by subtle and not so subtle changes of wording in a question.

From the Hirschmann framework of exit, voice, and loyalty, I have amalgamated four answers into two categories: "Use connections" and "bribe an official" are amalgamated into a broader voice and "nothing can be done" and "wait and hope" are amalgamated into a broader loyalty. Thus the response patterns move closer to the Hirschmann framework.

Chapter 3
Model Specification

To explain the individual choice of exit, voice, and loyalty, the following sets of variable clusters are examined. They are: lifestyles, exposure to globalization, trust in social institutions, assessment of government performance, and demographics. Next is a brief breakdown of what is included in each of the listed clusters.

Lifestyles are relevant in determining whether to choose exit, voice, or loyalty. They include: number of public utilities, home ownership, religiosity, participation in national elections, and patriotism.

Exposure to globalization includes use of Internet, living internationally (includes international friends and foreign travel), and ability to use English.

Satisfaction with aspects of daily life examines housing, friendships, standard of living, household income, health, education, job, neighbors, public safety, conditions of the environment, social welfare system, the democratic system, family life, leisure, spiritual life, your life as a whole, and happiness.

Trust in social institutions examines trust in institutions such as the central government, the army, the legal system, and the police. Assessment of government performance examines such items as duty to vote, widespread corruption, experience with bribery, and reliance on experts.

Demographics examine such items as gender, age, level of education, marital status, and income.

T. Inoguchi, *Exit, Voice and Loyalty in Asia*,
Quality of Life in Asia 10, DOI 10.1007/978-981-10-4724-4_3

Chapter 4
Exit, Voice, and Loyalty: State-Centered Versus Society-Centered Perspective

The original formulation of the exit, voice, and loyalty problematique by Hirschmann is organization-centered. The original formulation starts with the assumption of a situational decline. That is, if an organization one belongs to starts to exhibit the symptom of organizational stagnation and decay, then how does one proceed? As he develops this formulation from organization to society and political regime, the Hirschmann formulation can be labeled a society-centered scheme or a state-centered scheme. The society-centered approach can be called the approach as seen from the bottom up, whereas the state-centered approach can be called the approach as seen from the top down. In this chapter, I attempt to contrast the society-centered and state-centered approach. Needless to say, this volume adopts a society-centered approach.

4.1 Most Common in Political Theory Is the State-Centric Approach to Exit, Voice, and Loyalty

That starts normally from the loss of the mandate of heaven. By the mandate of heaven is meant either the loss of popular satisfaction, or the betrayal of the king's staff, or the defeat of a king in war, or the turtle's omen as in Asia it represents cosmic order, or some other sign or development. Once the loss of the mandate of heaven occurs, a new regime takes shape. Once a regime is shaped and consolidated, a large bulk of the theory of the state stops talking about its dynamics and focuses on regime types. Aristotle has monarchy, aristocracy, and democracy as a regime type. Once a regime type is determined, society is bound to align its nature to the spirit of a regime type. Nicolo Machiavelli notes two regime types: monarchy and republics. He focuses on monarchy whose sustenance depends on two components of a monarch's characteristics: virtue and fortune. By virtue is meant a monarch's moral power and by fortune is meant a monarch's luck or ability to grasp

T. Inoguchi, *Exit, Voice and Loyalty in Asia*,
Quality of Life in Asia 10, DOI 10.1007/978-981-10-4724-4_4

an opportunity once it arises. The decay and fall of a monarchy is explained by the combination of virtue and fortune. Machiavelli's eye never focuses on the grassroot level. After all, most states were monarchies at the time of his writing.

Modern democratic philosophers like John Locke and Jean-Jacque Rousseau start from individual citizens. Once they are awakened and form a majority, a democratic regime takes shape. The problem is how the aggregation of individual citizens' preferences is carried out. The interactions among individual citizens are not the focus of much attention. Modern democratic theorists like Robert Dahl are not that different. What Dahl is interested in is whether the three prerequisites of becoming democratic is more or less satisfied: freedom, tolerance, and trust. Freedom of expression needs to be fully respected. Tolerance must be assured when individual citizens' preference configuration requires some sort of aggregation. Even if aggregated collective will differs from one's own will, tolerance is a must as those out of power must trust those in power. Dahl was content with framing the nature of democracy in conceptual terms and not very interested in the interactions among individual citizens and competition among social groups sustaining a democratic state.

Marxist or post-Marxist state theorists concentrate on how the state's capitalist characteristics shape key features of capitalist democratic states. Class conflicts, ideological appeals, hegemony, multitudes are often discussed. Once regime types are determined, or once the state adopts its Marxist or post-Marxist requirements, the state is fixated by their regime type.

In other words, the state-centered perspective has dominated political theory since ancient times. Even after opinion polling has become a routine method of analyzing individual citizens' preferences in business, politics, and media, the state-centered perspective has dominated even in most democracies.

4.2 The Society-Centered Perspective Has not Been Highlighted at Least in Political Theory

Anthropological, sociological, and linguistic approaches have been dominant. Some noted examples of society-centered perspectives in political science are briefly summarized here: James Scott investigates the hill tribes in Southeast Asia (2010); Takeshi Matsui examines Afghanistan, and Baluchistan (2011); Itsuro Nakamura writes about deep Siberia (2005); and I examine twenty-nine Asian societies (2015 and 2017a).

Scott in his book, *The Art of Not Being Governed* (2010), gives us a very articulate study of a society-centered perspective with dense empirical illustrations that detail the history of upland Southeast Asian communities in their refusal to be governed through tax, war, and institutions. Scott posits their refusal to be governed in the conventional philosophical context of Thomas Hobbes' justification of leaving the state of nature for the yearning of the state. Scott argues that upland

Southeast Asian peoples want to depart from the state that taxes people, enslaves people for war, and constrains people with laws and institutions.

Matsui provides us with another anthropological study of a society-centered perspective but this time with detailed empirical descriptions of the Pushtun societies in Afghanistan and Baluchistan, Pakistan. Like upland Southeast Asian tribal peoples, Pushtuns do not like being constrained by tax, war, and state institutions. Unlike upland Southeast Asian tribes, Pushtuns form a majority in Afghanistan but the state in Kabul is dominated by a mixture of invaders/occupiers and collaborators from within the country. To abide by the traditional way of doing things, Pushtuns find it expedient to have distance from Kabul, sticking to the tribal principle of distrusting outsiders and trusting insiders in the most extreme, strict form and practice. For instance, Matsui was welcomed in a most lavish form when he visited a Pushtun tribe, and yet at night fully armed men were placed outside his tent. Whether it was meant as a cautious measure against him or a deterrence against a possible onslaught from outside was difficult to assess. Perhaps it was a combination of both reasons.

Nakamura, the third noted author of this section, gives us an anthropological description and analysis of Siberian life. In Siberia, the population is sparse. The climate is harsh. In the community, everyone knows each other but still at an adequate distance. Nature is serene and beautiful. Air and water are the purest while plants and animals live their lives without much outside intrusions. In a 2016 survey result on happiness in Russia, many were surprised that 87% of respondents in Tuva, a tiny autonomous republic in the middle of Siberia, registered either very happy or happy!

For my work in this area (2015 and 2017a, b), my writings represent what is most likely the first society-centered typology of Asian societies through a systematic, scientific, and evidence-based approach. Using factor-analysis of people's daily life satisfaction, I (2015 and 2017a) construct five types of Asian societies. In my second writing, the illustrations and justifications of the validity of such research is particularly strong.

This study of exit, voice, and loyalty in Asia represents a line of study on society-centered and evidence-based approaches as applied to 32 societies in broader Asia, including three of Asia's neighbors, that is, Russia, Australia, and the United States.

References

Inoguchi, Takashi. 2015. Multiple modes of well-being. In *Global Handbook of Quality of Life: Exploration of Well-Being of Nations and Continent*, eds. Wolfgang Glatzer et al., 597–607. Dordrecht: Springer.

Inoguchi, Takashi. 2017a. An evidence-based typology of Asian societies: what do societies look like from the bottom up instead of top down? *Japanese Journal of Political Science* 18(1) pp. 216–234.

Inoguchi, Takashi. 2017b. Asia inquiry: a continental analysis. *Seton Hall Journal of Diplomacy and International Relations* (forthcoming).
Matsui, Tekeshi. 2011. *Seinan Ajia no Sabaku Bunka (Desert culture in southwest Asia)*. Kyoto: Jinbun Shoten.
Nakamura, Itsuro. 2005. *Teikoku Minshushugi Kokka Russia—Putin no Jidai (Imperial democratic state of Russia—Putin's era)*. Tokyo, Japan: Iwanami Shoten.
Scott, James. 2010. *The art of not being governed: an anarchist history of upland southeast Asia*. New Haven, Connecticut: Yale University Press.

Chapter 5
Exit, Voice, and Loyalty: A Profile

5.1 A Profile of the 32 Societies on Exit, Voice, and Loyalty

We pose the question:

You have requested permission from an agency. What would you do when a bureaucrat replies to you, wait patiently?

1. Use connections
2. Nothing can be done
3. Wait and hope patiently
4. Write a letter
5. Act without a permit
6. Bribe an official
7. Don't know

The task of the analysis is to list the 32 societies according to the most popular responses and then interpret these choices.

1. Use Connections
   The societies that have the highest selection of this response were the Philippines, Nepal, Afghanistan, Uzbekistan, Russia, Kazakhstan, Mongolia, and Bangladesh. The societies that have the lowest rate of response for this selection include the Maldives, Hong Kong, Japan, Brunei, Singapore, Thailand, Indonesia, and Pakistan. It is interesting to find India, the United States, China, South Korea, and Australia in the intermediate group. After all, "use connections" is a vague and not well-defined phrase. The meaning of the word and its consequent action can vary widely from country to country.
2. Nothing Can Be Done
   The societies rating this choice as the highest consists of Brunei, Hong Kong, Pakistan, Japan, Taiwan, China, Bangladesh, and South Korea. The group of societies with the lowest rating of this response consists of Laos, Nepal,

T. Inoguchi, *Exit, Voice and Loyalty in Asia*,
Quality of Life in Asia 10, DOI 10.1007/978-981-10-4724-4_5

Uzbekistan, the United States, Vietnam, Australia, Cambodia, and Singapore. The intermediate group consists of Indonesia, Mongolia, Malaysia, Thailand, Afghanistan, Russia, the Philippines, and India. It is interesting to note that the United States, Australia, Singapore, Cambodia, Vietnam, Nepal, Laos, and Uzbekistan register the lowest frequency for this response. New settler societies where a large percentage of people move constantly seem to register "nothing can be done" far less frequently.

3. Wait Patiently and Hope
   The countries that rated this option the most, include Vietnam, Indonesia, Thailand, Malaysia, South Korea, the Maldives, Bhutan, and Laos. It is not surprising that five countries in this group belong to the Association of Southeast Asian Nations (ASEAN). Two key features of the ASEAN countries are: (1) they register between 5 and 8% in annual growth, and (2) their regimes tend to be authoritarian. These two features allow people to respond to the question with some benignancy and generosity. The lowest group in this category consists of Turkmenistan, Tajikistan, Nepal, Russia, Afghanistan, the United States, the Philippines, and Bangladesh. This group is mixed in terms of regime type: both authoritarian regimes and democratic regimes (the United States and the Philippines) are represented. The intermediate group for this response consists of Japan, Taiwan, Cambodia, Mongol, India, China, Singapore, Australia, Hong Kong, Pakistan, and Uzbekistan.
4. Write A Letter
   The societies that select this option the most consist of Australia, Singapore, the Maldives, Nepal, Laos, the United States, Hong Kong, China, and India. Except for Laos and China, all those in this grouping used to be a British colony, including the United States. "Writing a letter" is some sort of inherited tradition in Asia, especially for former British colonies. The group that least favored this option consists of Vietnam, Turkmenistan, Indonesia, Mongolia, Tajikistan, Uzbekistan, Kazakhstan, Afghanistan, and South Korea. All or most of these countries are former colonies of Russia and Japan. Indonesia was a Dutch colony and was briefly occupied by Japan.
5. Act Without A Permit
   The societies that select this category the most consist of Pakistan, Kyrgyzstan, Turkmenistan, Afghanistan, Taiwan, Russia, Japan, and Kazakhstan. What is the common thread that runs through them? Pakistan, Kyrgyzstan, Turkmenistan, Afghanistan, Kazakhstan, and parts of Russia are Islamic. Former Soviet Union members are Kyrgyzstan, Turkmenistan, and Kazakhstan. Taiwan was a former Japanese colony. It is noteworthy that Taiwan and Japan belong to this group. The group of societies that select this option the least, include Brunei, Singapore, Laos, Thailand, the Maldives, Nepal, Malaysia, and Vietnam. Six of the ASEAN members, the Maldives and Nepal have broadly authoritarian regimes with Laos and Vietnam being led by communist parties. For the group that least favored this option, to act without a permit is widely regarded as outrageous or at least very uncommon. The intermediate group

consists of Hong Kong, the Philippines, the United States, Indonesia, China, Australia, South Korea, India, Tajikistan, and Bangladesh. Although the percentages of respondents are either small or very small, the responses to this option illuminate the spot of freedom in fragmented and segmented society.

6. Bribe An Official

   The group to most frequently select this option consists of Tajikistan, Uzbekistan, Turkmenistan, Kazakhstan, Bangladesh, Cambodia, Kyrgyzstan, and Sri Lanka. From this list, one may conclude that the more bribe-lenient societies are found in Central Asia and South Asia. It is true to a certain extent. However, it is important to not forget that in rigorous authoritarian societies with effective oppressive mechanisms, societies tend to not register this response to the question because they know that the ever-present monitoring system does not encourage such a response. Candidly selecting such a response can be dangerous. Many polling companies or organizations in authoritarian regimes are closely linked with internal security organizations. The lowest response to this choice, includes Brunei, Singapore, the Maldives, Hong Kong, Japan, the United States, Taiwan, and Malaysia. The intermediate group consists of Australia, Thailand, South Korea, Indonesia, the Philippines, Pakistan, China, Vietnam, Russia, Afghanistan, and India.

7. Don't Know

   For this response, the societies that favored this option the most are Turkmenistan, Russia, the United States, Afghanistan, Japan, Pakistan, Brunei, Bhutan, and Singapore. Those respondents who believe that the phrase "open your mouth only for the dentist" tend to choose "don't know" as a response. Or one could interpret that choosing one out of seven options is too difficult. Some respondents may say that the definitions of bribing and using connections are often blurred in real situations. Some others may say that without a little more context-specific details, it is easier to select "don't know." The lowest rating of this choice, include Cambodia, Thailand. Nepal, Laos, the Philippines, China, Bangladesh, Hong Kong, India, and Vietnam.

5.2 Subregional Profiles

5.2.1 East Asia: China, Taiwan, Hong Kong, South Korea, and Japan

All five societies register four major responses: use connections, nothing can be done, wait patiently and hope, and write a letter. Hong Kong and Japan register a lower response rate to the "use connection" option than the other three societies. Similarly, Hong Kong and Japan register the lowest response rate to "bribe an official" option. Of the five societies, Hong Kong registers the highest response to the question by selecting "write a letter." Hong Kong appears to follow the former British colonial way. Japan appears to be less influenced by the Chinese *guanxi* (relations) practice than other Sinic societies. The option of "act without a permit" registers the highest choice for Japan, Taiwan, and Hong Kong. It makes sense that these three societies enjoy a fairly high degree of freedom. In this regard, South Korean respondents appear to be somewhat inhibited from choosing "bribe an official" response by their rigid Confucian interpretation of Confucian morals.

5.2.2 Southeast Asia: Cambodia, the Philippines, Laos, Vietnam, Malaysia, Thailand, Singapore, Brunei, and Indonesia

Two small societies, Brunei and Singapore, fairly frequently chose the "don't know" response. They are not only authoritarian but also reasonably effective in monitoring dissenters and dissidents. There are no less authoritarian societies in Southeast Asia than Brunei and Singapore. Two societies, Cambodia and Laos chose equally a trio of options: use connections, wait patiently and hope, and write a letter. Indonesia, Thailand, and Malaysia most frequently select the option of "wait patiently and hope," suggesting that the regimes are fairly authoritarian and yet citizens are adept to answering "correctly." Vietnam wears two faces as reflected in the fairly solid response choice: the solidly authoritarian face prompting the response "wait patiently and hope" and the second face of a guanxi-like response "use connections".

5.2.3 South Asia: Pakistan, Nepal, Bhutan, India, Sri Lanka, Bangladesh, and the Maldives

The Maldives is a small society with a fairly effective authoritarian regime, prompting a trio of responses: wait patiently and hope, write a letter, and nothing can be done. The South Asian pattern is the four-way response: use connections, wait patiently and hope, write a letter, and nothing can be done. The quartet set of responses is universal in South Asia. The option "bribe and official" is a less popular choice and the option "don't know" is more frequently selected, in particular, where effective authoritarian monitoring and measures are the norm, as in Pakistan and Bhutan.

5.2.4 *Central Asia: Uzbekistan, Kazakhstan, Kyrgyzstan, Turkmenistan, Afghanistan, Tajikistan, and Mongolia*

Kazakhstan represents Central Asia in the quintet response: use connections, nothing can be done, wait patiently and hope, write a letter, and bribe an official. Kazakhstan, Kyrgyzstan, Afghanistan, Tajikistan, and Mongolia belong to the quintet school. Tajikistan registers the most frequent selection of "bribe an official," whereas Afghanistan registers the least frequent selection of "bribe an official." Turkmenistan is an exception to this quintet rule of Central Asia: it represents the largest contingent of respondents to select the option "don't know," suggesting its authoritarian nature is solid.

5.2.5 *Russia, Australia, and the United States*

Australia and the United States register fairly similar response patterns: write a letter, wait patiently and hope, and use connections. Australian respondents select "use connections" less frequently than those in the United States. Respondents in the United States fairly frequently chose the option "don't know." Russian respondents select "use connections" very frequently and "write a letter" less frequently than those in Australia and the United States. Another notable difference is that Russians fairly frequently select "bribe an official" and "act without a permit," especially in comparison to data on the United States and Australia.

5.3 Exit, Broader Voice, Bureaucratic Voice, Broader Loyalty, and Don't Know

Voice and loyalty are not easy to distinguish from each other. Bribing an official and using connections also share the quality of not being easily distinguishable from each other. When these similar options are considered together, they are called a broader voice. The decision to "write a letter" is called a bureaucratic voice. And for those who choose to "wait patiently and hope," this is called broader loyalty.

5.3.1 *Exit (Act Without a Permit)*

The group of societies to most frequently make this choice consists of Pakistan, Kyrgyzstan, Turkmenistan, Afghanistan, Taiwan, Russia, Japan, and Kazakhstan.

5.3.2 Broader Voice (Use Connections and Bribe an Official Combined)

The group of societies that most frequently choose a broader voice consists of Tajikistan, Uzbekistan, the Philippines, Kazakhstan, Bangladesh, Nepal, Afghanistan, and Kyrgyzstan. This group can be categorized into two types. First, the moderately authoritarian regimes without a solid and effective internal monitoring capacity and, second, a relatively free society not equipped with a solid and effective internal monitoring capacity. The former includes Uzbekistan, Kazakhstan, Afghanistan, and Kyrgyzstan. The latter includes the Philippines, Bangladesh, and Nepal. The group of societies that ranked the lowest in this broader voice category consists of the Maldives, Hong Kong, Brunei, Japan, Singapore, Thailand, Indonesia, and Australia. Two categories exist. Tightly authoritarian regimes exist with effective internal monitoring capacity and relatively free society. The former includes the Maldives, Brunei, Hong Kong, and Singapore. The latter includes Japan and Australia. Thailand and Indonesia are a mixed regime, combining authoritarianism and democracy. They also have tightly authoritarian regimes with a moderately effective monitoring capacity. The intermediate group in this analysis consists of Sri Lanka, Mongolia, Russia, Cambodia, India, Turkmenistan, the United States, China, Vietnam, Taiwan, South Korea, Pakistan, and Malaysia. It is interesting that the United States is together with other societies in this intermediate group. The "use of connections" register a very high figure for this group.

5.3.3 Bureaucratic Voice (Write a Letter)

The bureaucratic voice is most robustly embraced by Australia, Singapore, the Maldives, Nepal, Laos, the United States, Hong Kong, and China. Seemingly salient is the former British colonial influence of writing a letter to express oneself. This is particularly true in Australia, Singapore, the Maldives, Nepal, the United States, and Hong Kong.

5.3.4 Broader Loyalty (Wait Patiently and Hope and Nothing Can Be Done)

The group of societies that choose forms of broader loyalty, include Indonesia, Vietnam, Thailand, Brunei, Hong Kong, Malaysia, South Korea, and Japan.

5.3.5 Don't Know

The choice of "don't know" as an option is most commonly selected by Turkmenistan, Russia, the United States, Afghanistan, Japan, Pakistan, Brunei, Bhutan, and Singapore.

Chapter 6
Exit, Voice, and Loyalty in Twenty-Nine Asian Societies

6.1 Country Profiles of Twenty-Nine Asian Societies: Logit Regression Analysis

This chapter attempts to reveals how values, views and demographics of respondents determine their choices using logit regression analysis. Yet it is very important to emphasize that "determine" means something more modest here than normally used in relation to logit regression analysis. Regression analysis is associated with "explanation" rather than "description". Explanation as used in regression analysis tends to mean strict causal relations. In this chapter, my use of logit regression analysis is to alert some salient views, values and demographics of respondents to readers when they try to understand the national characteristics of each of 29 societies in answering the Hirshmanite question.

6.2 Afghanistan

Afghanistan is a society with an authoritarian regime in Kabul and fragmented center-periphery relations, which exist on the basis of strong proud tribal clans who distrust outsiders. After all, for the last one and half centuries, three foreign intervenors, Britain, the Soviet Union and the United States, have delivered and suffered devastating blows. After the British difficulties in "taming" Afghans in Central Asia and Boers in South Africa, Britain entered a phase of a visible and tangible decline at the turn of the nineteenth century. The Soviet Union wanted to Sovietize Afghanistan when its Marxists took power away from the monarchy. However, the Soviet armed forces were forced to withdraw after little more than a

T. Inoguchi, *Exit, Voice and Loyalty in Asia*,
Quality of Life in Asia 10, DOI 10.1007/978-981-10-4724-4_6

decade. Its defeat accelerated the Soviet collapse in 1991. The United States, having retaliated against the September 11, 2001, terrorist attacks in New York and Washington, D.C., by launching its own invasion of Afghanistan in 2001 and Iraq in 2003. The fallout from these conflicts are widely viewed as accelerating its own decline. This victory of Donald Trump in the 2016 U.S. presidential election means isolationism and protectionism under the slogan "America First."

Based on demographics, regions, and city size, a basic picture emerges. First, the older the society is, the stronger the tendency to pursue a bureaucratic voice. Region-wise, Kabul manifests an exit tendency, whereas Southwestern, Western, and Northern regions of the country exhibit the tendency to show loyalty. Southwestern and Western regions are dominated by Pushtuns, a majority ethnic group. The Northern region is more mixed with Tajiks and other minorities who coexist. The Central/Hazarjat region exhibits also a strong tendency to show loyalty. In terms of city size, Kabul is mildly exit-prone, whereas cities are prone to expressing a broader voice. Cities other than Kabul tend to be located in the core of ethnic-linguistic groups with strong homogeneity. Kabul is the capital city where an authoritarian regime exerts authoritarian control with international actors providing legitimacy and financial assistance on the basis of military forces.

Which variables are more prone to exit? Residents of Kabul are most strongly exit prone. Those who worry about government corruption and those who worry about the right to criticize the government are two groups who are the most negative about exit. Which variables are more prone to a broader voice? Those who trust in the legal system are the most negative about a broader voice. In other words, they do not trust the legal system and, therefore, they remain silent. Which variables are more prone to a bureaucratic voice? Those who use Internet are prone to bureaucratic voice. In other words, they are politically correct in their responses. Those satisfied do not even express themselves in a bureaucratic voice.

Next is loyalty. The choice of broader loyalty stands out among those married and those who reside in Southwestern, Western, and Northern regions. The first two regions are dominated by Pushtuns, a majority ethnic group. The last region is an ethnically mixed region adjacent to Kabul, the capital. Not to be suspected of disloyalty and also not to miss the opportunity to join power once Pushtuns and international forces reach an accord on power sharing, the Northern region seems to show strong loyalty. In contrast, the Central/Hazarjat region has a heavy concentration of Hazars, an ethnic group heavily influenced by Mongol blood and by Shia Muslims. Hazars, similar to Kabul residents, they exhibit mild dissent.

Summary statistics of countries Afghanistan					
	n	Mean	SD	Min	Max
Exit	774	0.06	0.24	0	1
Broader voice	774	0.49	0.50	0	1
Bureaucratic voice	774	0.12	0.33	0	1
Broader loyalty	774	0.32	0.47	0	1
(A) Lifestyles					
Number of public utilities	874	2.13	1.12	0	5
Homeownership	871	0.74	0.44	0	1
Number of family members	874	8.79	3.13	2	20
Pray	872	4.96	0.27	2	5
Proud	871	3.83	0.51	1	4
Relative Standard of Living	868	2.95	0.97	1	5
(B) Exposure to globalization					
Internet	782	2.12	0.58	2	5
Living internationally	874	0.74	0.77	0	4
English ability	831	1.34	0.69	1	4
(C) Satisfaction with aspects of life					
Housing	870	4.55	0.85	1	5
Friendships	864	4.42	0.75	1	5
Household income	862	3.58	1.05	1	5
Health	867	4.11	0.98	1	5
Education	858	3.86	1.07	1	5
Job	817	3.52	1.22	1	5
Neighbors	866	4.25	0.89	1	5
Public safety	861	3.85	1.01	1	5
The condition of the environment	841	3.52	1.03	1	5
Social welfare system	831	3.21	1.13	1	5
The democratic system	792	3.43	1.20	1	5
Family life	853	4.30	0.88	1	5
Leisure	855	3.81	0.92	1	5
Spiritual life	856	4.05	0.96	1	5
Happiness	867	3.44	0.93	1	5
(D) Trust in social institution					
Trust generally	850	0.50	0.50	0	1
Trust the central government	869	3.44	0.68	1	4
Trust local governments	855	3.06	0.78	1	4
Trust the army	866	3.41	0.71	1	4
Trust the legal system	815	2.85	0.86	1	4
Trust the police	868	3.26	0.75	1	4
(E) Assessment of government performance					
Worry about corruption	874	0.44	0.50	0	1

(continued)

(continued)

Summary statistics of countries Afghanistan					
	n	Mean	SD	Min	Max
Worry about Economic inequality	874	0.27	0.45	0	1
Political corruption	817	2.52	0.82	1	4
Duty to vote	870	4.70	0.60	1	5
Widespread corruption	847	4.10	0.99	1	5
No power	829	4.00	0.97	1	5
Complicated	827	4.08	1.02	1	5
No matter whether vote	825	3.43	1.36	1	5
Stop thinking	816	4.01	1.03	1	5
Pay little attention	840	4.13	0.99	1	5
Powerful leader	825	2.02	0.79	1	3
Experts	821	2.36	0.68	1	3
Military government	833	1.88	0.75	1	3
Democratic political system	797	2.30	0.70	1	3
Bribe	851	9.18	2.18	1	10
(F) Satisfaction with rights					
Right to vote	866	3.68	0.56	1	4
Right to participate in any organizations	827	3.25	0.72	1	4
Right to gather and demonstrate	827	2.92	0.94	1	4
Right to be informed about government	845	2.93	0.89	1	4
Freedom of speech	856	3.28	0.84	1	4
Right to criticize the government	837	3.01	0.97	1	4
(H) Demographics					
Female	874	0.48	0.50	0	1
Age	874	35.0	12.1	20	69
Level of education	867	1.42	0.60	1	3
Married	871	0.77	0.42	0	1
Income	853	2.12	0.82	1	3
Unemployed	874	0.12	0.32	0	1
(I) Region (Base = Eastern)					
Central/Kabul	874	0.22	0.41	0	1
South Central	874	0.14	0.34	0	1
South Western	874	0.09	0.29	0	1
Western	874	0.10	0.30	0	1
Northern	874	0.30	0.46	0	1
Central/Hazarjat	874	0.07	0.25	0	1
(J) City size (Base = Villages)					
Towns	874	0.02	0.15	0	1
City	874	0.05	0.21	0	1
Kabul	874	0.14	0.34	0	1

Frequency Distribution of 7 Responses and Partially Aggregated 4 Responses Afghanistan

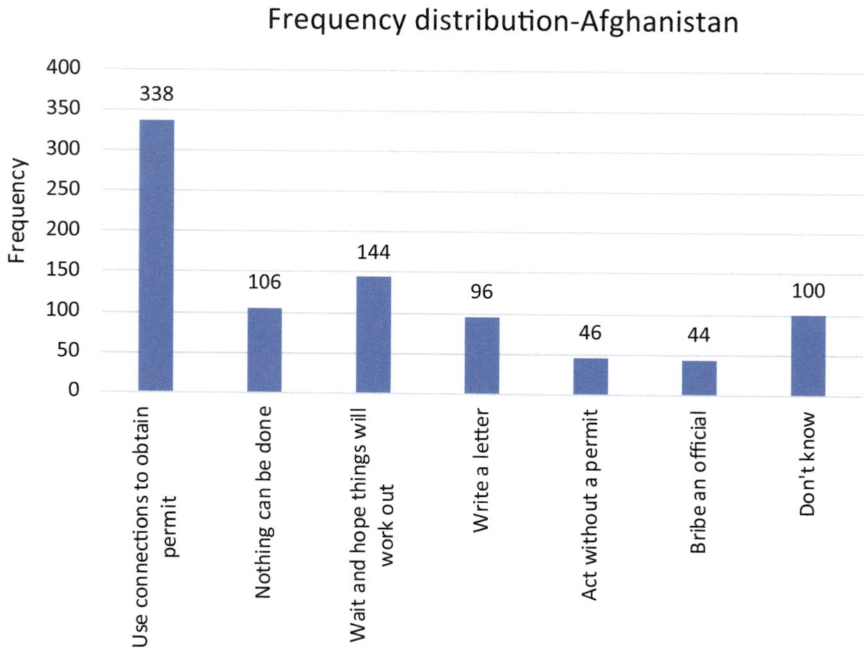

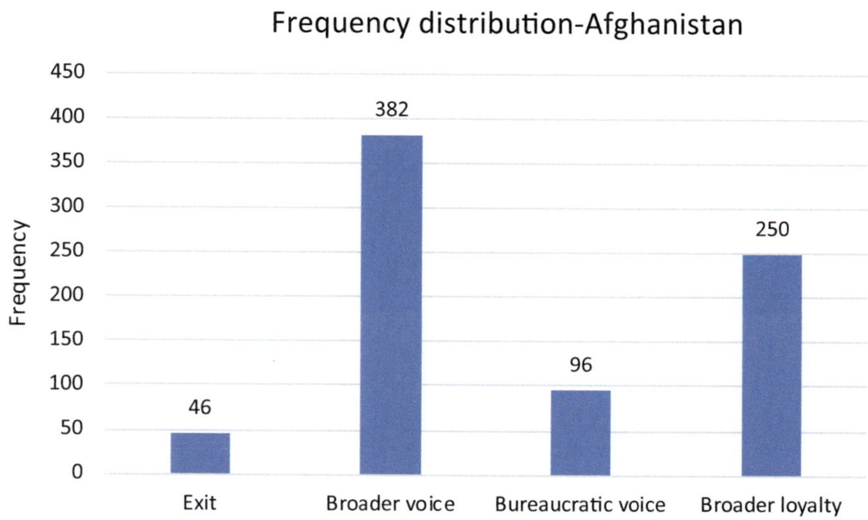

Logit regression analysis results by country Afghanistan								
Dependent variable	Exit		Broader voice		Bureaucratic voice		Broader Loyalty	
Independent variables	Coeff.	z-stat.	Coeff.	z-stat.	Coeff.	z-stat.	Coeff.	z-stat.
(A) Lifestyles								
Number of public utilities	–	–	−0.24	−1.34	0.12	0.31	0.01	0.03
Homeownership	–	–	−0.61	−1.54	0.71	0.93	0.56	1.35
Number of family members	–	–	−0.02	−0.46	0.03	0.31	0.01	0.21
Pray	–	–	1.26	1.17	−0.39	−0.28	−0.72	−0.92
Proud	–	–	−0.45	−1.15	−0.66	−0.65	0.79	1.77
Relative Standard of Living	–	–	0.25	1.42	−0.43	−1.03	−0.16	−0.77
(B) Exposure to globalization								
Internet	–	–	−0.39	−1.87	0.81	2.06[a]	0.04	0.19
Living internationally	–	–	0.22	0.95	−0.78	−1.66	0.07	0.29
English ability	–	–	−0.17	−0.65	0.77	1.24	−0.21	−0.69
(C) Satisfaction with aspects of life								
Housing	–	–	−0.31	−1.17	1.32	1.68	0.47	1.51
Friendships	–	–	0.15	0.63	−0.89	−1.68	0.13	0.53
Household income	–	–	−0.17	−1.09	0.47	1.35	0.14	0.75
Health	–	–	−0.10	−0.56	−0.31	−0.84	−0.09	−0.49
Education	–	–	0.21	1.19	−0.40	−0.86	0.02	0.08
Job	–	–	−0.03	−0.17	0.30	0.90	0.03	0.20
Neighbors	–	–	−0.07	−0.37	0.60	1.27	−0.06	−0.27
Public safety	–	–	−0.05	−0.23	0.10	0.22	0.06	0.26
The condition of the environment	–	–	−0.004	−0.02	−0.23	−0.58	0.07	0.38
Social welfare system	–	–	0.07	0.40	0.12	0.28	−0.02	−0.08
The democratic system	–	–	0.10	0.63	0.14	0.48	−0.31	−1.89
Family life	–	–	−0.08	−0.39	0.33	0.73	−0.07	−0.32
Leisure	–	–	0.33	1.76	0.13	0.34	−0.38	−1.89
Spiritual life	–	–	0.15	0.79	−0.25	−0.60	−0.08	−0.39
Happiness	–	–	0.07	0.38	−1.15	(−2.80)[b]	0.22	1.20
(D) Trust in social institution								
Trust generally	–	–	0.21	0.67	−0.55	−0.83	0.002	0.00
Trust the central government	–	–	0.15	0.47	1.12	1.76	−0.35	−1.01
Trust local governments	–	–	−0.32	−1.30	0.59	1.08	0.26	1.00
Trust the army	–	–	−0.35	−1.30	0.85	1.36	0.58	1.93
Trust the legal system	–	–	−0.42	(−2.02)[a]	−0.05	−0.11	0.46	2.08[a]
Trust the police	–	–	0.07	0.29	0.17	0.33	−0.21	−0.78

(continued)

(continued)

Logit regression analysis results by country Afghanistan								
Dependent variable	Exit		Broader voice		Bureaucratic voice		Broader Loyalty	
Independent variables	Coeff.	z-stat.	Coeff.	z-stat.	Coeff.	z-stat.	Coeff.	z-stat.
(E) Assessment of government performance								
Worry about corruption	–	–	0.24	0.76	0.60	0.87	−0.28	−0.85
Worry about Economic inequality	–	–	0.18	0.47	−0.06	−0.07	−0.09	−0.20
Political corruption	–	–	0.16	0.79	−0.37	−0.81	−0.09	−0.39
Duty to vote	–	–	−0.25	−1.04	0.32	0.65	−0.14	−0.57
Widespread corruption	–	–	0.33	1.83	−1.01	(−2.82)[b]	0.11	0.58
No power	–	–	0.35	1.96	−0.57	−1.51	−0.12	−0.62
Complicated	–	–	−0.13	−0.75	0.38	0.98	−0.25	−1.31
No matter whether vote	–	–	−0.18	−1.21	−0.13	−0.38	0.26	1.59
Stop thinking	–	–	−0.24	−1.16	0.18	0.40	0.06	0.28
Pay little attention	–	–	−0.28	−1.5	−0.06	−0.14	0.46	2.11[a]
Powerful leader	–	–	0.01	0.04	0.03	0.06	0.10	0.38
Experts	–	–	0.26	0.93	−0.84	−1.52	0.12	0.41
Military government	–	–	−0.35	−1.64	0.87	1.85	0.60	2.54[a]
Democratic political system	–	–	0.02	0.1	−0.57	−1.05	−0.12	−0.49
Bribe	–	–	0.002	0.02	−0.27	−1.57	0.11	1.30
(F) Satisfaction with rights								
Right to vote	–	–	0.18	0.46	−0.49	−0.60	−0.12	−0.29
Right to participate in any organizations	–	–	0.25	0.95	0.54	0.80	−0.34	−1.25
Right to gather and demonstrate	–	–	−0.24	−1.18	0.80	1.74	−0.10	−0.43
Right to be informed about government	–	–	−0.01	−0.06	−0.33	−0.72	0.05	0.25
Freedom of speech	–	–	−0.23	−1.07	0.48	0.78	0.09	0.38
Right to criticize the government	–	–	0.25	1.27	0.80	1.68	−0.33	−1.54
(H) Demographics								
Female	–	–	0.32	0.93	−0.50	−0.70	0.28	0.77
Age	–	–	−0.02	−1.28	0.05	2.12[a]	−0.01	−0.43
Level of education	–	–	−0.14	−0.49	−0.85	−1.16	0.51	1.62
Married	–	–	−0.31	−0.82	−0.99	−1.20	1.09	2.28[a]
Income	–	–	0.12	0.59	−0.79	−1.82	0.17	0.77
Unemployed	–	–	0.38	0.71	1.06	1.03	−0.52	−0.83
(I) Region (Base = Eastern)								
Central/Kabul	–	–	1.27	1.59	−19.3	−0.02	−0.36	−0.40
South Central	–	–	−0.58	−0.79	−2.54	−1.64	1.23	1.49

(continued)

(continued)

Logit regression analysis results by country Afghanistan								
Dependent variable	Exit		Broader voice		Bureaucratic voice		Broader Loyalty	
Independent variables	Coeff.	z-stat.	Coeff.	z-stat.	Coeff.	z-stat.	Coeff.	z-stat.
South Western	–	–	−2.82	(−3.03)[b]	0.94	0.48	2.58	2.49[a]
Western	–	–	−1.25	−1.63	1.69	1.09	1.89	2.16[a]
Northern	–	–	−1.49	(−2.32)[a]	−1.07	−0.83	1.87	2.51[a]
Central/Hazarjat	–	–	1.34	0.99	–	–	−0.84	−0.59
(J) City size (Base = Villages)								
Towns	–	–	−1.97	−1.6	1.10	0.81	1.46	1.58
City	–	–	2.04	2.35[a]	−0.55	−0.29	−1.89	(−2.02)[a]
Kabul	–	–	−1.20	−1.51	18.6	0.02	−0.92	−0.73
Constant	–	–	0.76	0.13	−7.14	−0.68	−7.50	−1.42
n	–		370		354		370	
Pseudo R squared	–		0.2596		0.4417		0.2676	

Note [a]5% significance level; [b]1% significance level

6.3 Australia

Of the four categories (exit, boarder voice, bureaucratic voice, and broader loyalty), the frequency of Australian exit is so low that we cannot discuss the Australian exit in a statistically meaningful way. Broader loyalty is salient among those who are healthy, are not highly educated, trust the army, are young, do not have a high income, and reside in Melbourne and Brisbane when Sydney is located as a sort of Greenwich Standard time. The choice of a broader voice is salient among those who have a small family, use Internet, are satisfied with their neighbors, are not satisfied about public safety, are worried about economic inequality, do not highly regard the democratic performance of government, and reside in Melbourne and Brisbane when Sydney is located as zero. Demographically, those who are employed, are not married, and have a high income tend to exhibit a high salience of a broader voice. Bureaucratic voice is salient to those who are satisfied with friendships, are highly educated, do not trust the army, do not worry about economic inequality, regard government economic performance as important, are not satisfied with their right to be informed about government, and earn a high income.

The Australian exit frequency is so low that statistical discussion cannot be carried out in a meaningful way. Of the respondents surveyed, 21 out of a sample size of 971 choose this option. The frequency of broader loyalty is 137. Broader voice registers 355, whereas bureaucratic voice registers 458. Similar to the Australian low exit frequency, Australian high bureaucratic voice frequency is somewhat of a surprise. As a non-Australian who was surprised that heated parliamentary debates could descend into shouting matches between adversarial MPs, we should remind ourselves that Australian citizens are more a product of classical education in responding to interviewers.

Summary statistics of countries Australia					
	n	Mean	SD	Min	Max
Exit	971	0.02	0.15	0	1
Broader voice	971	0.14	0.35	0	1
Bureaucratic voice	971	0.47	0.50	0	1
Broader loyalty	971	0.37	0.48	0	1
(A) Lifestyles					
Number of public utilities	1000	4.78	1.02	1	7
Homeownership	995	0.57	0.50	0	1
Number of family members	1000	2.85	1.50	1	10
Pray	993	2.69	1.63	1	5
National elections	898	4.76	0.87	1	5
Proud	921	3.76	0.50	1	4
Relative Standard of Living	993	3.38	0.83	1	5
(B) Exposure to globalization					
Internet	997	3.65	1.68	1	5
Living internationally	1000	2.39	1.66	0	6
English ability	998	3.94	0.29	1	4
(C) Satisfaction with aspects of life					
Housing	998	4.03	1.09	1	5
Friendships	998	4.49	0.73	1	5
Household income	996	3.65	1.16	1	5
Health	999	4.03	1.05	1	5
Education	992	4.11	0.88	1	5
Job	926	3.74	1.08	1	5
Neighbors	985	3.97	1.04	1	5
Public safety	996	3.59	1.07	1	5
The condition of the environment	996	3.10	1.16	1	5
Social welfare system	962	3.00	1.15	1	5
The democratic system	958	3.60	1.03	1	5
Family life	993	4.35	0.83	1	5
Leisure	996	4.15	0.87	1	5
Spiritual life	963	3.98	0.89	1	5
Happiness	999	4.17	0.81	1	5
(D) Trust in social institution					
Trust generally	988	0.52	0.50	0	1
Trust the central government	966	2.64	0.82	1	4
Trust the army	950	3.22	0.74	1	4
Trust the legal system	967	2.63	0.85	1	4
Trust the police	982	3.08	0.79	1	4
(E) Assessment of government performance					
Worry about corruption	1000	0.33	0.47	0	1

(continued)

(continued)

Summary statistics of countries Australia					
	n	Mean	SD	Min	Max
Worry about Economic inequality	1000	0.23	0.42	0	1
Political corruption	892	2.55	0.76	1	4
Duty to vote	993	4.45	0.84	1	5
Widespread corruption	941	3.13	1.04	1	5
No power	990	3.39	1.12	1	5
Complicated	994	3.45	1.14	1	5
No matter whether vote	990	2.38	1.16	1	5
Pay little attention	988	3.43	1.02	1	5
Powerful leader	940	1.21	0.46	1	3
Experts	932	1.58	0.64	1	3
Military government	951	1.18	0.46	1	3
Democratic political system	950	2.59	0.57	1	3
Bribe	988	9.36	1.50	1	10
(F) Satisfaction with rights					
Right to vote	983	3.76	0.50	1	4
Right to participate in any organizations	985	3.62	0.58	1	4
Right to gather and demonstrate	974	3.42	0.70	1	4
Right to be informed about government	979	3.36	0.70	1	4
Freedom of speech	989	3.54	0.64	1	4
Right to criticize the government	980	3.43	0.76	1	4
(G) Political spectrum					
Political spectrum	761	5.21	1.91	1	10
(H) Demographics					
Female	1000	0.61	0.49	0	1
Age	1000	42.5	15.1	20	69
Level of education	996	2.38	0.71	1	3
Married	997	0.55	0.50	0	1
Unemployed	998	0.09	0.28	0	1
Income	759	4.35	2.59	1	8
No religion	995	0.36	0.48	0	1
(I) Region (Base = Sydney)					
Melbourne	1000	0.30	0.46	0	1
Brisbane	1000	0.15	0.35	0	1
Adelaide	1000	0.09	0.29	0	1
Perth	1000	0.12	0.32	0	1

Frequency Distribution of 7 Responses and Partially Aggregated 4 Responses Australia

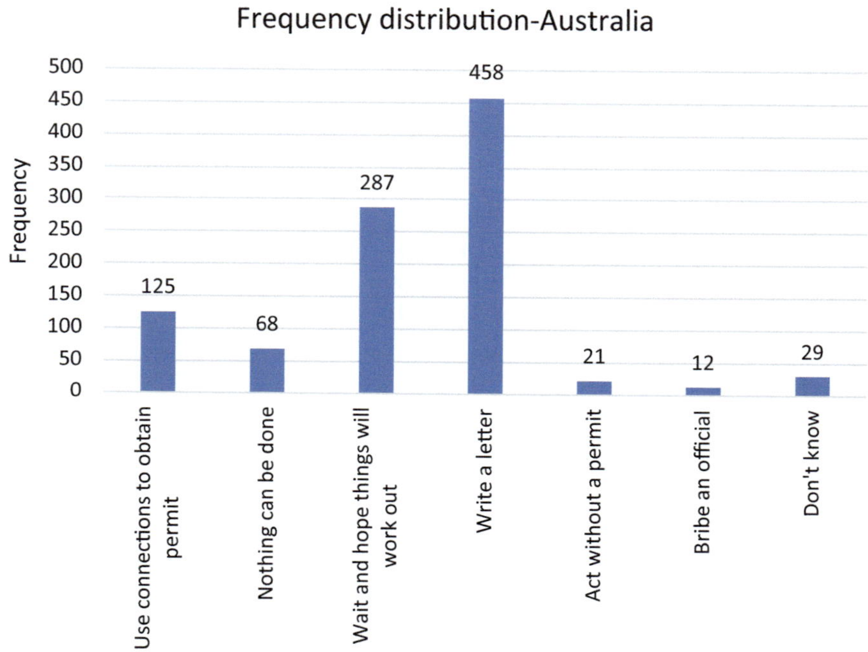

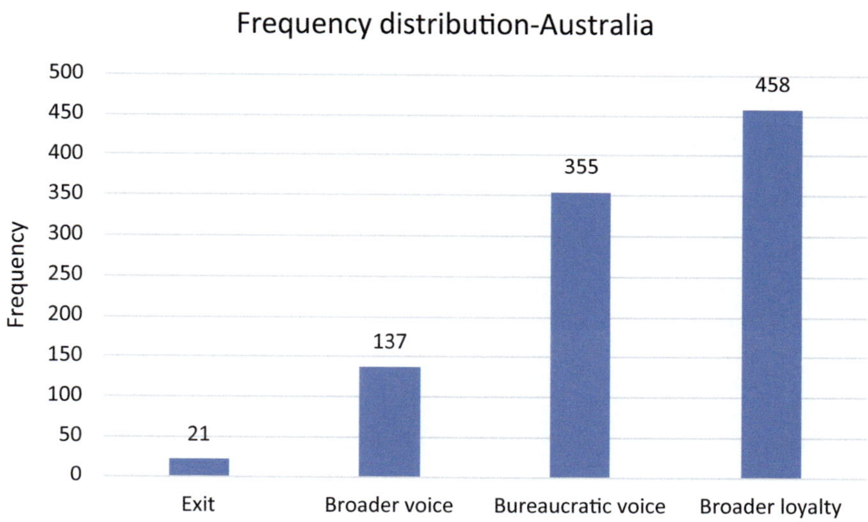

Logit regression analysis results by country Australia								
Dependent variable	Exit		Broader voice		Bureaucratic voice		Broader loyalty	
Independent variables	Coeff.	z-stat.	Coeff.	z-stat.	Coeff.	z-stat.	Coeff.	z-stat.
(A) Lifestyles								
Number of public utilities	–	–	0.44	1.48	−0.08	−0.48	−0.09	−0.54
Homeownership	–	–	0.49	0.88	0.13	0.38	−0.34	−0.96
Number of family members	–	–	−0.36	−1.71	0.04	0.34	0.13	1.08
Pray	–	–	0.30	1.68	0.03	0.29	−0.17	−1.58
National elections	–	–	0.29	0.82	−0.43	(−2.11)[a]	0.24	1.22
Proud	–	–	0.22	0.40	0.01	0.05	−0.06	−0.22
Relative Standard of Living	–	–	0.39	1.11	0.15	0.68	−0.43	−1.87
(B) Exposure to globalization								
Internet	–	–	0.53	2.84[b]	−0.11	−0.96	−0.10	−0.85
Living internationally	–	–	−0.03	−0.18	0.10	1.01	−0.07	−0.70
English ability	–	–	–	–	0.63	1.20	−0.58	−1.09
(C) Satisfaction with aspects of life								
Housing	–	–	0.43	1.43	−0.30	−1.79	0.12	0.73
Friendships	–	–	−0.68	−1.76	0.75	2.93[b]	−0.36	−1.45
Household income	–	–	0.12	0.36	−0.12	−0.68	0.23	1.25
Health	–	–	−0.30	−0.94	−0.24	−1.35	0.39	2.05[a]
Education	–	–	−0.12	−0.34	0.51	2.30[a]	−0.58	(−2.46)[a]
Job	–	–	−0.44	−1.69	0.22	1.45	−0.13	−0.87
Neighbors	–	–	0.69	2.10[a]	−0.12	−0.77	−0.06	−0.39
Public safety	–	–	−0.61	−1.93	0.14	0.78	0.03	0.14
The condition of the environment	–	–	0.04	0.14	0.09	0.53	−0.18	−1.07
Social welfare system	–	–	0.11	0.40	−0.09	−0.54	0.15	0.83
The democratic system	–	–	0.08	0.27	0.09	0.49	−0.17	−0.91
Family life	–	–	−0.11	−0.30	−0.16	−0.78	0.13	0.58
Leisure	–	–	0.38	0.81	−0.16	−0.64	−0.02	−0.06
Spiritual life	–	–	0.02	0.06	−0.30	−1.60	0.37	1.88
Happiness	–	–	−0.18	−0.50	−0.09	−0.40	0.20	0.76
(D) Trust in social institution								
Trust generally	–	–	0.08	0.15	−0.07	−0.21	−0.06	−0.20
Trust the central government	–	–	−0.24	−0.76	0.15	0.78	0.09	0.45
Trust the army	–	–	0.75	1.81	−0.70	(−3.09)[b]	0.49	2.13[a]
Trust the legal system	–	–	−0.45	−1.25	0.33	1.60	−0.05	−0.23
Trust the police	–	–	−0.11	−0.30	−0.07	−0.34	−0.01	−0.03
(E) Assessment of government performance								
Worry about corruption	–	–	−0.08	−0.15	0.14	0.47	−0.39	−1.20
Worry about Economic inequality	–	–	0.38	0.68	−0.77	(−2.22)[a]	0.61	1.73

(continued)

(continued)

Logit regression analysis results by country Australia								
Dependent variable	Exit		Broader voice		Bureaucratic voice		Broader loyalty	
Independent variables	Coeff.	z-stat.	Coeff.	z-stat.	Coeff.	z-stat.	Coeff.	z-stat.
Political corruption	–	–	1.27	3.21[b]	−0.06	−0.30	−0.37	−1.61
Duty to vote	–	–	−0.43	−1.21	−0.12	−0.59	0.34	1.55
Widespread corruption	–	–	−0.07	−0.25	0.11	0.67	−0.15	−0.87
No power	–	–	−0.02	−0.06	−0.09	−0.60	0.28	1.74
Complicated	–	–	0.22	0.94	−0.10	−0.67	0.13	0.80
No matter whether vote	–	–	−0.25	−0.97	−0.06	−0.42	0.09	0.59
Pay little attention	–	–	−0.06	−0.22	0.24	1.44	−0.34	(−2.00)[a]
Powerful leader	–	–	0.64	0.99	−0.48	−1.14	0.40	0.94
Experts	–	–	0.44	1.20	0.03	0.11	−0.36	−1.47
Military government	–	–	0.78	1.44	−0.34	−0.84	−0.13	−0.33
Democratic political system	–	–	−1.44	(−2.75)[b]	0.76	2.46[a]	−0.16	−0.53
Bribe	–	–	−0.07	−0.41	0.20	1.66	−0.19	−1.69
(F) Satisfaction with rights								
Right to vote	–	–	−0.70	−1.05	1.00	2.37[a]	−0.93	(−2.17)’
Right to participate in any organizations	–	–	0.49	0.79	−0.37	−1.13	0.23	0.70
Right to gather and demonstrate	–	–	−0.19	−0.39	0.10	0.37	−0.09	−0.35
Right to be informed about government	–	–	0.68	1.40	−0.62	(−2.22)[a]	0.49	1.78
Freedom of speech	–	–	0.95	1.74	−0.01	−0.04	−0.27	−0.83
Right to criticize the government	–	–	−0.83	−1.89	0.10	0.38	0.05	0.17
(G) Political spectrum								
Political spectrum	–	–	0.07	0.52	0.01	0.15	−0.07	−0.94
(H) Demographics								
Female	–	–	0.23	0.44	0.53	1.71	−0.47	−1.47
Age	–	–	0.04	1.70	0.02	1.54	−0.04	(−2.66)[a]
Level of education	–	–	0.02	0.04	−0.05	−0.21	0.18	0.72
Married	–	–	−0.13	−0.24	0.48	1.42	−0.55	−1.56
Unemployed	–	–	−2.21	−1.18	1.33	1.94	−0.72	−1.06
Income	–	–	0.04	0.26	0.20	2.44[a]	−0.17	−1.96
No religion	–	–	0.83	1.49	−0.43	−1.30	0.02	0.05
(I) Region (Base = Sydney)								
Melbourne	–	–	1.32	2.22[a]	0.21	0.59	−0.80	(−2.10)[a]
Brisbane	–	–	1.32	1.85	−0.16	−0.35	−0.65	−1.44
Adelaide	–	–	–	–	−0.50	−0.68	1.12	1.48
Perth	–	–	0.30	0.35	−0.33	−0.71	0.21	0.43

(continued)

(continued)

Logit regression analysis results by country Australia								
Dependent variable	Exit		Broader voice		Bureaucratic voice		Broader loyalty	
Independent variables	Coeff.	z-stat.	Coeff.	z-stat.	Coeff.	z-stat.	Coeff.	z-stat.
Constant	–	–	−12.1	−2.58	−6.28	−1.85	8.61	2.48[a]
n	–		321		343		343	
Pseudo R squared	–		0.3204		0.2150		0.2058	

Note [a]5% significance level; [b]1% significance level

6.4 Bangladesh

In terms of the reorganized four categories to the question, let us look at frequency distribution. Exit is very small, that is, 12 respondents out of the sample size of 997 respondents. This means that we cannot discuss the Bangladesh exit in a statistically meaningful way. Broader loyalty and bureaucratic voice are both high. The former registers 465, whereas the latter registers 368. Both numbers suggest that under a regime that has not been consistently democratic, citizens are cautious to open their mouth when their views are not necessarily supportive of the government.

Broader loyalty are salient to those who own a home, pray, are satisfied with income, are satisfied with neighbors, trust local governments, regard government performance on political corruption as high, regard government democratic performance as high, and regard government performance on freedom of speech as high. Demographically, those who are married exhibit broader loyalty. In terms of region, those who reside in Dhaka are less likely to belong to this category. They are more vocal. Those who reside in the confluence of the Brahmaputra, the Ganges, and the Meghna split, that is, provinces of Khulna, Barisal, and Chittagong, are more loyal than the two provinces that are located in the upper low steams as Dhaka. When urban is set to zero, rural exhibits high non-loyalty. It appears that the degree of flood-related disasters makes a big difference to citizens' attitudes.

Broader voice is salient to those who have a small family, do not have high household income, are not satisfied with public safety, do not have a high level of trust in general, have a high level of trust in central government, regard government performance as producing powerful leadership, regard government democratic performance as high, are satisfied with the right to vote, are satisfied with freedom of speech, are not satisfied with the right to participate in any organizations, and have high income. Those who are not married and are unemployed belong to this category as well. In terms of region, those who reside in the two provinces adjacent to Dhaka, that is, Rajshahi and Barisal, register more vocal than other provinces.

Bureaucratic voice is salient to those who register participation in national elections, live internationally, are satisfied with the democratic system, and negatively regard government performance of keeping duty to vote high.

Summary statistics of countries Bangladesh					
	n	Mean	SD	Min	Max
Exit	997	0.01	0.11	0	1
Broader voice	997	0.47	0.50	0	1
Bureaucratic voice	997	0.15	0.36	0	1
Broader loyalty	997	0.37	0.48	0	1
(A) Lifestyles					
Number of public utilities	1008	2.02	1.60	0	6
Homeownership	1008	0.62	0.49	0	1
Number of family members	1008	5.04	2.24	1	19
Pray	1007	4.44	0.84	1	5
National elections	953	4.35	1.20	1	5
Proud	1006	3.84	0.43	1	4
Relative Standard of Living	1007	2.93	0.80	1	5
(B) Exposure to globalization					
Internet	612	1.09	0.47	1	5
Living internationally	1008	0.63	0.75	0	4
English ability	714	1.86	0.86	1	4
(C) Satisfaction with aspects of life					
Housing	1008	3.89	1.09	1	5
Friendships	940	4.04	0.85	1	5
Household income	1007	3.66	1.08	1	5
Health	1008	3.87	1.04	1	5
Education	988	3.45	1.26	1	5
Job	848	3.22	1.24	1	5
Neighbors	1005	4.17	0.84	1	5
Public safety	983	3.56	1.08	1	5
The condition of the environment	990	3.66	1.02	1	5
Social welfare system	932	3.48	0.97	1	5
The democratic system	923	3.54	1.06	1	5
Family life	993	4.24	0.89	1	5
Leisure	974	3.90	0.96	1	5
Spiritual life	791	3.83	1.01	1	5
Happiness	1008	3.77	0.90	1	5
(D) Trust in social institution					
Trust generally	1006	0.24	0.43	0	1
Trust the central government	976	3.00	0.82	1	4
Trust local governments	986	2.97	0.81	1	4
Trust the army	984	3.41	0.76	1	4
Trust the legal system	996	2.90	0.87	1	4
Trust the police	1005	2.02	1.00	1	4

(continued)

(continued)

Summary statistics of countries Bangladesh					
	n	Mean	SD	Min	Max
(E) Assessment of government performance					
Worry about corruption	1008	0.65	0.48	0	1
Worry about Economic inequality	1008	0.19	0.39	0	1
Political corruption	972	2.27	0.87	1	4
Duty to vote	1008	4.95	0.22	3	5
Widespread corruption	1001	4.41	0.80	1	5
No power	963	4.09	0.97	1	5
Complicated	967	4.09	1.08	1	5
No matter whether vote	1004	1.95	1.32	1	5
Stop thinking	1006	4.45	0.88	1	5
Pay little attention	992	4.39	0.83	1	5
Powerful leader	958	1.64	0.80	1	3
Experts	959	2.42	0.64	1	3
Military government	958	1.96	0.78	1	3
Democratic political system	957	2.32	0.70	1	3
(F) Satisfaction with rights					
Right to vote	993	3.53	0.69	1	4
Right to participate in any organizations	899	2.84	0.78	1	4
Right to gather and demonstrate	916	2.81	0.89	1	4
Right to be informed about government	960	2.81	0.88	1	4
Freedom of speech	952	2.99	0.95	1	4
Right to criticize the government	955	2.84	0.90	1	4
(H) Demographics					
Female	1008	0.50	0.50	0	1
Age	1008	34.4	10.0	20	59
Level of education	1008	1.37	0.68	1	3
Married	1008	0.87	0.34	0	1
Unemployed	1008	0.01	0.12	0	1
Income	1008	7.59	4.38	1	20
(I) Region (Base = Dhaka)					
Chittagong	1008	0.18	0.38	0	1
Rajshahi	1008	0.19	0.39	0	1
Barisal	1008	0.11	0.31	0	1
Khulna	1008	0.17	0.37	0	1
Sylhet	1008	0.11	0.31	0	1
(K) Rural					
Rural	1008	0.21	0.41	0	1

Frequency Distribution of 7 Responses and Partially Aggregated 4 Responses Bangladesh

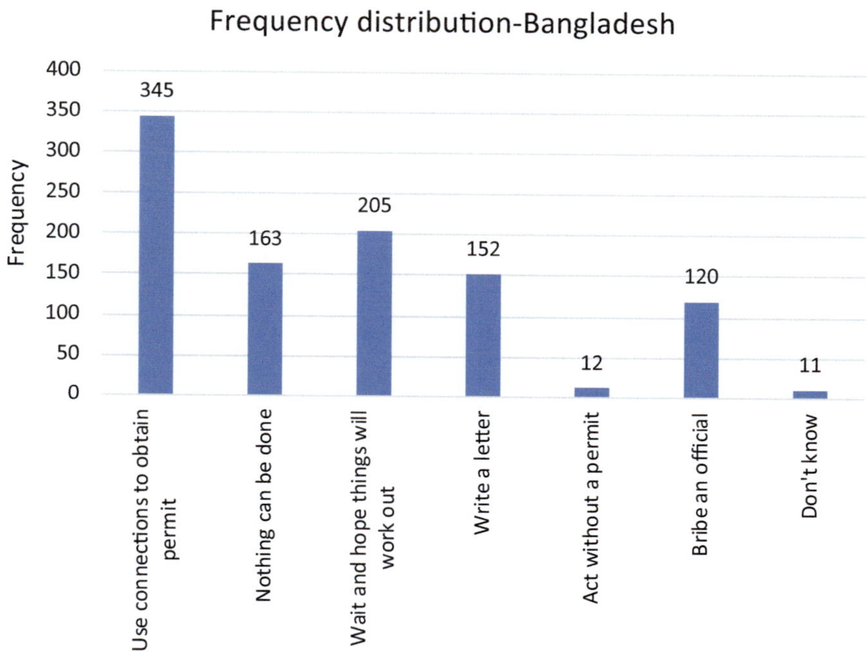

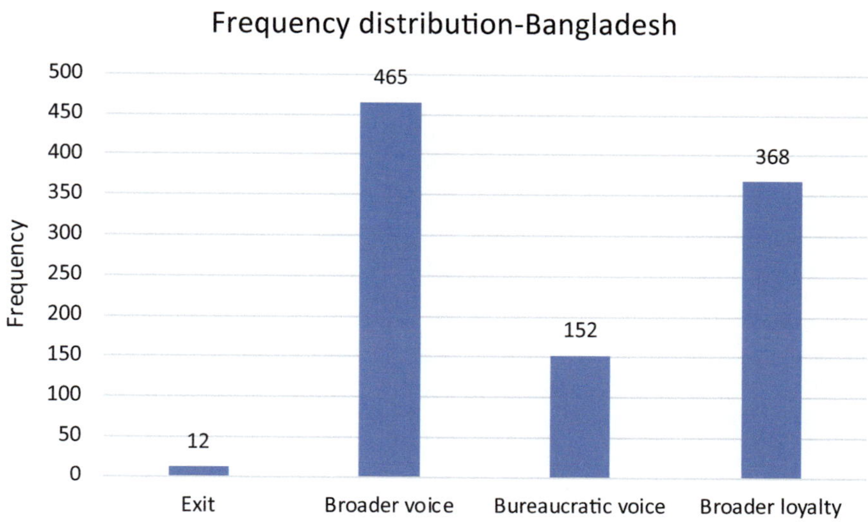

Logit regression analysis results by country Bangladesh								
Dependent variable	Exit		Broader voice		Bureaucratic voice		Broader loyalty	
Independent variables	Coeff.	z-stat.	Coeff.	z-stat.	Coeff.	z-stat.	Coeff.	z-stat.
(A) Lifestyles								
Number of public utilities	–	–	0.04	0.27	0.36	1.60	−0.11	−0.80
Homeownership	–	–	−0.37	−1.02	−0.78	−1.24	1.17	2.97[b]
Number of family members	–	–	−0.04	−0.54	0.20	1.64	−0.03	−0.40
Pray	–	–	−0.82	(−3.09)[b]	0.44	1.13	0.84	3.09[b]
National elections		–	−0.11	−0.77	0.33	1.24	−0.04	−0.28
Proud	– –	–	0.08	0.17	1.65	1.75	−0.50	−1.15
Relative Standard of Living	–	–	0.30	1.17	−1.01	(−2.46)[a]	0.18	0.67
(B) Exposure to globalization								
Internet	–	–	0.32	0.90	0.69	1.42	−0.38	−0.98
Living internationally	–	–	−0.47	(−1.97)[a]	0.59	1.56	−0.09	−0.36
English ability	–	–	−0.29	−1.09	−0.07	−0.14	0.46	1.64
(C) Satisfaction with aspects of life								
Housing	–	–	0.26	1.18	−0.17	−0.46	−0.28	−1.26
Friendships	–	–	0.19	0.94	0.44	1.24	−0.36	−1.63
Household income	–	–	−0.56	(−2.50)[a]	0.25	0.68	0.58	2.42[a]
Health	–	–	0.13	0.66	−0.42	−1.39	−0.05	−0.22
Education	–	–	0.22	1.03	0.16	0.44	−0.19	−0.83
Job	–	–	−0.07	−0.41	−0.15	−0.61	0.04	0.24
Neighbors	–	–	−0.25	−1.04	−0.13	−0.34	0.39	1.59
Public safety	–	–	−0.50	(−2.40)[a]	0.08	0.26	0.39	1.87
The condition of the environment	–	–	0.03	0.13	0.02	0.07	−0.03	−0.16
Social welfare system	–	–	0.28	1.19	0.36	0.92	−0.36	−1.44
The democratic system	–	–	−0.35	−1.85	0.51	1.62	0.17	0.81
Family life	–	–	0.17	0.62	−0.45	−0.97	−0.33	−1.08
Leisure	–	–	−0.12	−0.53	0.52	1.45	−0.13	−0.54
Spiritual life	–	–	0.05	0.26	−0.61	−1.90	0.18	0.85

(continued)

(continued)

Logit regression analysis results by country Bangladesh								
Dependent variable	Exit		Broader voice		Bureaucratic voice		Broader loyalty	
Independent variables	Coeff.	z-stat.	Coeff.	z-stat.	Coeff.	z-stat.	Coeff.	z-stat.
Happiness	–	–	0.10	0.39	−0.78	−1.69	−0.09	−0.34
(D) Trust in social institution								
Trust generally	–	–	−0.59	−1.33	0.67	0.79	0.34	0.79
Trust the central government	–	–	0.69	2.50[a]	−0.46	−1.14	−0.51	−1.84
Trust local governments	–	–	0.46	1.68	0.22	0.57	−0.48	−1.83
Trust the army	–	–	0.20	0.81	−0.91	(−2.08)[a]	0.11	0.43
Trust the legal system	–	–	0.25	1.08	0.31	0.83	−0.40	−1.66
Trust the police	–	–	0.001	0.01	−0.03	−0.08	0.19	0.87
(E) Assessment of government performance								
Worry about corruption	–	–	−0.12	−0.29	0.58	0.87	−0.17	−0.38
Worry about Economic inequality	–	–	−0.06	−0.17	0.003	0.00	0.15	0.37
Political corruption	–	–	−0.30	−1.29	−0.25	−0.62	0.57	2.21[a]
Duty to vote	–	–	0.17	0.21	−2.00	−1.64	0.72	0.83
Widespread corruption	–	–	0.20	0.81	0.29	0.67	−0.14	−0.54
No power	–	–	−0.24	−1.43	−0.46	−1.75	0.35	1.99[a]
Complicated	–	–	0.28	1.51	0.26	0.89	−0.37	−1.96
No matter whether vote	–	–	−0.20	−1.38	0.30	1.33	0.12	0.80
Stop thinking	–	–	−0.07	−0.34	0.37	1.19	−0.03	−0.15
Pay little attention	–	–	−0.001	−0.01	0.38	1.04	−0.33	−1.53
Powerful leader	–	–	0.78	3.23[b]	−1.78	(−3.28)[b]	−0.33	−1.37
Experts	–	–	−0.15	−0.58	0.25	0.62	0.07	0.26
Military government	–	–	−0.22	−0.87	0.27	0.60	0.06	0.24
Democratic political system	–	–	0.86	3.07[b]	0.55	1.15	−0.97	(−3.33)[b]

(continued)

(continued)

Logit regression analysis results by country Bangladesh								
Dependent variable	Exit		Broader voice		Bureaucratic voice		Broader loyalty	
Independent variables	Coeff.	z-stat.	Coeff.	z-stat.	Coeff.	z-stat.	Coeff.	z-stat.
(F) Satisfaction with rights								
Right to vote	–	–	0.72	2.61[b]	−0.81	−1.91	−0.27	−0.97
Right to participate in any organizations	–	–	−0.62	(−2.18)[a]	0.62	1.32	0.35	1.21
Right to gather and demonstrate	–	–	−0.03	−0.13	0.07	0.19	−0.15	−0.64
Right to be informed about government	–	–	0.34	1.34	−0.31	−0.75	−0.18	−0.69
Freedom of speech	–	–	0.50	2.06[a]	0.29	0.80	−0.61	(−2.43)[a]
Right to criticize the government	–	–	−0.58	(−2.29)[a]	1.02	2.26[a]	0.38	1.42
(H) Demographics								
Female	–	–	0.76	1.72	0.39	0.53	−1.18	(−2.55)[a]
Age	–	–	0.01	0.36	0.02	0.56	−0.03	−1.43
Level of education	–	–	0.03	0.12	0.53	1.28	−0.46	−1.68
Married	–	–	−0.13	−0.24	0.72	0.74	0.31	0.57
Unemployed	–	–	0.17	0.11	−1.62	−0.69	−1.13	−0.75
Income	–	–	0.08	1.61	−0.16	−1.93	-0.001	−0.02
(I) Region (Base = Dhaka)								
Chittagong	–	–	−0.37	−0.63	0.46	0.46	0.48	0.80
Rajshahi	–	–	−0.12	−0.18	−0.11	−0.11	−0.03	−0.05
Barisal	–	–	−0.70	−1.08	−0.80	−0.69	0.87	1.29
Khulna	–	–	−0.53	−0.88	−0.19	−0.19	0.94	1.44
Sylhet	–	–	−0.09	−0.09	0.04	0.02	0.14	0.14
(K) Rural								
Rural	–	–	1.35	2.23[a]	−0.51	−0.43	−1.72	(−2.66)[b]
Constant	–	–	−5.13	−1.04	−4.31	−0.55	3.45	0.66
n	–		304		304		304	
Pseudo R squared	–		0.2698		0.3820		0.2776	

Note [a]5% significance level; [b]1% significance level

6.5 Bhutan

Again, so few respondents in Bhutan choose the exit option that it is not possible to statistically examine the results with reliability. Therefore, no analysis is provided on exit. Respondents who choose the broader voice option also do not participate in national elections, are not proud, do not have job, do not trust the legal system, and are not satisfied with their right to participate in any organization. For those who exhibit bureaucratic voice, they also share features such as prayer, not having a good English ability, not satisfied with the social welfare system, worried about corruption, negatively assess the government performance on political corruption, view the government as powerful, view the government performance as complicated, satisfied with the right to gather and demonstrate, and are not satisfied with freedom of speech. Broader loyalty is contributed to by those who are not satisfied with the social welfare system, trust the police, assess government performance on political corruption as high, view government as powerless, and are older in age.

Summary statistics of countries Bhutan

	n	Mean	SD	Min	Max
Exit	731	0.03	0.17	0	1
Broader voice	731	0.22	0.41	0	1
Bureaucratic voice	731	0.16	0.37	0	1
Broader loyalty	731	0.60	0.49	0	1
(A) Lifestyles					
Number of public utilities	801	5.21	0.95	1	7
Homeownership	788	0.19	0.39	0	1
Number of family members	801	4.54	2.31	1	19
Pray	795	3.84	1.40	1	5
National elections	660	1.22	0.72	1	5
Local elections	678	1.42	0.89	1	5
Proud	793	3.82	0.45	1	4
Relative Standard of Living	797	3.19	0.57	1	5
(B) Exposure to globalization					
Internet	788	2.89	1.63	1	5
Living internationally	801	1.90	1.33	0	6
English ability	794	3.09	0.88	1	4
(C) Satisfaction with aspects of life					
Housing	799	4.15	0.90	1	5
Friendships	797	4.52	0.62	1	5
Household income	789	3.96	0.84	1	5
Health	795	4.38	0.81	1	5
Education	783	3.95	1.03	1	5
Job	731	4.01	0.89	1	5
Neighbors	787	4.05	0.83	1	5

(continued)

(continued)

Summary statistics of countries Bhutan					
	n	Mean	SD	Min	Max
Social welfare system	743	3.90	0.79	1	5
Family life	764	4.49	0.71	1	5
Leisure	781	4.16	0.87	1	5
Spiritual life	777	4.38	0.75	1	5
Happiness	792	4.13	0.81	1	5
(D) Trust in social institution					
Trust generally	699	0.35	0.48	0	1
Trust the central government	771	3.54	0.57	2	4
Trust local governments	750	3.30	0.63	1	4
Trust the legal system	741	3.26	0.65	1	4
Trust the police	746	3.22	0.69	1	4
(E) Assessment of government performance					
Worry about corruption	801	0.53	0.50	0	1
Worry about Economic inequality	801	0.42	0.49	0	1
Political corruption	691	2.90	0.73	1	4
Duty to vote	768	4.35	0.81	1	5
Widespread corruption	705	3.25	0.93	1	5
No power	738	3.26	1.11	1	5
Complicated	726	3.28	1.02	1	5
No matter whether vote	729	2.65	1.05	1	5
Stop thinking	703	3.09	1.12	1	5
Pay little attention	696	3.01	1.09	1	5
Powerful leader	680	2.00	0.74	1	3
Experts	655	1.87	0.61	1	3
Military government	650	1.60	0.72	1	3
Democratic political system	643	2.10	0.68	1	3
Bribe	749	8.16	2.79	1	10
(F) Satisfaction with rights					
Right to vote	726	3.24	0.75	1	4
Right to participate in any organizations	720	3.09	0.71	1	4
Right to gather and demonstrate	641	2.80	0.85	1	4
Right to be informed about government	725	3.06	0.77	1	4
Freedom of speech	714	2.95	0.89	1	4
Right to criticize the government	636	2.47	0.95	1	4
(H) Demographics					
Female	801	0.48	0.50	0	1
Age	801	35.5	10.8	20	69
Level of education	797	2.22	0.82	1	3
Married	800	0.72	0.45	0	1
Income	691	6.49	2.48	1	11

Frequency Distribution of 7 Responses and Partially Aggregated 4 Responses
Bhutan

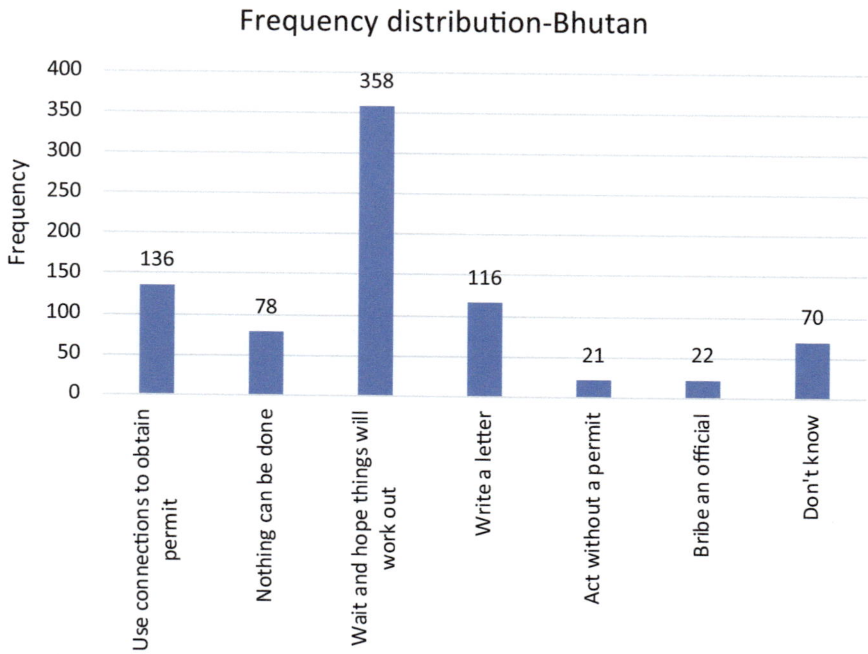

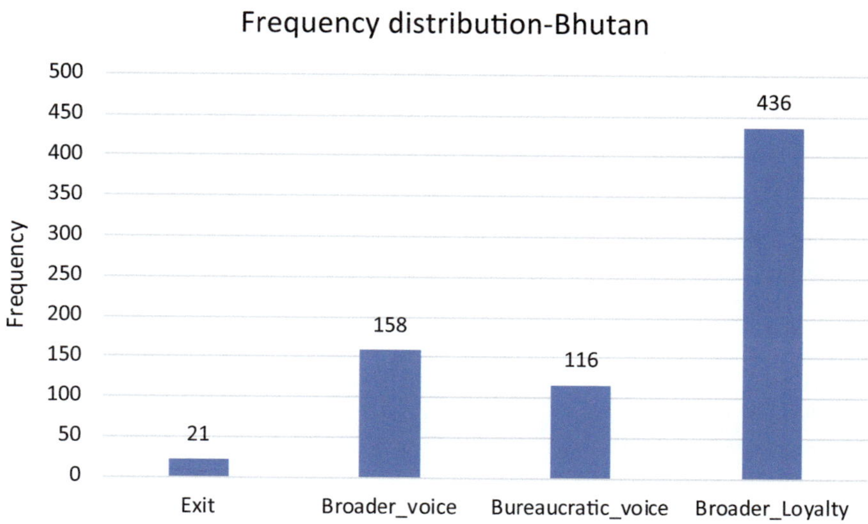

Logit regression analysis results by country Bhutan								
Dependent variables	Exit		Broader voice		Bureaucratic voice		Broader loyalty	
Independent variables	Coeff.	z-stat.	Coeff.	z-stat.	Coeff.	z-stat.	Coeff.	z-stat.
(A) Lifestyles								
Number of public utilities	–	–	−0.22	−0.81	−0.38	−1.35	0.20	0.91
Homeownership	–	–	0.47	0.76	−1.71	−1.93	0.57	1.10
Number of family members	–	–	−0.13	−1.11	0.02	0.11	−0.03	−0.30
Pray	–	–	−0.30	−1.65	0.44	2.01[a]	−0.09	−0.61
National elections	–	–	−2.55	(−2.49)[a]	0.28	0.45	0.43	1.02
Local elections	–	–	0.55	1.29	−0.32	−0.72	−0.32	−0.94
Proud	–	–	−1.47	(−2.16)[a]	0.13	0.17	0.65	1.22
Relative Standard of Living	–	–	0.08	0.18	0.63	1.16	−0.29	−0.79
(B) Exposure to globalization								
Internet	–	–	−0.02	−0.11	0.27	1.23	−0.02	−0.10
Living internationally	–	–	−0.32	−1.35	0.36	1.33	−0.14	−0.78
English ability	–	–	0.42	1.08	−1.10	(−2.51)[b]	0.35	1.14
(C) Satisfaction with aspects of life								
Housing	–	–	0.09	0.25	−0.45	−1.16	0.07	0.25
Friendships	–	–	−0.51	−1.12	0.44	0.85	0.34	0.93
Household income	–	–	−0.04	−0.10	0.58	1.23	−0.42	−1.31
Health	–	–	0.17	0.44	−0.45	−1.23	0.14	0.53
Education	–	–	0.13	0.40	0.14	0.42	−0.07	−0.27
Job	–	–	−0.73	(−2.29)[a]	−0.34	−0.91	0.41	1.53
Neighbors	–	–	−0.20	−0.47	0.05	0.10	0.08	0.23
Social welfare system	–	–	0.27	0.66	0.86	2.00[a]	−0.77	(−2.43)[a]
Family life	–	–	−0.20	−0.58	−0.13	−0.33	0.49	1.47
Leisure	–	–	0.42	1.26	−0.13	−0.42	−0.17	−0.64
Spiritual life	–	–	0.31	0.75	0.47	1.04	−0.66	−1.93
Happiness	–	–	0.07	0.18	−0.56	−1.26	0.43	1.22
(D) Trust in social institution								
Trust generally	–	–	0.42	0.84	0.63	1.11	−0.60	−1.48
Trust the central government	–	–	0.21	0.40	−0.58	−1.08	0.19	0.47
Trust local governments	–	–	1.06	1.88	0.24	0.45	−0.68	−1.61
Trust the legal system	–	–	−1.14	(−2.22)[a]	0.34	0.66	0.43	1.08
Trust the police	–	–	−0.30	−0.65	−0.50	−1.04	0.69	2.00[a]
(E) Assessment of government performance								
Worry about corruption	–	–	0.30	0.61	1.22	2.16[a]	−0.58	−1.47

(continued)

(continued)

Logit regression analysis results by country Bhutan								
Dependent variables	Exit		Broader voice		Bureaucratic voice		Broader loyalty	
Independent variables	Coeff.	z-stat.	Coeff.	z-stat.	Coeff.	z-stat.	Coeff.	z-stat.
Worry about Economic inequality	–	–	−0.13	−0.24	−0.12	−0.22	0.19	0.46
Political corruption	–	–	0.05	0.11	−1.04	(−2.25)[a]	0.68	2.08[a]
Duty to vote	–	–	0.84	1.95	−0.30	−0.69	−0.17	−0.55
Widespread corruption	–	–	−0.21	−0.56	0.58	1.40	−0.11	−0.37
No power	–	–	−0.09	−0.26	−1.57	(−3.63)[b]	0.85	2.98[b]
Complicated	–	–	−0.40	−1.08	1.06	2.73[b]	−0.33	−1.23
No matter whether vote	–	–	0.15	0.49	−0.04	−0.13	−0.10	−0.40
Stop thinking	–	–	0.06	0.21	−0.08	−0.27	0.07	0.30
Pay little attention	–	–	0.23	0.71	−0.65	−1.62	0.10	0.37
Powerful leader	–	–	−0.52	−1.47	−0.07	−0.18	0.38	1.28
Experts	–	–	−0.25	−0.55	−0.07	−0.13	−0.09	−0.24
Military government	–	–	0.45	1.28	0.19	0.50	−0.36	−1.26
Democratic political system	–	–	−0.26	−0.62	0.26	0.64	−0.01	−0.03
Bribe	–	–	0.10	1.00	0.06	0.65	0.01	0.13
(F) Satisfaction with rights								
Right to vote	–	–	−0.02	−0.04	−0.05	−0.09	0.47	1.19
Right to participate in any organizations	–	–	1.35	(2.53)[a]	−0.28	−0.51	−0.51	−1.26
Right to gather and demonstrate	–	–	−0.57	−1.30	1.19	2.16[a]	−0.35	−0.99
Right to be informed about government	–	–	−0.07	−0.13	0.30	0.54	−0.15	−0.38
Freedom of speech	–	–	0.45	1.06	−1.02	(−2.14)[a]	−0.01	−0.03
Right to criticize the government	–	–	0.11	0.39	−0.01	−0.02	−0.02	−0.09
(H) Demographics								
Female	–	–	−0.95	−1.85	−0.60	−1.17	0.70	1.82
Age	–	–	−0.05	−1.87	−0.02	−0.66	0.05	2.21[a]
Level of education	–	–	0.10	0.23	0.25	0.51	−0.07	−0.22
Married	–	–	0.07	0.12	−0.92	−1.54	0.68	1.35
Income	–	–	0.08	0.68	0.00	−0.03	−0.02	−0.25
Constant	–	–	4.06	0.79	2.92	0.49	−7.61	−1.87
n	–		221		221		221	
Pseudo R squared	–		0.2711		0.2995		0.2421	

Note [a]5% significance level; [b]1% significance level

6.6 Brunei

As so few respondents choose the exit option, it is not possible to statistically analyze it. For the broader voice option, respondents shared the following attributes: prayer, are satisfied with leisure, assessment of government performance is high on combatting bribery practices, are male, and are not old. For those selecting the bureaucratic voice, they as a group trust in general, assess government performance as high for worrying about economic inequality, are older in age, have a high level of education, are not married, and are rural. In the category of broader loyalty, the respondents pray, have a relatively high standard of living, are proficient in English, are satisfied with leisure, trust generally, assess of government performances on economic equality as high, and are female. To sum up, the citizens are one of the most satisfied among this group of 32 societies, who predominantly exhibit broader loyalty. In descending order, bureaucratic voice comes second. Bureaucratic voice is one-tenth of broader loyalty.

Summary statistics of countries Brunei

	n	Mean	SD	Min	Max
Exit	727	0.00	0.04	0	1
Broader voice	727	0.07	0.26	0	1
Bureaucratic voice	727	0.15	0.36	0	1
Broader loyalty	727	0.77	0.42	0	1
(A) Lifestyles					
Public water supply	804	1.00	0.04	0	1
Electricity	804	0.99	0.08	0	1
LPG	804	0.11	0.32	0	1
Homeownership	802	0.55	0.50	0	1
Number of family members	804	7.63	4.15	1	30
Pray	799	4.29	1.18	1	5
Proud	774	3.84	0.40	1	4
Relative Standard of Living	803	3.12	0.46	1	5
(B) Exposure to globalization					
Living internationally	804	2.85	1.24	0	6
English ability	801	2.54	0.84	1	4
(C) Satisfaction with aspects of life					
Housing	803	4.56	0.67	2	5

(continued)

(continued)

Summary statistics of countries Brunei					
	n	Mean	SD	Min	Max
Friendships	804	4.64	0.52	2	5
Household income	804	4.42	0.73	2	5
Health	804	4.62	0.57	2	5
Education	800	4.54	0.64	2	5
Job	755	4.38	0.77	1	5
Neighbors	801	4.54	0.59	1	5
Public safety	803	4.56	0.59	2	5
The condition of the environment	804	4.52	0.58	2	5
Social welfare system	798	4.54	0.57	2	5
Family life	802	4.63	0.50	3	5
Leisure	801	4.50	0.66	1	5
Happiness	804	4.45	0.64	2	5
(D) Trust in social institution					
Trust generally	794	0.20	0.40	0	1
Trust the army	789	3.56	0.55	1	4
Trust the legal system	795	3.57	0.53	2	4
(E) Assessment of government performance					
Worry about corruption	804	0.19	0.39	0	1
Worry about Economic inequality	804	0.21	0.41	0	1
Bribe	774	9.62	1.08	1	10
(H) Demographics					
Female	804	0.50	0.50	0	1
Age	804	34.4	10.0	20	59
Level of education	804	1.91	0.63	1	3
Married	802	0.67	0.47	0	1
Unemployed	801	0.07	0.26	0	1
Income	708	2.60	1.43	1	9
No religion	803	0.01	0.08	0	1
(K) Urban					
Urban	804	0.80	0.40	0	1

Frequency Distribution of 7 Responses and Partially Aggregated 4 Responses

Brunei

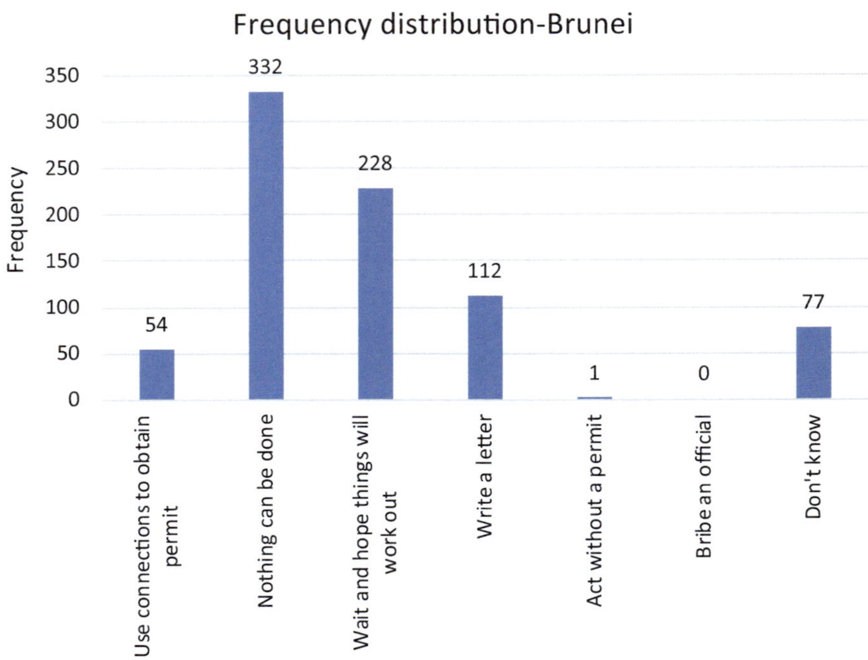

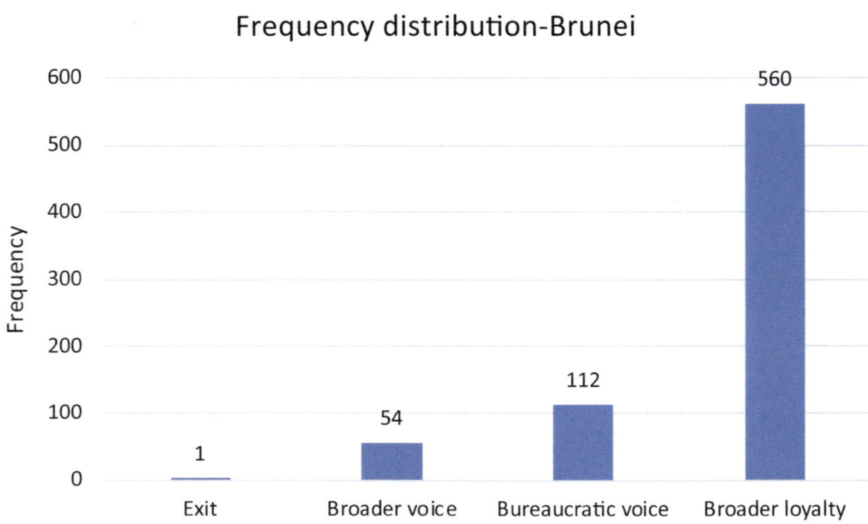

Logit regression analysis results by country Brunei								
Dependent variable	Exit		Broader voice		Bureaucratic voice		Broader loyalty	
Independent variables	Coeff.	z-stat.	Coeff.	z-stat.	Coeff.	z-stat.	Coeff.	z-stat.
(A) Lifestyles								
LPG	–	–	−0.35	−0.50	0.07	0.15	0.20	0.48
Homeownership	–	–	0.65	1.49	0.09	0.32	−0.34	−1.35
Number of family members	–	–	−0.01	−0.25	−0.01	−0.21	0.01	0.30
Pray	–	–	−0.39	(−2.49)[a]	−0.23	−1.89	0.34	3.22[b]
Proud	–	–	−0.38	−0.87	−0.09	−0.24	0.17	0.54
Relative Standard of Living	–	–	0.63	1.75	0.26	0.81	−0.55	(−2.19)[a]
(B) Exposure to globalization								
Living internationally	–	–	0.22	1.27	−0.03	−0.26	−0.06	−0.60
English ability	–	–	−0.33	−1.13	−0.37	−1.65	0.41	2.19[a]
(C) Satisfaction with aspects of life								
Housing	–	–	0.27	0.62	−0.07	−0.25	−0.10	−0.41
Friendships	–	–	−0.02	−0.03	0.05	0.11	0.04	0.11
Household income	–	–	0.04	0.12	0.47	1.60	−0.36	−1.50
Health	–	–	0.07	0.14	−0.09	−0.28	0.13	0.46
Education	–	–	0.35	0.92	0.05	0.14	−0.13	−0.50
Job	–	–	−0.25	−0.73	0.12	0.46	−0.03	−0.15
Neighbors	–	–	−0.07	−0.14	0.18	0.54	−0.26	−0.88
Public safety	–	–	−0.05	−0.12	−0.51	−1.58	0.34	1.20
The condition of the environment	–	–	0.69	1.38	0.03	0.07	−0.40	−1.24
Social welfare system	–	–	−0.24	−0.46	−0.41	−1.05	0.48	1.46
Family life	–	–	−0.31	−0.58	0.29	0.68	−0.10	−0.27
Leisure	–	–	−0.81	(−2.57)[a]	−0.10	−0.32	0.62	2.60[b]
Happiness	–	–	−0.24	−0.70	−0.12	−0.51	0.16	0.81
(D) Trust in social institution								
Trust generally	–	–	−0.58	−1.12	−0.87	(−2.06)[a]	0.91	2.65[b]
Trust the army	–	–	−0.31	−0.69	0.15	0.41	0.11	0.35
Trust the legal system	–	–	0.65	1.37	−0.64	−1.85	0.20	0.66
(E) Assessment of government performance								
Worry about corruption	–	–	−0.31	−0.58	0.63	1.92	−0.41	−1.42
Worry about Economic inequality	–	–	0.19	0.38	1.57	5.25[b]	−1.36	(−5.08)[b]
Bribe	–	–	−0.26	(−2.04)[a]	−0.06	−0.50	0.19	1.96

(continued)

(continued)

Logit regression analysis results by country Brunei								
Dependent variable	Exit		Broader voice		Bureaucratic voice		Broader loyalty	
Independent variables	Coeff.	z-stat.	Coeff.	z-stat.	Coeff.	z-stat.	Coeff.	z-stat.
(H) Demographics								
Female	–	–	−0.99	(−2.37)[a]	−0.43	−1.56	0.67	2.76[b]
Age	–	–	−0.05	(−2.10)[a]	0.05	2.89[b]	−0.01	−0.89
Level of education	–	–	−0.03	−0.08	0.73	(2.55)[a]	−0.46	−1.95
Married	–	–	0.95	1.91	−0.92	(−2.66)[b]	0.35	1.18
Unemployed	–	–	–	–	−0.59	−0.89	1.14	1.73
Income	–	–	0.14	0.92	0.08	0.72	−0.09	−0.97
No religion	–	–	–	–	0.47	0.28	−0.51	−0.32
(K) Urban								
Urban	–	–	0.65	1.10	−0.73	(−2.25)[a]	0.33	1.12
Constant	–	–	2.79	0.89	0.19	0.07	−3.48	−1.61
n	–		520		552		552	
Pseudo R squared	–		0.2022		0.1989		0.1792	

Note [a]5% significance level; [b]1% significance level

6.7 Cambodia

Among the Cambodians who choose the exit option, their general attributes are living internationally and being not satisfied with public safety. Those who selected the broader voice option, also share similar views on enjoying the public water supply, having a relatively high standard of living, living internationally, assessing government as powerless, assessing government performance as not complicated, residing in the Palin region, and not residing in the Tongle Sap region. In the category of bureaucratic voice, respondents enjoy housing, enjoy public safety, assess government as having power, and assess government as best run by experts. This group is also not satisfied with their right to be informed about government, is not satisfied with their right to criticize government, is not married, and does not reside in the Palin region. For those who choose the broader loyalty option, they enjoy the public water supply, assess government performance as complicated, assess government as best run by experts, are female, and reside in the Tongle Sap region. To sum up, citizens opt for broader loyalty and bureaucratic voice. Exit and broader voice are relatively small. This may well be because expressing broader voice and exit is considered potentially dangerous. Those who reside in the Tongle Sap region are vulnerable to floods in the wet season, and they tend to not express a "voice" and to remain loyalty. The Tongle Sap is Cambodia's heartland. The lake grows from 2,590 square kilometers in the dry season to 24,605 square kilometers in the wet season. But it produces rice and fish, two dietary staples for Cambodians.

Summary statistics of countries Cambodia

	n	Mean	SD	Min	Max
Exit	1817	0.012	0.11	0	1
Broader voice	1817	0.389	0.49	0	1
Bureaucratic voice	1817	0.180	0.38	0	1
Broader loyalty	1817	0.419	0.49	0	1
(A) Lifestyles					
Public water supply	1824	0.59	0.49	0	1
Electricity	1824	0.87	0.33	0	1
LPG	1824	0.16	0.37	0	1
Homeownership	1824	0.85	0.36	0	1
Number of family members	1824	5.43	2.31	1	20
Pray	1824	2.91	1.43	1	5
National elections	1736	4.50	1.12	1	5
Local elections	1811	4.25	1.47	1	5
Proud	1824	3.80	0.45	1	4
Relative Standard of Living	1824	2.88	0.60	1	5
(B) Exposure to globalization					
Living internationally	1824	1.51	0.84	0	6
English ability	1819	1.55	0.74	1	4
(C) Satisfaction with aspects of life					
Housing	1824	3.81	1.08	1	5
Friendships	1824	3.74	0.87	1	5
Household income	1823	3.12	1.02	1	5
Health	1824	3.33	1.06	1	5
Education	1823	3.61	1.07	1	5
Job	1754	3.51	1.07	1	5
Neighbors	1823	3.72	0.88	1	5
Public safety	1822	3.05	1.07	1	5
The condition of the environment	1817	3.00	0.94	1	5
Social welfare system	1811	3.25	1.06	1	5
The democratic system	1788	3.43	1.03	1	5
Family life	1824	4.00	0.97	1	5
Leisure	1823	3.55	0.98	1	5
Happiness	1824	3.17	0.71	1	5
(D) Trust in social institution					
Trust generally	1824	0.04	0.21	0	1
Trust the central government	1779	2.83	0.74	1	4
Trust local governments	1804	2.79	0.75	1	4
Trust the army	1767	2.85	0.83	1	4

(continued)

(continued)

Summary statistics of countries Cambodia					
	n	Mean	SD	Min	Max
Trust the legal system	1802	2.53	0.91	1	4
Trust the police	1811	2.42	0.83	1	4
(E) Assessment of government performance					
Worry about corruption	1824	0.83	0.38	0	1
Worry about Economic inequality	1824	0.32	0.47	0	1
Political corruption	1787	1.84	0.72	1	4
Duty to vote	1823	4.65	0.54	1	5
Widespread corruption	1812	3.53	1.30	1	5
No power	1818	3.62	1.02	1	5
Complicated	1803	3.63	0.97	1	5
No matter whether vote	1819	2.46	1.21	1	5
Stop thinking	1808	3.17	1.26	1	5
Pay little attention	1812	3.53	1.03	1	5
Powerful leader	1801	1.17	0.42	1	3
Experts	1813	2.42	0.59	1	3
Military government	1766	1.39	0.58	1	3
Democratic political system	1799	2.49	0.56	1	3
Bribe	1820	8.91	1.94	1	10
(F) Satisfaction with rights					
Right to vote	1823	3.62	0.61	1	4
Right to participate in any organizations	1810	3.35	0.63	1	4
Right to gather and demonstrate	1803	2.24	0.91	1	4
Right to be informed about government	1799	3.09	0.78	1	4
Freedom of speech	1819	3.19	0.86	1	4
Right to criticize the government	1802	2.58	0.97	1	4
(H) Demographics					
Female	1824	0.52	0.50	0	1
Age	1824	36.09	11.48	20	69
Level of education	1824	1.51	0.69	1	3
Married	1824	0.67	0.47	0	1
Unemployed	1823	0.06	0.23	0	1
Income	1824	4.66	2.52	1	12
(I) Region (Base = Plain region)					
Coastal region	1824	0.14	0.35	0	1
Tonle Sap region	1824	0.39	0.49	0	1
(L) Yearly dummy variable (Base = 2004)					
2007	1824	0.55	0.50	0	1

Frequency Distribution of 7 Responses and Partially Aggregated 4 Responses Cambodia

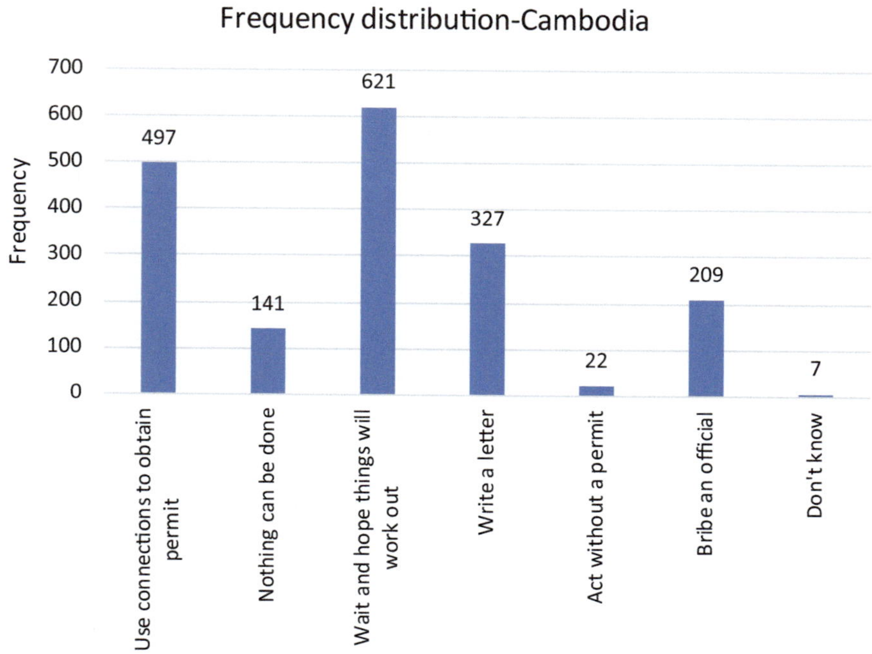

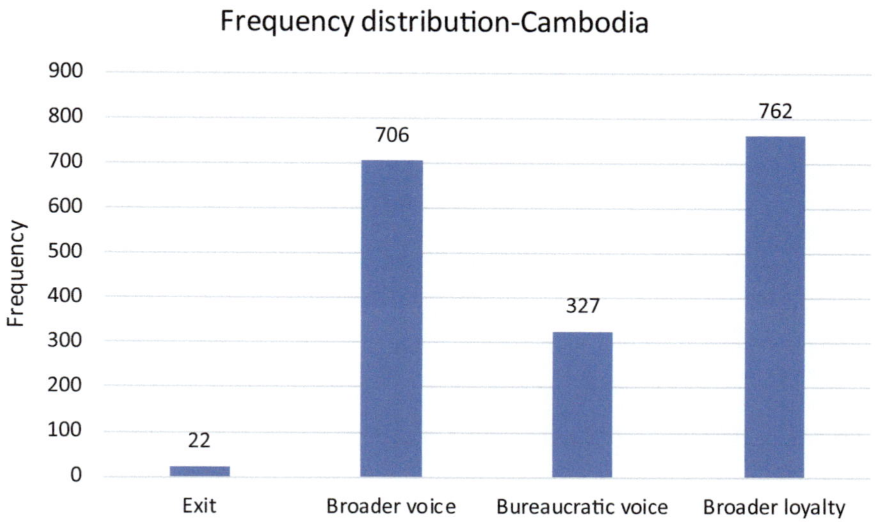

Logit regression analysis results by country Cambodia								
Dependent variable	Exit		Broader voice		Bureaucratic voice		Broader loyalty	
Independent variables	Coeff.	z-stat.	Coeff.	z-stat.	Coeff.	z-stat.	Coeff.	z-stat.
(A) Lifestyles								
Public water supply	0.14	0.16	0.36	2.08[a]	0.22	0.99	−0.46	(−2.74)[b]
Electricity	−1.52	−1.76	0.04	0.18	−0.13	−0.51	0.12	0.6
LPG	0.59	0.71	−0.25	−1.30	0.31	1.48	0.02	0.09
Homeownership	−0.47	−0.63	−0.14	−0.82	−0.06	−0.28	0.21	1.24
Number of family members	0.22	1.86	0.02	0.82	−0.05	−1.36	0.00	0.02
Pray	0.39	1.40	0.03	0.59	−0.06	−0.78	0.00	−0.05
National elections	−0.07	−0.23	−0.09	−1.36	0.10	1.19	0.03	0.43
Local elections	0.20	0.65	0.00	0.04	0.01	0.09	−0.01	−0.17
Proud	−0.01	−0.01	0.20	1.46	−0.11	−0.63	−0.15	−1.08
Relative Standard of Living	−0.54	−1.19	0.31	2.67[b]	−0.18	−1.22	−0.13	−1.22
(B) Exposure to globalization								
Living internationally	−1.03	(−2.32)[a]	0.17	2.16[a]	−0.04	−0.45	−0.12	−1.50
English ability	0.09	0.17	−0.17	−1.42	0.16	1.15	0.03	0.30
(C) Satisfaction with aspects of life								
Housing	−0.18	−0.64	−0.12	−1.94	0.18	2.19[a]	0.02	0.38
Friendships	−0.62	−1.51	0.03	0.44	0.03	0.36	−0.03	−0.43
Household income	−0.33	−1.08	−0.05	−0.77	0.02	0.21	0.05	0.73
Health	0.24	0.81	−0.01	−0.23	0.07	0.87	−0.04	−0.61
Education	0.42	1.28	−0.06	−0.94	0.02	0.24	0.03	0.49
Job	0.26	0.90	0.00	−0.04	−0.04	−0.55	0.03	0.42
Neighbors	0.004	0.01	−0.05	−0.60	−0.08	−0.90	0.10	1.32
Public safety	−0.80	(−2.46)[a]	−0.08	−1.26	0.20	2.50[a]	0.00	−0.04
The condition of the environment	0.50	1.43	0.03	0.38	−0.12	−1.28	0.01	0.16
Social welfare system	0.24	0.83	−0.12	−1.78	0.08	0.96	0.04	0.69
The democratic system	−0.22	−0.78	0.10	1.49	−0.07	−0.84	−0.04	−0.69
Family life	0.63	1.71	−0.04	−0.64	0.05	0.60	−0.02	−0.33
Leisure	−0.36	−1.15	0.02	0.35	−0.01	−0.11	0.00	−0.01
Happiness	0.38	0.87	−0.13	−1.41	0.18	1.55	−0.01	−0.09
(D) Trust in social institution								
Trust generally	−0.17	−0.13	0.44	1.63	−0.45	−1.17	−0.23	−0.85
Trust the central government	0.15	0.32	−0.05	−0.50	−0.03	−0.21	0.06	0.59
Trust local governments	−0.08	−0.18	0.04	0.40	−0.21	−1.73	0.10	1.02
Trust the army	−0.35	−0.97	0.05	0.61	0.02	0.19	−0.05	−0.58
Trust the legal system	−0.49	−1.33	−0.03	−0.38	0.03	0.26	0.05	0.66
Trust the police	0.18	0.43	0.07	0.75	−0.03	−0.31	−0.05	−0.54

(continued)

(continued)

Logit regression analysis results by country Cambodia								
Dependent variable	Exit		Broader voice		Bureaucratic voice		Broader loyalty	
Independent variables	Coeff.	z-stat.	Coeff.	z-stat.	Coeff.	z-stat.	Coeff.	z-stat.
(E) Assessment of government performance								
Worry about corruption	0.55	0.62	0.004	0.03	0.13	0.64	−0.08	−0.49
Worry about Economic inequality	−0.10	−0.17	0.17	1.33	0.09	0.57	−0.22	−1.72
Political corruption	0.31	0.80	−0.10	−1.14	0.01	0.08	0.12	1.34
Duty to vote	0.60	0.88	0.01	0.09	−0.12	−0.82	0.02	0.17
Widespread corruption	−0.09	−0.40	0.07	1.39	−0.001	−0.02	−0.07	−1.30
No power	0.46	1.49	0.14	2.21[a]	−0.19	(−2.41)[a]	−0.03	−0.52
Complicated	−0.45	−1.36	−0.20	(−2.75)[b]	0.01	0.06	0.21	2.92[b]
No matter whether vote	−0.60	−1.98	−0.06	−1.04	−0.06	−0.88	0.12	2.39[a]
Stop thinking	−0.46	−1.72	0.04	0.70	0.03	0.41	−0.03	−0.60
Pay little attention	0.27	0.90	−0.005	−0.07	−0.04	−0.47	0.02	0.31
Powerful leader	−0.09	−0.12	−0.21	−1.39	0.19	1.09	0.10	0.73
Experts	0.31	0.63	0.13	1.28	0.28	2.14[a]	−0.32	(−3.17)[b]
Military government	0.47	0.96	−0.04	−0.38	0.12	0.92	−0.08	−0.77
Democratic political system	0.20	0.38	−0.02	−0.16	−0.18	−1.29	0.11	0.93
Bribe	0.03	0.19	−0.04	−1.45	0.02	0.60	0.03	0.86
(F) Satisfaction with rights								
Right to vote	−0.42	−0.88	−0.18	−1.66	0.17	1.22	0.12	1.03
Right to participate in any organizations	−0.58	−1.09	−0.04	−0.35	−0.05	−0.39	0.07	0.65
Right to gather and demonstrate	0.20	0.59	−0.02	−0.35	0.10	1.11	−0.06	−0.83
Right to be informed about government	−0.25	−0.52	0.13	1.42	−0.31	(−2.54)[a]	0.05	0.59
Freedom of speech	0.58	1.27	−0.02	−0.26	0.09	0.77	−0.05	−0.60
Right to criticize the government	0.43	1.10	−0.04	−0.52	0.21	2.34[a]	−0.09	−1.25
(H) Demographics								
Female	−0.44	−0.70	−0.43	(−3.34)[b]	−0.08	−0.49	0.47	3.77[b]
Age	−0.02	−0.75	−0.01	−0.78	0.0003	0.04	0.00	0.76
Level of education	0.64	1.05	0.11	0.92	−0.11	−0.72	−0.07	−0.62
Married	0.52	0.70	0.30	1.98	−0.56	(−3.25)[b]	0.08	0.53
Unemployed			0.12	0.40	−0.11	−0.30	0.06	0.20
Income	0.12	1.01	−0.01	−0.48	0.01	0.33	0.00	0.12
(I) Region (Base = Coastal region)								
Plain region	−0.65	−0.52	0.72	3.35[b]	−0.75	(−2.62)[b]	−0.24	−1.08
Tonle Sap region	−0.36	−0.41	−0.45	(−2.42)[a]	−0.13	−0.57	0.54	3.04[b]

(continued)

(continued)

Logit regression analysis results by country Cambodia								
Dependent variable	Exit		Broader voice		Bureaucratic voice		Broader loyalty	
Independent variables	Coeff.	z-stat.	Coeff.	z-stat.	Coeff.	z-stat.	Coeff.	z-stat.
(L) Yearly dummy variable (Base = 2004)								
2007	−0.68	−0.72	−0.95	(−4.83)[b]	0.72	2.96[b]	0.48	2.55[a]
Constant	−6.84	−1.14	1.13	0.96	−1.94	−1.33	−1.88	−1.64
n	1428		1427		1427		1427	
Pseudo R squared	0.2987		0.1171		0.0936		0.0970	

Note [a]5% significance level; [b]1% significance level

6.8 China

Those who choose the exit option include those who have a relatively high standard of living, are not living internationally, are highly educated, do not trust others generally, trust local government, do not trust the legal system, and are not very old. The number of respondents who choose the exit option is high enough to do statistical testing. Those who register a broader voice include those who do not participate in local elections, are not highly educated, are satisfied with their job, do not assess negatively corruption, do not assess negatively bribery, are male, and are married. Those who choose a bureaucratic voice include those who have a large family, do not participate in national elections, participate in local elections, do not trust the police, assess positively government efforts to deal with political corruption, agree that government pays attention, have lukewarm assessment of government action to halt bribery, and are satisfied about the right to gather and demonstrate. Those who choose broader loyalty include those whose family is small and have members who are very old in years,

The profiles of each option make sense: Exit is attractive to poor, young, low risk, males. Broader voice is attractive to those without employment, do not participate in local elections, and are strongly negative about political corruption and bribery. Those who are male and married are among those who are attracted to the broader voice option. Bureaucratic voice is attractive to those who have a big family, participate in local elections, do not trust the police, and have a lukewarm view of corruption and bribery. Broader loyalty is attractive to those whose family is small in size (alone), and who are old. All four options have good profiles. Those who choose bureaucratic voice, ironically, seem to convey some Chinese characteristics of popular behavior patterns at the grassroot level.

Summary Statistics of Countries China

	n	Mean	SD	Min	Max
Exit	2975	0.026	0.16	0	1
Broader voice	2975	0.286	0.45	0	1
Bureaucratic voice	2975	0.237	0.43	0	1
Broader loyalty	2975	0.450	0.50	0	1
(A) Lifestyles					
Number of public utilities	3000	5.13	1.20	0	7
Homeownership	2972	0.74	0.44	0	1
Number of family members	3000	3.61	1.49	1	13
Pray	2996	1.53	1.00	1	5
National elections	2034	2.57	1.39	1	5
Local elections	2447	2.83	1.43	1	5
Proud	2986	3.39	0.75	1	4
Relative Standard of Living	2994	2.86	0.67	1	5
(B) Exposure to globalization					
Internet	2967	2.27	1.60	1	5
Living internationally	3000	0.46	0.74	0	6
English ability	2994	1.51	0.65	1	4
(C) Satisfaction with aspects of life					
Housing	2991	3.38	1.00	1	5
Friendships	2984	3.85	0.80	1	5
Household income	2988	3.12	0.87	1	5
Health	2991	3.72	0.94	1	5
Education	2977	3.25	0.93	1	5
Job	2932	3.17	0.99	1	5
Neighbors	2986	3.61	0.83	1	5
Public safety	2981	3.09	0.98	1	5
The condition of the environment	2980	3.22	0.92	1	5
Social welfare system	2961	2.72	1.05	1	5
The democratic system	2956	3.00	0.95	1	5
Family life	2984	3.65	0.88	1	5
Leisure	2977	3.20	0.93	1	5
Spiritual life	2977	3.40	0.93	1	5
Happiness	2997	3.72	0.86	1	5
(D) Trust in social institution					
Trust generally	2987	0.64	0.48	0	1
Trust the central government	2946	3.28	0.74	1	4
Trust local governments	2927	2.75	0.78	1	4
Trust the army	2909	3.20	0.77	1	4
Trust the legal system	2929	2.79	0.75	1	4
Trust the police	2949	2.72	0.74	1	4

(continued)

(continued)

Summary Statistics of Countries China					
	n	Mean	SD	Min	Max
(E) Assessment of government performance					
Worry about corruption	3000	0.41	0.49	0	1
Worry about Economic inequality	3000	0.35	0.48	0	1
Political corruption	2979	1.95	0.76	1	4
Duty to vote	2988	4.19	0.71	1	5
Widespread corruption	2987	3.70	1.16	1	5
No power	2975	3.59	0.95	1	5
Complicated	2973	3.53	0.85	1	5
No matter whether vote	2970	2.99	1.00	1	5
Stop thinking	2978	3.20	1.04	1	5
Pay little attention	2971	3.38	1.01	1	5
Powerful leader	2959	1.26	0.52	1	3
Experts	2965	2.13	0.60	1	3
Military government	2957	1.70	0.70	1	3
Democratic political system	2955	2.32	0.58	1	3
Bribe	2993	9.12	1.87	1	10
(F) Satisfaction with rights					
Right to vote	2988	2.67	0.88	1	4
Right to participate in any organizations	2965	2.56	0.81	1	4
Right to gather and demonstrate	2767	2.39	0.86	1	4
Right to be informed about government	2959	2.24	0.87	1	4
Freedom of speech	2971	2.76	0.85	1	4
Right to criticize the government	2897	2.29	0.87	1	4
(H) Demographics					
Female	3000	0.49	0.50	0	1
Age	3000	40.27	12.43	20	69
Level of education	3000	1.84	0.83	1	3
Married	3000	0.79	0.41	0	1
Unemployed	3000	0.07	0.26	0	1
Income	2986	3.09	3.10	1	20
No religion	2965	0.80	0.40	0	1
(K) Rural					
Rural	3000	0.44	0.50	0	1
(L) Yearly dummy variable (Base = 2006)					
2008	3000	0.33	0.47	0	1

Frequency Distribution of 7 Responses and Partially Aggregated 4 Responses China

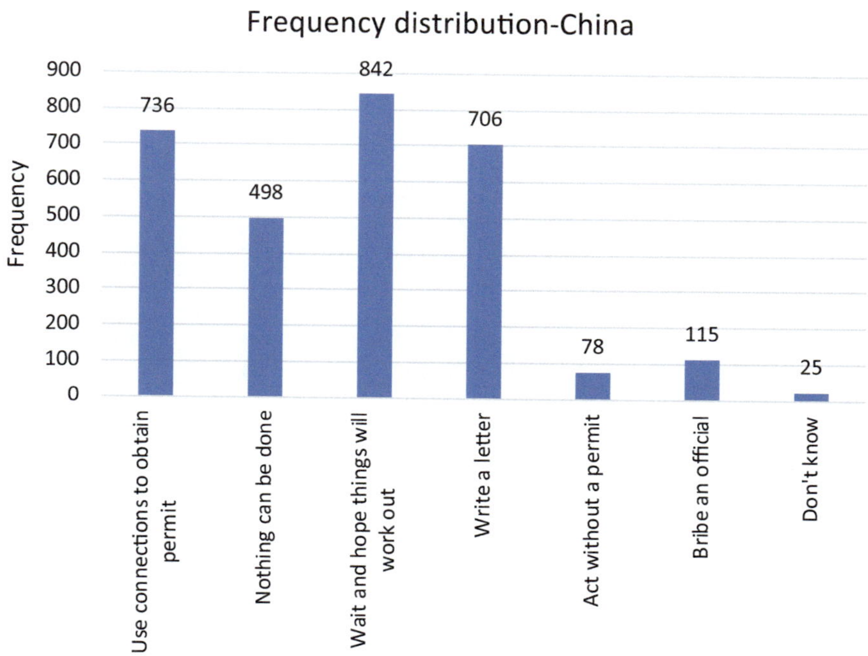

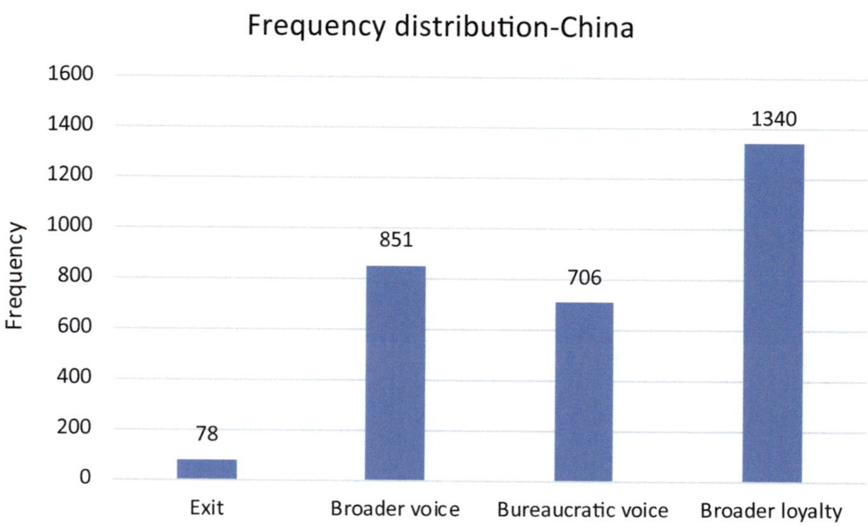

Logit regression analysis results by country China								
Dependent variable	Exit		Broader voice		Bureaucratic voice		Broader loyalty	
Independent variables	Coeff.	z-stat.	Coeff.	z-stat.	Coeff.	z-stat.	Coeff.	z-stat.
(A) Lifestyles								
Number of public utilities	0.24	1.05	0.08	1.17	0.02	0.31	−0.07	−1.19
Homeownership	0.17	0.30	−0.16	−1.08	−0.08	−0.43	0.18	1.32
Number of family members	0.07	0.48	−0.02	−0.39	0.13	2.59[b]	−0.09	(−2.09)[a]
Pray	−0.03	−0.13	−0.09	−1.21	−0.02	−0.21	0.09	1.42
National elections	0.22	1.11	0.09	1.60	−0.17	(−2.59)[b]	0.03	0.52
Local elections	0.16	0.82	−0.19	(−3.20)[b]	0.31	4.60[b]	−0.06	−1.10
Proud	0.24	0.73	−0.17	−1.87	0.12	1.07	0.06	0.76
Relative Standard of Living	1.03	2.46[a]	0.01	0.09	0.03	0.22	−0.08	−0.78
(B) Exposure to globalization								
Internet	−0.35	−1.54	0.01	0.20	0.07	1.00	−0.03	−0.64
Living internationally	−1.26	(−2.56)[a]	−0.04	−0.44	0.08	0.77	0.04	0.44
English ability	−0.42	−0.85	−0.20	−1.46	0.05	0.30	0.14	1.14
(C) Satisfaction with aspects of life								
Housing	0.28	1.07	−0.02	−0.31	0.07	0.77	−0.04	−0.64
Friendships	0.43	1.23	−0.04	−0.41	0.06	0.50	−0.04	−0.41
Household income	−0.78	(−2.20)[a]	0.18	1.78	−0.19	−1.63	0.03	0.36
Health	0.04	0.15	−0.03	−0.34	0.06	0.61	−0.01	−0.12
Education	1.13	3.47[b]	0.09	0.95	−0.01	−0.11	−0.15	−1.78
Job	−0.03	−0.10	−0.18	(−2.08)[a]	0.09	0.99	0.09	1.15
Neighbors	0.09	0.28	0.05	0.61	0.02	0.19	−0.07	−0.83
Public safety	−0.21	−0.73	−0.03	−0.33	0.04	0.43	0.01	0.17
The condition of the environment	−0.25	−0.94	−0.15	−1.62	0.06	0.55	0.08	0.93
Social welfare system	−0.23	−0.74	0.13	1.52	−0.03	−0.33	−0.06	−0.75
The democratic system	0.04	0.13	−0.07	−0.82	−0.13	−1.33	0.14	1.79
Family life	−0.56	−1.71	0.13	1.43	0.07	0.63	−0.12	−1.45
Leisure	−0.41	−1.27	−0.04	−0.41	0.09	0.88	−0.01	−0.07
Spiritual life	0.11	0.32	−0.04	−0.36	0.13	1.22	−0.08	−0.89
Happiness	−0.29	−1.01	0.01	0.15	−0.004	−0.04	0.02	0.27
(D) Trust in social institution								
Trust generally	−1.28	(−2.64)[b]	−0.11	−0.84	0.20	1.21	0.10	0.80
Trust the central government	−0.11	−0.30	−0.03	−0.32	0.12	1.03	−0.06	−0.67

(continued)

(continued)

Logit regression analysis results by country China								
Dependent variable	Exit		Broader voice		Bureaucratic voice		Broader loyalty	
Independent variables	Coeff.	z-stat.	Coeff.	z-stat.	Coeff.	z-stat.	Coeff.	z-stat.
Trust local governments	1.02	2.64[b]	−0.07	−0.70	−0.0003	0.00	−0.01	−0.14
Trust the army	−0.41	−1.18	−0.13	−1.43	0.07	0.61	0.10	1.13
Trust the legal system	−0.73	(−2.07)[a]	−0.07	−0.71	−0.01	−0.06	0.13	1.43
Trust the police	0.49	1.20	0.17	1.66	−0.27	(−2.21)[a]	0.01	0.09
(E) Assessment of government performance								
Worry about corruption	0.47	1.00	−0.03	−0.24	0.27	1.81	−0.17	−1.38
Worry about Economic inequality	0.26	0.55	−0.12	−0.86	−0.10	−0.61	0.16	1.26
Political corruption	0.28	0.79	−0.30	(−2.93)[b]	0.31	2.76[b]	0.04	0.47
Duty to vote	0.10	0.29	0.04	0.44	−0.21	−1.86	0.08	0.92
Widespread corruption	0.12	0.53	0.00	0.06	0.06	0.85	−0.06	−1.09
No power	−0.31	−1.05	0.05	0.66	−0.04	−0.41	−0.04	−0.53
Complicated	−0.22	−0.68	0.13	1.54	−0.12	−1.23	−0.02	−0.24
No matter whether vote	0.08	0.30	−0.11	−1.45	0.02	0.25	0.04	0.61
Stop thinking	−0.004	−0.01	0.17	2.08[a]	−0.01	−0.16	–	–
Pay little attention	0.02	0.05	0.02	0.24	−0.28	(−2.91)[b]	0.12	1.76
Powerful leader	−0.38	−0.70	−0.02	−0.19	−0.06	−0.37	0.07	0.59
Experts	0.28	0.68	−0.06	−0.51	−0.02	−0.12	0.01	0.10
Military government	0.31	0.97	−0.18	−1.77	0.01	0.12	0.09	1.00
Democratic political system	−0.71	−1.73	0.02	0.16	0.10	0.74	−0.03	−0.25
Bribe	−0.01	−0.06	−0.11	(−3.07)[b]	0.16	3.04[b]	0.01	0.32
(F) Satisfaction with rights								
Right to vote	−0.40	−1.05	−0.15	−1.45	0.13	1.05	0.08	0.87
Right to participate in any organizations	−0.23	−0.58	0.08	0.73	−0.02	−0.14	−0.03	−0.28
Right to gather and demonstrate	−0.10	−0.25	−0.07	−0.67	0.26	2.09[a]	−0.09	−0.92
Right to be informed about government	0.07	0.20	−0.07	−0.70	−0.13	−1.18	0.16	1.87

(continued)

(continued)

Logit regression analysis results by country China								
Dependent variable	Exit		Broader voice		Bureaucratic voice		Broader loyalty	
Independent variables	Coeff.	z-stat.	Coeff.	z-stat.	Coeff.	z-stat.	Coeff.	z-stat.
Freedom of speech	−0.49	−1.60	−0.05	−0.60	0.06	0.63	0.04	0.49
Right to criticize the government	0.69	1.65	0.10	0.95	−0.09	−0.74	−0.08	−0.81
(H) Demographics								
Female	−0.01	−0.03	−0.30	(−2.29)[a]	0.20	1.33	0.16	1.40
Age	−0.06	(−2.32)[a]	−0.01	−1.74	−0.01	−0.72	0.02	2.56[a]
Level of education	0.12	0.29	0.10	0.82	−0.09	−0.66	−0.03	−0.24
Married	−0.79	−1.35	0.38	2.04[a]	−0.12	−0.59	−0.15	−0.86
Unemployed	1.05	1.42	−0.30	−1.10	0.42	1.45	−0.18	−0.77
Income	0.09	1.13	0.04	1.50	−0.01	−0.25	−0.04	−1.57
No religion	−1.02	−1.83	−0.06	−0.33	−0.02	−0.08	0.19	1.09
(K) Rural								
Rural	−0.71	−1.25	0.04	0.27	−0.35	−1.84	0.21	1.42
(L) Yearly dummy variable (Base = 2006)								
2008	−0.82	−1.36	−0.25	−1.57	−0.0001	0.00	0.29	2.00[a]
Constant	−1.30	−0.34	2.20	2.18[a]	−4.58	(−3.73)[b]	−1.46	−1.59
n	1382		1382		1382		1382	
Pseudo R squared	0.3015		0.0925		0.0999		0.0460	

Note [a]5% significance level; [b]1% significance level

6.9 Hong Kong

A glance at the frequency distribution of the options reveals that in Hong Kong, broader loyalty is overwhelming, registering 64.5%. Among the voice options, the bureaucratic voice option dominates the broader voice option.

The broader loyalty option is contributed to by those who do not participate in national elections, do not use Internet, those are not satisfied with friendships, are satisfied with family life, assess government performance as complicated, are satisfied with the right to vote. The bureaucratic voice option is contributed to by those who use Internet, have proficiency in English, are not satisfied with family life, are lukewarm about corruption, regard politics as complicated, are not satisfied with the right to vote, and do not have a high level of education.

The exit option is contributed to by those who yearn for a powerful leader, prefer a democratic political system, and have a high level of education.

Summary statistics of countries Hong Kong					
	n	Mean	SD	Min	Max
Exit	987	0.041	0.20	0	1
Broader voice	987	0.064	0.24	0	1
Bureaucratic voice	987	0.250	0.43	0	1
Broader loyalty	987	0.645	0.48	0	1
(A) Lifestyles					
Number of public utilities	1000	5.41	0.72	3	7
Homeownership	1000	0.57	0.50	0	1
Number of family members	1000	3.61	1.31	1	9
Pray	999	1.50	1.14	1	5
National elections	743	2.84	1.68	1	5
Proud	988	2.81	0.65	1	4
Relative Standard of Living	1000	3.02	0.55	1	5
(B) Exposure to globalization					
Internet	1000	3.17	1.75	1	5
Living internationally	1000	1.13	1.33	0	6
English ability	998	2.03	0.82	1	4
(C) Satisfaction with aspects of life					
Housing	1000	3.48	0.77	1	5
Friendships	1000	3.81	0.65	1	5
Household income	996	3.18	0.73	1	5
Health	1000	3.57	0.71	1	5
Education	998	3.25	0.72	1	5
Job	990	3.35	0.70	1	5
Neighbors	994	3.28	0.63	1	5
Public safety	1000	3.49	0.68	2	5
The condition of the environment	1000	3.36	0.65	1	5
Social welfare system	994	3.18	0.70	1	5
The democratic system	985	3.26	0.72	1	5
Family life	999	3.60	0.64	1	5
Leisure	999	3.49	0.73	1	5
Spiritual life	996	3.41	0.68	1	5
Happiness	999	3.53	0.70	1	5
(D) Trust in social institution					
Trust generally	993	0.34	0.47	0	1
Trust the central government	972	2.60	0.67	1	4
Trust local governments	983	2.68	0.64	1	4
Trust the army	890	2.44	0.68	1	4
Trust the legal system	938	2.61	0.72	1	4
Trust the police	981	2.81	0.73	1	4
(E) Assessment of government performance					

(continued)

(continued)

Summary statistics of countries Hong Kong					
	n	Mean	SD	Min	Max
Worry about corruption	1000	0.08	0.27	0	1
Worry about Economic inequality	1000	0.20	0.40	0	1
Political corruption	922	2.57	0.61	1	4
Duty to vote	1000	3.90	0.76	2	5
Widespread corruption	984	3.22	0.82	1	5
No power	999	3.36	0.98	1	5
Complicated	996	3.48	0.95	1	5
No matter whether vote	998	2.87	0.96	1	5
Stop thinking	994	3.19	0.89	1	5
Pay little attention	996	3.20	0.85	1	5
Powerful leader	950	1.24	0.44	1	3
Experts	968	1.91	0.69	1	3
Military government	921	1.28	0.49	1	3
Democratic political system	980	2.25	0.64	1	3
Bribe	998	9.76	0.72	4	10
(F) Satisfaction with rights					
Right to vote	987	2.94	0.60	1	4
Right to participate in any organizations	986	3.00	0.54	1	4
Right to gather and demonstrate	992	2.87	0.62	1	4
Right to be informed about government	982	2.54	0.67	1	4
Freedom of speech	996	2.88	0.63	1	4
Right to criticize the government	995	2.78	0.64	1	4
(H) Demographics					
Female	1000	0.52	0.50	0	1
Age	1000	40.92	12.81	20	69
Level of education	998	1.74	0.72	1	3
Married	1000	0.63	0.48	0	1
Unemployed	998	0.06	0.24	0	1
Income	937	7.63	3.65	1	20
No religion	998	0.73	0.44	0	1

Frequency Distribution of 7 Responses and Partially Aggregated 4 Responses
Hong Kong

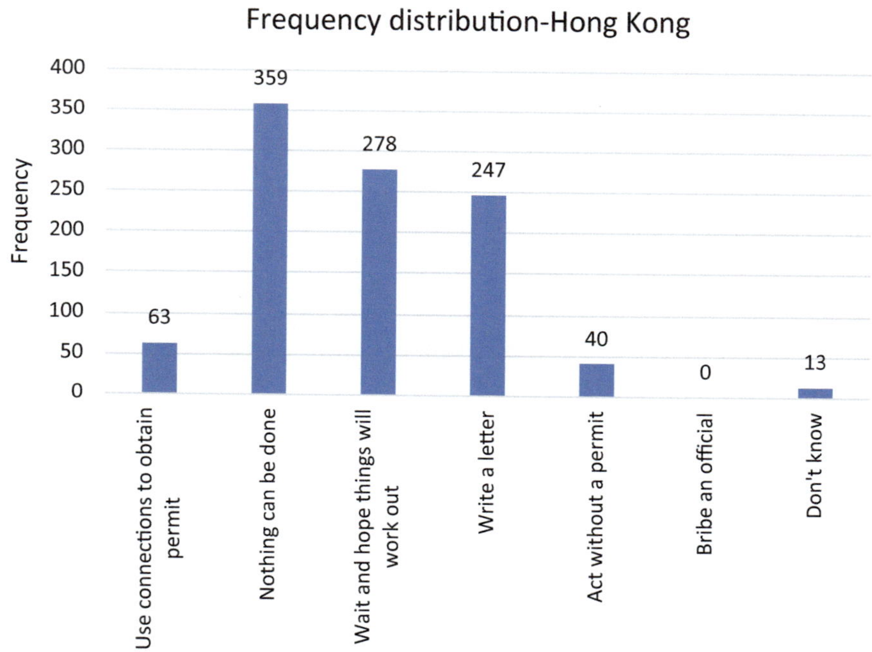

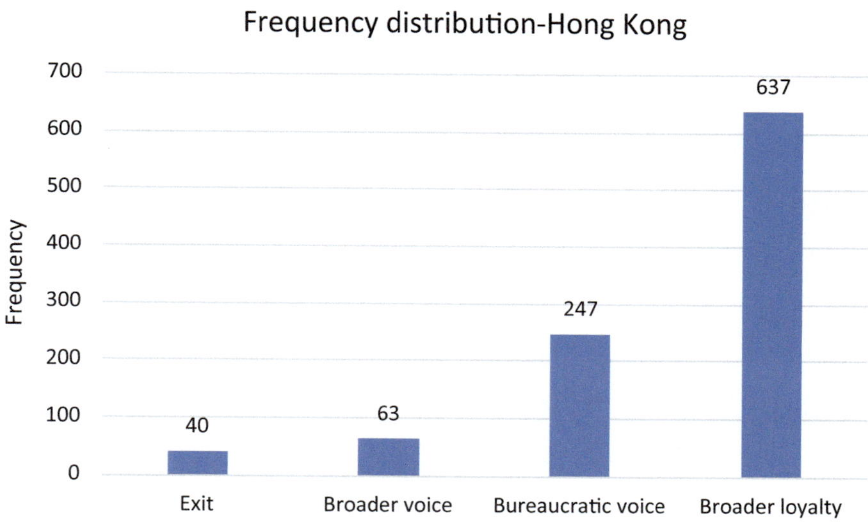

Logit regression analysis results by country Hong Kong								
Dependent variable	Exit		Broader voice		Bureaucratic voice		Broader loyalty	
Independent variables	Coeff.	z-stat.	Coeff.	z-stat.	Coeff.	z-stat.	Coeff.	z-stat.
(A) Lifestyles								
Number of public utilities	–	–	0.38	0.95	0.15	0.87	−0.17	−1.09
Homeownership	–	–	0.18	0.30	−0.15	−0.57	0.12	0.52
Number of family members	–	–	−0.41	−1.61	0.03	0.28	0.07	0.75
Pray	–	–	−0.18	−0.69	−0.15	−1.22	0.15	1.37
National elections	–	–	0.30	1.43	0.14	1.60	−0.17	(−2.14)[a]
Proud	–	–	0.52	1.00	−0.09	−0.42	0.01	0.05
Relative Standard of Living	–	–	0.02	0.03	0.06	0.20	0.13	0.50
(B) Exposure to globalization								
Internet	–	–	−0.21	−0.80	0.29	2.94[b]	−0.22	(−2.45)[a]
Living internationally	–	–	−0.35	−1.40	0.02	0.19	0.07	0.73
English ability	–	–	−1.09	−1.89	0.49	2.12[a]	−0.11	−0.54
(C) Satisfaction with aspects of life								
Housing	–	–	−0.10	−0.19	−0.007	−0.04	0.08	0.46
Friendships	–	–	0.39	0.65	0.15	0.60	−0.16	−0.69
Household income	–	–	0.86	1.46	0.17	0.66	−0.46	(−2.10)[a]
Health	–	–	0.26	0.50	0.44	1.87	−0.32	−1.57
Education	–	–	−0.88	−1.66	0.01	0.06	0.03	0.18
Job	–	–	0.08	0.16	−0.18	−0.77	0.37	1.86
Neighbors	–	–	0.22	0.46	0.21	0.96	−0.26	−1.35
Public safety	–	–	−0.08	−0.16	−0.25	−1.12	0.14	0.72
The condition of the environment	–	–	0.39	0.69	−0.15	−0.65	0.06	0.30
Social welfare system	–	–	0.30	0.66	0.13	0.59	−0.10	−0.52
The democratic system	–	–	−0.35	−0.78	0.09	0.44	−0.06	−0.36
Family life	–	–	−0.35	−0.63	0.48	1.84	−0.19	−0.85
Leisure	–	–	0.38	0.68	−0.99	(−3.53)[b]	0.72	2.96[b]

(continued)

(continued)

Logit regression analysis results by country Hong Kong								
Dependent variable	Exit		Broader voice		Bureaucratic voice		Broader loyalty	
Independent variables	Coeff.	z-stat.	Coeff.	z-stat.	Coeff.	z-stat.	Coeff.	z-stat.
Spiritual life	–	–	0.27	0.47	0.16	0.57	−0.39	−1.53
Happiness	–	–	−0.02	−0.03	0.01	0.05	0.08	0.38
(D) Trust in social institution								
Trust generally	–	–	−0.12	−0.19	−0.36	−1.22	0.21	0.84
Trust the central government	–	–	−0.32	−0.63	0.08	0.34	−0.05	−0.27
Trust local governments	–	–	0.82	1.39	0.19	0.80	−0.26	−1.20
Trust the army	–	–	0.37	0.84	0.28	1.31	−0.28	−1.48
Trust the legal system	–	–	0.32	0.64	−0.19	−0.86	0.08	0.40
Trust the police	–	–	−0.05	−0.12	−0.14	−0.70	0.13	0.70
(E) Assessment of government performance								
Worry about corruption	–	–	–	–	1.06	2.61[b]	−0.70	−1.87
Worry about Economic inequality	–	–	−0.43	−0.61	0.26	0.92	−0.29	−1.15
Political corruption	–	–	0.61	1.29	0.18	0.82	−0.20	−1.01
Duty to vote	–	–	−0.31	−0.63	0.16	0.77	−0.12	−0.65
Widespread corruption	–	–	0.74	1.69	−0.13	−0.74	0.01	0.08
No power	–	–	0.46	1.22	0.10	0.62	−0.13	−0.91
Complicated	–	–	0.12	0.30	−0.40	(−2.34)[a]	0.33	2.17[a]
No matter whether vote	–	–	0.12	0.32	−0.09	−0.52	−0.05	−0.37
Stop thinking	–	–	0.18	0.43	0.03	0.16	−0.05	−0.34
Pay little attention	–	–	−0.65	−1.60	−0.22	−1.26	0.23	1.48
Powerful leader	–	–	2.45	3.46[b]	−0.56	−1.76	0.04	0.13
Experts	–	–	−0.32	−0.77	0.29	1.47	−0.25	−1.45
Military government	–	–	0.74	1.42	−0.40	−1.43	0.16	0.70
Democratic political system	–	–	1.70	3.07	−0.02	−0.08	−0.23	−1.15
Bribe	–	–	0.63	0.80	0.25	1.27	−0.30	−1.58

(continued)

(continued)

Logit regression analysis results by country Hong Kong								
Dependent variable	Exit		Broader voice		Bureaucratic voice		Broader loyalty	
Independent variables	Coeff.	z-stat.	Coeff.	z-stat.	Coeff.	z-stat.	Coeff.	z-stat.
(F) Satisfaction with rights								
Right to vote	–	–	0.06	0.11	−0.62	(−2.75)[b]	0.47	2.32[a]
Right to participate in any organizations	–	–	0.47	0.74	−0.29	−1.06	0.21	0.86
Right to gather and demonstrate	–	–	0.27	0.60	−0.02	−0.07	−0.001	−0.01
Right to be informed about government	–	–	−0.85	−1.83	−0.16	−0.73	0.17	0.87
Freedom of speech	–	–	−0.63	−1.44	0.44	1.92	−0.23	−1.16
Right to criticize the government	–	–	0.09	0.22	−0.16	−0.74	0.08	0.42
(H) Demographics								
Female	–	–	0.31	0.51	0.35	1.30	−0.36	−1.51
Age	–	–	−0.01	−0.29	0.003	0.18	0.01	0.85
Level of education	–	–	1.29	1.91	−0.97	(−3.55)[b]	0.41	1.72
Married	–	–	−0.81	−1.17	−0.24	−0.77	0.10	0.37
Unemployed	–	–	0.08	0.05	0.38	0.71	−0.36	−0.75
Income	–	–	0.22	2.04[a]	0.04	0.80	−0.06	−1.62
No religion	–	–	−0.77	−1.06	−0.67	(−1.98)[a]	0.56	1.89
Constant	–	–	−30.4	(−2.84)[b]	−2.22	−0.73	5.01	1.76
n	–		489		489		489	
Pseudo R squared	–		0.4608		0.1923		0.1462	

Note [a]5% significance level; [b]1% significance level

6.10 India

The frequency distribution of exit, broader voice, bureaucratic voice and broader loyalty shows that those who opt for the exit option is very small, that those who opt for the broader voice option is about as large as those who opt for the broader loyalty option, and that those who opt for the bureaucratic voice option is far less than either the broader voice option or the bureaucratic loyalty option.

Those who choose the exit option are characterized as those who yearn for a powerful leader, are satisfied with the right to criticize government, and are from Hyderabad. Why Hyderabad? Compared to other large cities, Hyderabad is of lower income level and geographically farther away from Delhi. Those states whose exit coefficients are higher are Kolkata (z-stat is not significant, though) and Hyderabad (z-stat is significant).

Those who choose the broader voice option are characterized as having a relatively low standard of living, being not satisfied with their neighbors, not trusting the central government, assessing government performance as low in terms of widespread corruption, assessing government as having no power, assessing government performance as bribe-ridden, being satisfied with the right to vote, not being satisfied with the right to gather and demonstrate, and assessing high government performance on freedom of speech. Regionally, this group of respondents is from Hyderabad, Chennai, and Mumbai. These large cities are known for their focus on information technology. Nurturing and advancing information technology requires government deregulation in many domains and that must help them to have more voice-prone citizens in the highly bureaucratically regulated Indian society.

Those who choose the bureaucratic option are characterized by those who are not satisfied with family life, are happy, do not trust people in general, worry about government low performance on issues of inequality, yearn for a powerful leader, highly assess government performance in running the democratic political system, and are married. Regionally, those from Kolkata and Hyderabad are prone to bureaucratic voice as well as broader voice.

Those who choose the broader loyalty option are characterized as those who use Internet, do not have a command of English, are not satisfied with housing, trust the central government, assess government performance as low on issues of inequality, assess government as having no power, trust the central government, and are not satisfied with the right to vote and freedom of speech. Regionally, those from Mumbai register the highest in this loyalty option, compared to those from Kolkata who register the lowest.

To sum up, the voice option appears to focus on inequality, ineffective governance, and government regulation.

Summary statistics of countries India					
	n	Mean	SD	Min	Max
Exit	2243	0.018	0.13	0	1
Broader voice	2243	0.402	0.49	0	1
Bureaucratic voice	2243	0.168	0.37	0	1
Broader loyalty	2243	0.412	0.49	0	1
(A) Lifestyles					
Number of public utilities	2290	5.05	1.00	1	7
Homeownership	2243	0.68	0.47	0	1
Number of family members	2290	4.59	1.81	1	15
Pray	2287	4.69	0.88	1	5
National elections	2256	4.44	1.00	1	5
Proud	2288	3.89	0.34	1	4
Relative Standard of Living	2289	3.46	0.83	1	5
(B) Exposure to globalization					
Internet	2166	1.55	1.19	1	5
Living internationally	2290	0.47	0.81	0	6
English ability	2271	2.45	1.01	1	4
(C) Satisfaction with aspects of life					
Housing	2289	4.46	0.83	1	5
Friendships	2274	4.42	0.75	1	5
Household income	2286	4.05	0.89	1	5
Health	2289	4.33	0.87	1	5
Education	2278	4.15	0.88	1	5
Job	1745	3.88	1.02	1	5
Neighbors	2278	4.23	0.83	1	5
Public safety	2262	3.51	1.05	1	5
The condition of the environment	2270	3.24	1.13	1	5
Social welfare system	2204	3.46	0.96	1	5
The democratic system	2194	3.46	0.99	1	5
Family life	2275	4.20	0.82	1	5
Leisure	2261	4.05	0.86	1	5
Spiritual life	2239	4.04	0.85	1	5
Happiness	2290	4.13	0.87	1	5
(D) Trust in social institution					
Trust generally	2224	0.37	0.48	0	1
Trust the central government	2251	2.92	0.92	1	4
Trust the army	2259	3.50	0.80	1	4
Trust the legal system	2232	2.71	0.91	1	4
Trust the police	2223	2.40	1.01	1	4
(E) Assessment of government performance					
Worry about corruption	2290	0.71	0.45	0	1

(continued)

(continued)

Summary statistics of countries India					
	n	Mean	SD	Min	Max
Worry about Economic inequality	2290	0.40	0.49	0	1
Political corruption	2232	2.00	0.92	1	4
Duty to vote	2288	4.64	0.60	1	5
Widespread corruption	2275	4.22	0.79	1	5
No power	2256	3.70	1.09	1	5
Complicated	2261	3.98	0.90	1	5
No matter whether vote	2280	2.64	1.40	1	5
Stop thinking	2268	4.06	0.92	1	5
Pay little attention	2262	3.97	0.92	1	5
Powerful leader	2216	1.82	0.77	1	3
Experts	2154	2.07	0.67	1	3
Military government	2189	2.16	0.74	1	3
Democratic political system	2210	2.32	0.65	1	3
Bribe	2274	9.28	1.50	1	10
(F) Satisfaction with rights					
Right to vote	2263	3.48	0.67	1	4
Right to participate in any organizations	2161	3.11	0.75	1	4
Right to gather and demonstrate	2155	2.93	0.85	1	4
Right to be informed about government	2152	2.98	0.82	1	4
Freedom of speech	2240	3.21	0.80	1	4
Right to criticize the government	2181	2.99	0.83	1	4
(H) Demographics					
Female	2290	0.48	0.50	0	1
Age	2290	36.28	12.37	20	69
Level of education	2284	2.27	0.70	1	3
Married	2289	0.75	0.43	0	1
Unemployed	2275	0.05	0.21	0	1
Income	2245	1.92	0.84	1	3
(I) City (Base = Delhi)					
Mumbai	2290	0.29	0.45	0	1
Chennai	2290	0.09	0.28	0	1
Kolkata	2290	0.09	0.28	0	1
Bangalore	2290	0.11	0.32	0	1
Hyderabad	2290	0.07	0.26	0	1
Ahmedabad	2290	0.11	0.31	0	1
(L) Yearly dummy variable (Base = 2005)					
2008	2290	0.46	0.50	0	1

Frequency Distribution of 7 Responses and Partially Aggregated 4 Responses India

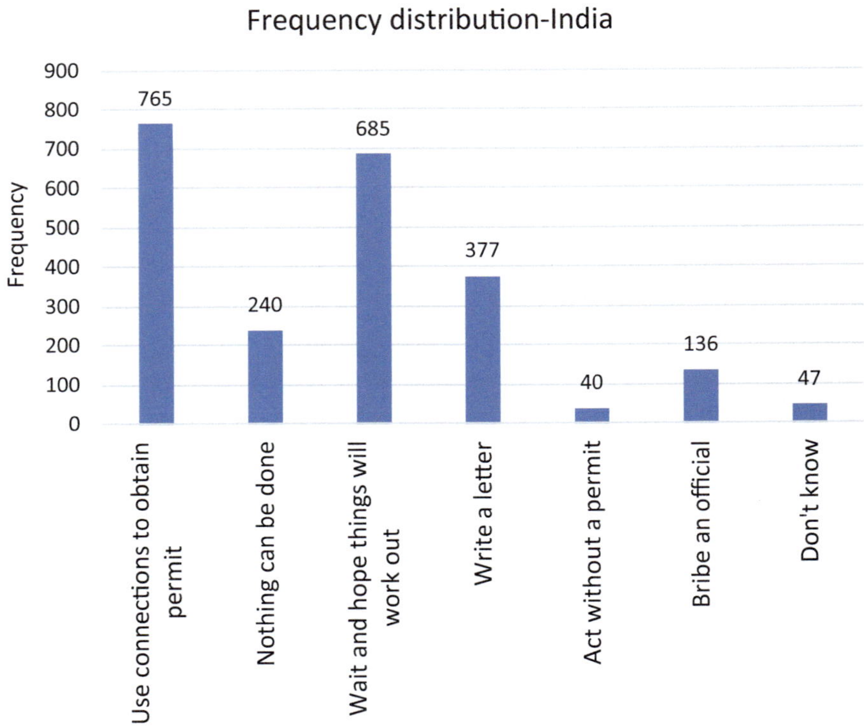

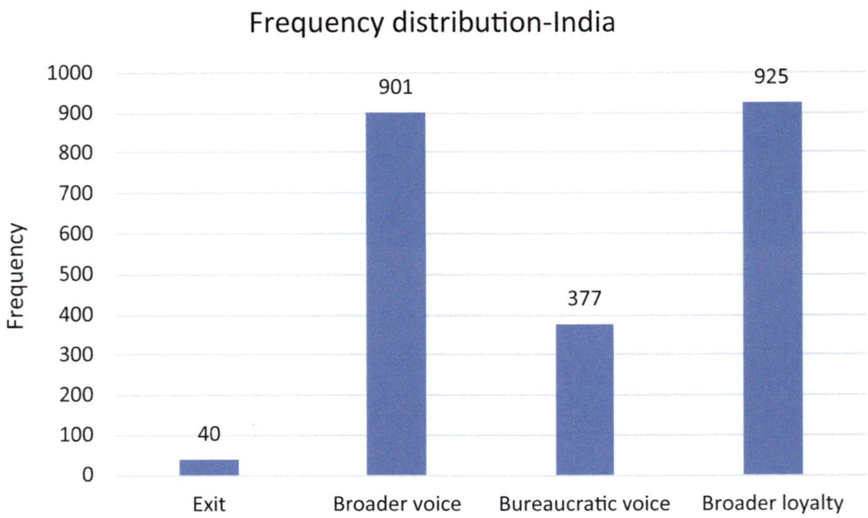

Logit regression analysis results by country India								
Dependent variable	Exit		Broader voice		Bureaucratic voice		Broader loyalty	
Independent variables	Coeff.	z-stat.	Coeff.	z-stat.	Coeff.	z-stat.	Coeff.	z-stat.
(A) Lifestyles								
Number of public utilities	−0.52	−1.52	−0.08	−0.87	0.11	0.94	0.03	0.35
Homeownership	0.66	0.98	0.03	0.17	−0.01	−0.04	0.03	0.18
Number of family members	0.35	2.55[b]	0.03	0.92	0.01	0.29	−0.07	−1.79
Pray	0.63	1.15	−0.03	−0.32	−0.17	−1.67	0.18	1.94
National elections	0.14	0.45	0.05	0.60	−0.18	−1.85	0.06	0.81
Proud	–	–	0.02	0.11	0.04	0.14	−0.19	−0.85
Relative Standard of Living	0.55	1.54	−0.24	(−2.35)[a]	0.13	0.97	0.12	1.26
(B) Exposure to globalization								
Internet	0.05	0.19	−0.11	−1.62	−0.10	−1.06	0.16	2.43[a]
Living internationally	0.21	0.54	0.03	0.36	−0.03	−0.26	−0.02	−0.19
English ability	−0.55	−1.34	0.18	1.77	0.16	1.22	−0.24	(−2.37)[a]
(C) Satisfaction with aspects of life								
Housing	1.04	1.62	0.21	1.83	0.19	1.30	−0.32	(−2.98)[a]
Friendships	−0.12	−0.32	−0.05	−0.43	0.13	0.90	−0.03	−0.25
Household income	−0.003	−0.01	0.06	0.56	−0.001	0.00	−0.04	−0.44
Health	0.08	0.20	−0.06	−0.62	−0.10	−0.77	0.13	1.30
Education	−0.39	−1.01	0.01	0.09	0.09	0.70	−0.07	−0.65
Job	0.43	1.33	0.13	1.52	−0.12	−1.05	−0.12	−1.35
Neighbors	0.71	1.63	−0.23	(−2.17)[a]	0.18	1.32	0.08	0.77
Public safety	−0.32	−0.92	0.14	1.61	−0.09	−0.84	−0.04	−0.49
The condition of the environment	−0.01	−0.02	−0.13	−1.64	0.09	0.82	0.09	1.15
Social welfare system	−0.13	−0.35	0.04	0.40	−0.16	−1.27	0.03	0.34
The democratic system	−0.27	−0.76	0.09	1.03	0.11	0.89	−0.07	−0.79
Family life	−0.08	−0.21	0.03	0.25	−0.29	(−2.11)[a]	0.20	1.79
Leisure	−0.04	−0.10	0.06	0.58	0.05	0.40	−0.09	−0.93

(continued)

(continued)

Logit regression analysis results by country India								
Dependent variable	Exit		Broader voice		Bureaucratic voice		Broader loyalty	
Independent variables	Coeff.	z-stat.	Coeff.	z-stat.	Coeff.	z-stat.	Coeff.	z-stat.
Spiritual life	−0.44	−1.08	0.09	0.85	−0.25	−1.83	0.08	0.79
Happiness	0.39	0.81	−0.13	−1.38	0.25	1.98[a]	−0.03	−0.33
(D) Trust in social institution								
Trust generally	−0.11	−0.20	0.00	0.01	−0.42	(−2.03)[a]	0.28	1.88
Trust the central government	−0.04	−0.10	−0.22	(−2.46)[a]	−0.12	−1.03	0.34	3.60[b]
Trust the army	0.09	0.24	−0.20	−1.93	−0.12	−0.94	0.27	2.50[a]
Trust the legal system	0.23	0.57	−0.14	−1.50	0.10	0.82	0.10	1.10
Trust the police	0.26	0.79	−0.02	−0.28	−0.14	−1.27	0.06	0.74
(E) Assessment of government performance								
Worry about corruption	−0.15	−0.24	−0.13	−0.79	0.24	1.06	0.003	0.02
Worry about Economic inequality	−0.46	−0.67	0.64	4.16	−0.61	(−2.78)[b]	−0.31	(−2.05)[a]
Political corruption	−0.06	−0.20	−0.12	−1.50	−0.06	−0.51	0.17	2.21[a]
Duty to vote	−0.83	−1.77	0.13	1.02	0.18	0.97	−0.17	−1.24
Widespread corruption	0.61	1.48	−0.27	(−2.53)[a]	0.11	0.78	0.18	1.60
No power	−0.55	−1.81	0.17	2.27[a]	0.06	0.66	−0.15	(−2.02)[a]
Complicated	0.20	0.55	0.02	0.19	−0.19	−1.71	0.09	1.08
No matter whether vote	0.36	1.48	−0.04	−0.60	0.05	0.61	−0.04	−0.65
Stop thinking	−0.55	−1.48	−0.08	−0.89	0.08	0.63	0.06	0.61
Pay little attention	−0.17	−0.52	0.13	1.44	−0.23	−1.93	0.04	0.42
Powerful leader	0.97	2.09[a]	0.20	1.85	−0.42	(−2.72)[b]	−0.01	−0.09
Experts	−0.02	−0.05	−0.22	−1.82	0.32	2.10[a]	0.04	0.32
Military government	0.16	0.31	0.07	0.63	0.10	0.65	−0.14	−1.35
Democratic political system	−0.56	−1.08	−0.23	−1.98	0.40	2.55[a]	−0.04	−0.31
Bribe	−0.04	−0.23	−0.10	(−2.16)[a]	0.08	1.17	0.10	1.97[a]
(F) Satisfaction with rights								
Right to vote	0.49	0.89	0.33	2.47[a]	−0.10	−0.61	−0.28	(−2.16)[a]

(continued)

(continued)

Logit regression analysis results by country India								
Dependent variable	Exit		Broader voice		Bureaucratic voice		Broader loyalty	
Independent variables	Coeff.	z-stat.	Coeff.	z-stat.	Coeff.	z-stat.	Coeff.	z-stat.
Right to participate in any organizations	0.20	0.43	0.10	0.85	−0.17	−1.14	−0.07	−0.60
Right to gather and demonstrate	−0.69	−1.64	−0.22	(−2.04)[a]	0.11	0.78	0.17	1.65
Right to be informed about government	0.36	0.87	0.03	0.26	0.04	0.25	−0.03	−0.26
Freedom of speech	0.37	0.80	0.39	3.23[b]	−0.13	−0.88	−0.31	(−2.59)[a]
Right to criticize the government	1.56	3.40[b]	−0.03	−0.32	−0.13	−0.95	−0.002	−0.02
(H) Demographics								
Female	0.24	0.38	0.13	0.82	−0.20	−0.92	−0.11	−0.72
Age	−0.01	−0.47	−0.002	−0.34	0.01	1.22	−0.01	−0.75
Level of education	−0.01	−0.02	0.20	1.44	−0.27	−1.43	−0.04	−0.26
Married	−1.10	−1.47	−0.36	−1.88	0.59	2.07[a]	0.07	0.37
Unemployed	0.67	0.50	0.24	0.62	−0.65	−1.03	−0.14	−0.34
Income	−0.61	−1.33	−0.01	−0.13	0.05	0.36	0.02	0.17
(I) City (Base = Delhi)								
Mumbai	0.82	0.54	−0.63	(−2.52)[a]	−0.15	−0.46	0.77	3.08[b]
Chennai	–	–	−1.27	(−3.32)[b]	0.31	0.65	0.86	2.51[a]
Kolkata	3.34	1.66	0.12	0.33	1.18	2.54[a]	−1.18	(−2.77)[a]
Bangalore	−0.09	−0.05	0.20	0.63	−1.84	(−2.30)[a]	0.07	0.21
Hyderabad	3.17	1.97[a]	−1.36	(−3.84)[b]	1.13	2.63[b]	0.16	0.48
Ahmedabad	−0.36	−0.20	0.67	2.05[a]	−0.22	−0.50	−0.62	−1.78
(L) Yearly dummy variable (Base = 2005)								
2008	2.42	2.52[a]	−0.04	−0.23	0.05	0.21	−0.25	−1.47
Constant	−18.6	(−2.80)[b]	0.38	0.26	−2.26	−1.14	−1.44	−0.98
n	1053		1138		1138		1138	
Pseudo R squared	0.4327		0.1542		0.1752		0.1321	

Note [a]5% significance level; [b]1% significance level

6.11 Indonesia

A glance at the frequency distribution of exit, voice, and loyalty options gives a small surprise as the surveys were carried out after the democratization of Indonesia. The broader loyalty option dominates the other two choices.

Those who choose the exit option represent only a tiny portion of the sample size. They are characterized by those who do not participate in local elections, are not satisfied with work, do not trust the legal system, assess government as lacking a powerful leader, are not satisfied with the right to vote, and are male.

Those who choose the broader voice option are characterized by those who do not trust the legal system, do not highly assess government performance on economic inequality, assess government performance as having no power, highly assess government performance in curtailing bribery, are satisfied with the right to vote, and are highly educated.

Those who choose the bureaucratic voice option are characterized by those who do not enjoy public water supply and electricity, do not have a command of English, do not trust the police, assess government as not paying much attention, and are unemployed.

Those who choose the broader loyalty option are characterized by those who enjoy electricity supply, are proud of their country, do not have a high relative standard of living, are not satisfied with neighbors, trust the legal system, do not trust the police, negatively assess government performance with regard to duty to vote, assess government performance as high with regard to addressing widespread corruption, are satisfied with the right to criticize the government. Demographically, this group is not highly educated and is unemployed.

In sum, poverty looms large in citizens' perception and behavior. The exit option is related to no job, no political participation, not trusting the legal system, not satisfied with the right to vote, and being male. The exit option appears to come from a place of poverty and alienation. The broader voice option is related to those that are highly educated, do not trust the legal system, and are critical of government performance. This option represents those who are highly educated and critical of government. The genesis of the bureaucratic voice grows out of being disgruntled about little government attention, not having a command of English, and trusting the police. The broader loyalty option is shared by the vast majority, about 90% of the population. Therefore the characterization by demographics, daily life satisfaction, assessment of government, etc. is not simple.

Summary statistics of countries Indonesia					
	n	Mean	SD	Min	Max
Exit	1741	0.029	0.17	0	1
Broader voice	1741	0.136	0.34	0	1
Bureaucratic voice	1741	0.066	0.25	0	1
Broader loyalty	1741	0.770	0.42	0	1
(A) Lifestyles					
Public water supply	1825	0.21	0.41	0	1
Electricity	1825	0.98	0.12	0	1
LPG	1825	0.07	0.25	0	1
Homeownership	1824	0.88	0.32	0	1
Number of family members	1825	4.61	1.80	1	15
Pray	1821	4.74	0.76	1	5
National elections	1823	4.59	0.79	1	5
Local elections	1625	3.78	1.48	1	5
Proud	1822	3.85	0.41	1	4
Relative Standard of Living	1825	2.73	0.71	1	5
(B) Exposure to globalization					
Living internationally	1825	0.44	0.63	0	6
English ability	1779	1.45	0.56	1	4
(C) Satisfaction with aspects of life					
Housing	1825	4.14	0.98	1	5
Friendships	1813	4.50	0.67	1	5
Household income	1813	3.53	1.00	1	5
Health	1820	4.35	0.82	1	5
Education	1814	3.79	1.05	1	5
Job	1785	3.53	1.12	1	5
Neighbors	1821	4.48	0.70	1	5
Public safety	1820	4.42	0.74	1	5
The condition of the environment	1823	4.31	0.83	1	5
Social welfare system	1805	3.81	0.95	1	5
The democratic system	1774	3.95	0.86	1	5
Family life	1824	4.37	0.77	1	5
Leisure	1821	4.18	0.80	1	5
Happiness	1824	3.80	0.79	1	5
(D) Trust in social institution					
Trust generally	1816	0.23	0.42	0	1
Trust the central government	1795	3.04	0.74	1	4
Trust local governments	1811	3.10	0.71	1	4
Trust the army	1765	3.10	0.72	1	4

(continued)

(continued)

Summary statistics of countries Indonesia					
	n	Mean	SD	Min	Max
Trust the legal system	1735	2.99	0.75	1	4
Trust the police	1801	2.67	0.84	1	4
(E) Assessment of government performance					
Worry about corruption	1825	0.32	0.47	0	1
Worry about Economic inequality	1825	0.46	0.50	0	1
Political corruption	1771	1.89	0.74	1	4
Duty to vote	1824	4.46	0.61	1	5
Widespread corruption	1772	3.41	1.28	1	5
No power	1797	3.20	1.05	1	5
Complicated	1791	3.65	0.93	1	5
No matter whether vote	1798	2.95	1.05	1	5
Pay little attention	1802	3.62	1.03	1	5
Powerful leader	1664	1.46	0.65	1	3
Experts	1642	1.87	0.65	1	3
Military government	1636	1.77	0.65	1	3
Democratic political system	1757	2.40	0.60	1	3
Bribe	1817	8.85	1.56	1	10
(F) Satisfaction with rights					
Right to vote	1818	3.51	0.66	1	4
Right to gather and demonstrate	1734	3.05	0.75	1	4
Right to be informed about government	1746	2.59	0.89	1	4
Right to criticize the government	1724	2.71	0.88	1	4
(H) Demographics					
Female	1825	0.54	0.50	0	1
Age	1825	35.45	10.91	20	69
Level of education	1825	1.47	0.62	1	3
Married	1823	0.81	0.39	0	1
Unemployed	1824	0.10	0.29	0	1
Income	1804	4.15	2.16	1	9
(K) Urban/Rural					
Rural	1825	0.58	0.49	0	1
(L) Yearly dummy variable (Base = 2004)					
2007	1825	0.55	0.50	0	1

Frequency Distribution of 7 Responses and Partially Aggregated 4 Responses Indonesia

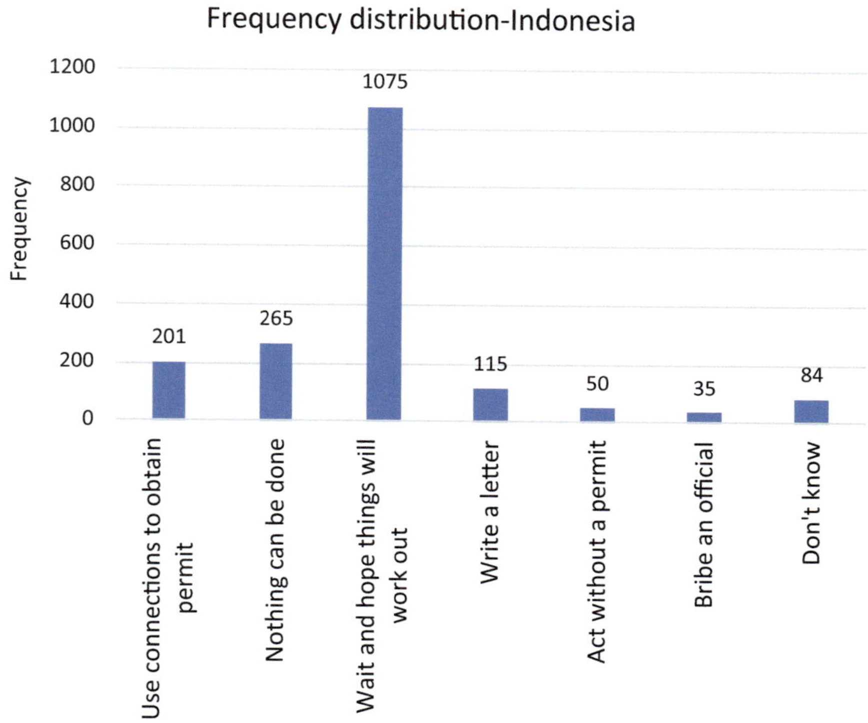

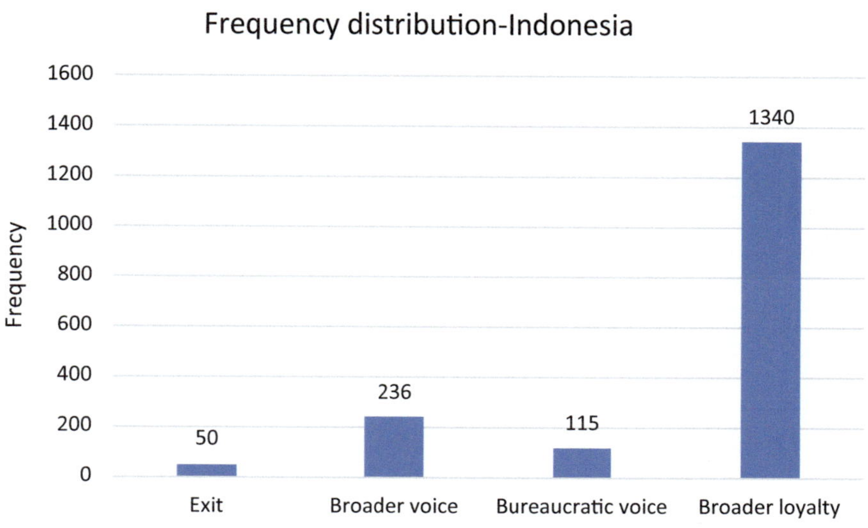

Logit regression analysis results by country Indonesia								
Dependent variable	Exit		Broader voice		Bureaucratic voice		Broader loyalty	
Independent variables	Coeff.	z-stat.	Coeff.	z-stat.	Coeff.	z-stat.	Coeff.	z-stat.
(A) Lifestyles								
Public water supply	−1.03	−1.51	0.22	0.86	−1.29	(−2.96)[b]	0.38	1.79
Electricity	−2.01	−1.48	−0.66	−0.76	−2.00	(−2.10)[a]	1.56	2.34[a]
LPG	−0.27	−0.28	0.03	0.09	0.48	0.97	−0.14	−0.45
Homeownership	0.99	0.87	0.07	0.22	0.31	0.58	−0.31	−1.05
Number of family members	−0.06	−0.44	−0.02	−0.40	−0.10	−1.14	0.07	1.44
Pray	−0.24	−0.87	−0.17	−1.29	0.02	0.09	0.08	0.76
National elections	0.34	1.02	0.20	1.15	−0.14	−0.70	−0.10	−0.84
Local elections	−0.40	(−2.32)[a]	−0.03	−0.40	0.13	1.16	0.03	0.38
Proud	−0.74	−1.57	−0.18	−0.66	−0.27	−0.78	0.45	2.17[a]
Relative Standard of Living	0.37	1.03	0.33	1.75	0.06	0.25	−0.30	(−2.05)[a]
(B) Exposure to globalization								
Living internationally	0.18	0.50	0.27	1.66	−0.24	−1.00	−0.04	−0.33
English ability	−0.34	−0.66	0.04	0.18	0.58	1.98[a]	−0.21	−1.12
(C) Satisfaction with aspects of life								
Housing	−0.13	−0.48	0.08	0.59	0.26	1.27	−0.19	−1.68
Friendships	0.03	0.08	0.29	1.49	0.06	0.21	−0.23	−1.45
Household income	0.25	0.87	−0.07	−0.48	−0.30	−1.57	0.09	0.81
Health	−0.12	−0.43	−0.10	−0.71	0.24	0.99	−0.003	−0.02
Education	0.20	0.79	−0.08	−0.67	0.07	0.39	−0.03	−0.30
Job	−0.55	(−2.35)[a]	−0.15	−1.30	0.16	0.92	0.13	1.35
Neighbors	0.70	1.55	0.17	0.88	0.52	1.65	−0.40	(−2.44)[a]
Public safety	−0.16	−0.49	0.19	1.05	−0.22	−0.98	−0.06	−0.46
The condition of the environment	0.04	0.11	−0.19	−1.19	0.24	0.97	0.09	0.70
Social welfare system	−0.29	−0.99	0.13	0.86	0.05	0.25	−0.02	−0.21
The democratic system	−0.12	−0.39	−0.08	−0.54	0.33	1.47	−0.01	−0.10
Family life	0.09	0.28	−0.12	−0.69	−0.11	−0.41	0.12	0.87

(continued)

(continued)

Logit regression analysis results by country Indonesia								
Dependent variable	Exit		Broader voice		Bureaucratic voice		Broader loyalty	
Independent variables	Coeff.	z-stat.	Coeff.	z-stat.	Coeff.	z-stat.	Coeff.	z-stat.
Leisure	0.36	1.13	0.30	1.95	−0.37	−1.72	−0.09	−0.74
Happiness	0.12	0.43	−0.10	−0.68	−0.06	−0.30	0.08	0.64
(D) Trust in social institution								
Trust generally	0.21	0.44	0.33	1.36	0.15	0.46	−0.25	−1.30
Trust the central government	0.16	0.37	0.24	1.14	−0.14	−0.50	−0.11	−0.66
Trust local governments	−0.28	−0.57	−0.19	−0.85	−0.37	−1.24	0.29	1.66
Trust the army	0.44	1.21	0.20	1.15	−0.27	−1.17	−0.13	−0.97
Trust the legal system	−0.67	(−2.03)[a]	−0.44	(−2.73)[b]	−0.28	−1.27	0.52	4.05[b]
Trust the police	0.25	0.73	−0.05	−0.37	0.72	3.32[b]	−0.26	(−2.16)[a]
(E) Assessment of government performance								
Worry about corruption	−0.81	−1.58	0.30	1.35	−0.41	−1.32	0.13	0.75
Worry about Economic inequality	−0.32	−0.73	−0.47	(−2.17)[a]	0.44	1.60	0.09	0.53
Political corruption	−0.23	−0.72	0.002	0.02	−0.01	−0.06	0.10	0.87
Duty to vote	0.39	0.98	0.42	2.13[a]	0.06	0.29	−0.42	(−2.87)[b]
Widespread corruption	0.06	0.29	−0.05	−0.48	−0.20	−1.56	0.17	2.23[a]
No power	0.13	0.50	0.31	2.63[a]	−0.11	−0.70	−0.18	−1.91
Complicated	−0.05	−0.17	−0.06	−0.49	−0.21	−1.25	0.18	1.76
No matter whether vote	−0.39	−1.54	0.05	0.43	0.18	1.18	−0.07	−0.74
Pay little attention	0.32	1.18	−0.12	−1.02	0.33	2.12[a]	−0.13	−1.40
Powerful leader	−1.46	(−2.27)[a]	0.31	1.81	−0.48	−1.66	0.09	0.62
Experts	0.21	0.56	0.08	0.47	0.02	0.06	−0.07	−0.46
Military government	−0.08	−0.22	0.09	0.52	−0.05	−0.22	−0.02	−0.18
Democratic political system	0.71	1.79	−0.18	−0.92	0.09	0.37	−0.09	−0.63
Bribe	0.21	1.32	−0.23	(−3.61)[b]	0.14	1.22	0.08	1.50

(continued)

(continued)

Logit regression analysis results by country Indonesia								
Dependent variable	Exit		Broader voice		Bureaucratic voice		Broader loyalty	
Independent variables	Coeff.	z-stat.	Coeff.	z-stat.	Coeff.	z-stat.	Coeff.	z-stat.
(F) Satisfaction with rights								
Right to vote	−0.97	(−2.49)[a]	0.72	3.07[b]	−0.51	−1.96	−0.03	−0.19
Right to gather and demonstrate	−0.56	−1.60	−0.16	−0.98	0.22	0.98	0.08	0.66
Right to be informed about government	0.37	1.24	−0.22	−1.45	0.07	0.35	0.09	0.76
Right to criticize the government	0.33	1.04	0.06	0.45	0.33	1.68	−0.27	(−2.38)[a]
(H) Demographics								
Female	−0.92	(−2.02)[a]	−0.10	−0.47	−0.16	−0.59	0.27	1.62
Age	0.03	1.66	−0.001	−0.09	0.01	0.38	−0.01	−1.43
Level of education	0.44	1.00	0.46	2.13[a]	0.08	0.29	−0.35	(−2.10)[a]
Married	0.18	0.31	−0.09	−0.29	−0.22	−0.58	0.12	0.55
Unemployed	0.20	0.26	−0.53	−1.28	0.24	0.48	0.15	0.48
Income	−0.13	−1.14	0.09	1.61	0.15	2.03[a]	−0.10	(−2.18)[a]
(K) Urban/Rural								
Rural	−0.19	−0.39	−0.21	−0.86	−0.56	−1.84	0.30	1.64
(L) Yearly dummy variable (Base = 2004)								
2007	1.41	2.48[a]	−0.25	−0.93	0.07	0.20	−0.15	−0.74
Constant	−3.30	−0.73	−5.43	(−2.39)[a]	−4.45	−1.59	3.09	1.81
n	1005		1005		1005		1005	
Pseudo R squared	0.3282		0.1618		0.2450		0.1300	

Note [a]5% significance level; [b]1% significance level

6.12 Japan

A glance at the frequency distribution of options reveals that Japanese love loyalty. Of the sample population, 67% choose loyalty. That corroborates findings of anthropology, sociology, and social psychology.

Those who choose the exit option have been exposed to globalization, are those highly educated, yearn for a powerful leader, and are from Kyushu, a southern island. It looks as if the more southern, the more exit-prone the sample population is.

Those who choose the broader voice option are satisfied with friendships in daily life, believe that his/her vote does not make much difference, negatively assess government on issues related to bribery, and are satisfied with the government for maintaining the right to criticize the government.

Those who choose the bureaucratic voice option live internationally, have a command of English, are not satisfied with the social welfare system, are not happy, are not satisfied with the democratic system, negatively assess government performance with regard to its power, believe that his/her vote does not make much difference, are female, and are highly educated.

Those who choose broader loyalty, the vast majority, can be characterized as immensely diverse populations. As a group, they do not enjoy access to a LPG fuel facility, do not pray, do not live internationally, do not trust the local government, believe government to be very complicated, believe that his/her vote does not make much difference, and are from northern regions (Hokkaido/Tohoku and Chubu).

In all, 67% are loyalists. They are diverse. Yet shared traits include that many are from northern regions, are not interested in politics, are not international, and do not speak English. Those who choose the exit option are saliently from the south, live internationally, are highly educated, and yearn for a powerful leader.

Those who choose the broader voice option enjoy friendships, regard government as too complicated to engage or understand, are satisfied with the government's efforts to maintain the right to criticize the government. Those who choose the bureaucratic voice are highly educated, live internationally, are proficient in English, do not pay much attention to politics, and are female.

Summary statistics of countries Japan					
	n	Mean	SD	Min	Max
Exit	2459	0.049	0.22	0	1
Broader voice	2459	0.078	0.27	0	1
Bureaucratic voice	2459	0.197	0.40	0	1
Broader loyalty	2459	0.676	0.47	0	1
(A) Lifestyles					
Public water supply	2840	0.96	0.20	0	1
Electricity	2840	1.00	0.02	0	1
LPG	2840	0.80	0.40	0	1
Homeownership	2839	0.75	0.43	0	1
Number of family members	2836	3.59	1.53	1	11
Pray	2811	2.42	1.54	1	5
National elections	2813	4.22	1.10	1	5
Proud	2758	3.12	0.75	1	4
(B) Exposure to globalization					
Living internationally	2840	0.71	1.09	0	6
English ability	2832	1.82	0.68	1	4
(C) Satisfaction with aspects of life					
Housing	2838	3.72	1.01	1	5
Friendships	2835	4.04	0.75	1	5
Household income	2805	3.26	1.01	1	5
Health	2837	3.78	0.96	1	5
Education	2789	3.54	0.82	1	5
Job	2708	3.47	0.91	1	5
Neighbors	2797	3.60	0.78	1	5
Public safety	2825	3.52	0.97	1	5
The condition of the environment	2830	3.72	0.87	1	5
Social welfare system	2749	3.01	0.93	1	5
The democratic system	2721	3.18	0.85	1	5
Family life	2819	3.95	0.75	1	5
Leisure	2832	3.63	0.91	1	5
Happiness	2821	3.72	0.81	1	5
(D) Trust in social institution					
Trust generally	2722	0.46	0.50	0	1
Trust the central government	2716	2.27	0.68	1	4
Trust local governments	2706	2.54	0.63	1	4
Trust the army	2676	2.69	0.69	1	4
Trust the legal system	2664	2.61	0.65	1	4
Trust the police	2768	2.67	0.70	1	4
(E) Assessment of government performance					
Worry about corruption	2840	0.15	0.36	0	1
Worry about Economic inequality	2840	0.25	0.43	0	1

(continued)

(continued)

Summary statistics of countries Japan					
	n	Mean	SD	Min	Max
Political corruption	2706	1.79	0.63	1	4
Duty to vote	2829	4.22	0.70	1	5
Widespread corruption	2738	3.79	1.00	1	5
No power	2758	3.32	0.97	1	5
Complicated	2777	3.48	0.90	1	5
No matter whether vote	2811	2.25	1.02	1	5
Stop thinking	2791	3.68	0.93	1	5
Pay little attention	2755	3.62	0.93	1	5
Powerful leader	2526	1.63	0.64	1	3
Experts	2471	1.82	0.59	1	3
Military government	2575	1.16	0.38	1	3
Democratic political system	2584	2.22	0.55	1	3
Bribe	2802	9.31	1.51	1	10
(F) Satisfaction with rights					
Right to vote	2763	3.18	0.62	1	4
Right to gather and demonstrate	2471	2.97	0.61	1	4
Right to be informed about government	2616	2.66	0.76	1	4
Freedom of speech	2691	2.99	0.66	1	4
Right to criticize the government	2597	2.83	0.75	1	4
(H) Demographics					
Female	2840	0.53	0.50	0	1
Age	2840	45.06	13.31	20	69
Level of education	2825	2.37	0.64	1	3
Married	2840	0.75	0.43	0	1
Unemployed	2817	0.04	0.21	0	1
Income	2156	5.78	3.80	1	20
No religion	2802	0.65	0.48	0	1
(I) Region (Base = Kanto)					
Hokkaido/Tohoku	2840	0.13	0.33	0	1
Chubu	2840	0.19	0.39	0	1
Kinki	2840	0.17	0.38	0	1
Chugoku/Shikoku	2840	0.10	0.30	0	1
Kyushu	2840	0.11	0.32	0	1
(J) City cize					
City cize	2840	2.64	1.02	1	4
(L) Yearly dummy variable (Base = 2004)					
2006	2840	0.35	0.48	0	1
2008	2840	0.36	0.48	0	1

Frequency Distribution of 7 Responses and Partially Aggregated 4 Responses

Japan

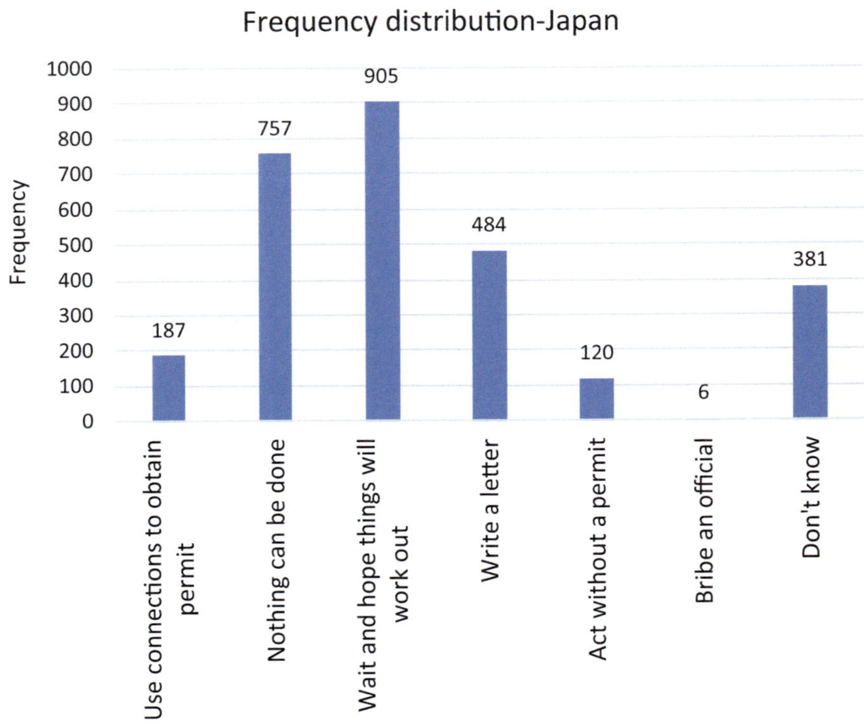

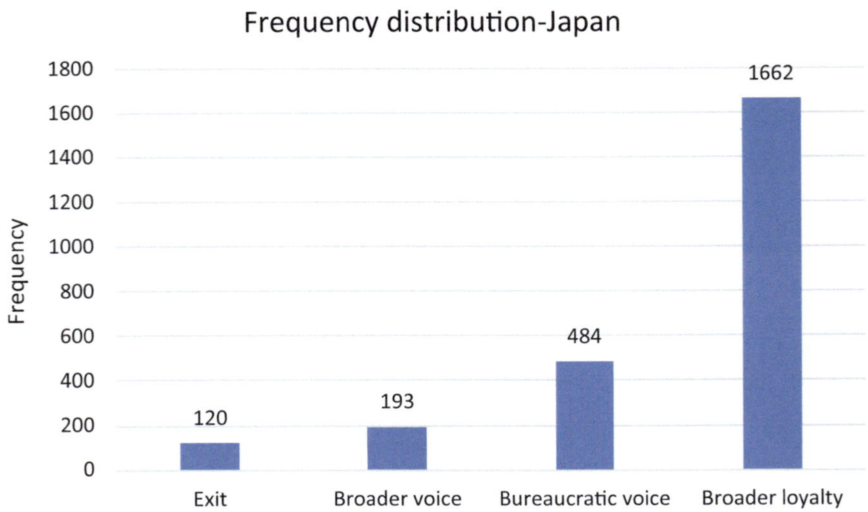

Logit regression analysis results by country Japan								
Dependent variable	Exit		Broader voice		Bureaucratic voice		Broader loyalty	
Independent variables	Coeff.	z-stat.	Coeff.	z-stat.	Coeff.	z-stat.	Coeff.	z-stat.
(A) Lifestyles								
Public water supply	−1.20	−1.92	1.28	1.17	−0.51	−1.18	0.42	1.12
Electricity	–	–	–	–	–	–	–	–
LPG	0.74	1.66	−0.03	−0.09	0.46	1.95	−0.53	(−2.55)[a]
Homeownership	0.04	0.12	0.07	0.21	−0.38	−1.81	0.24	1.37
Number of family members	−0.18	−1.53	0.12	1.25	0.04	0.74	−0.03	−0.65
Pray	−0.08	−0.72	0.12	1.34	0.11	1.89	−0.10	(−2.06)[a]
National elections	−0.02	−0.12	−0.04	−0.33	−0.18	−1.85	0.14	1.69
Proud	0.02	0.10	−0.30	−1.78	0.004	0.04	0.07	0.78
(B) Exposure to globalization								
Living internationally	0.31	2.61[b]	0.06	0.58	0.16	2.30[a]	−0.24	(−3.88)[b]
English ability	−0.42	−1.77	−0.03	−0.13	0.27	2.07[a]	−0.10	−0.91
(C) Satisfaction with aspects of life								
Housing	−0.04	−0.24	−0.22	−1.57	0.18	1.86	−0.04	−0.53
Friendships	0.004	0.02	0.44	2.14[a]	−0.24	−1.89	0.02	0.21
Household income	−0.18	−1.06	0.20	1.33	0.06	0.59	−0.07	−0.83
Health	−0.20	−1.21	−0.07	−0.48	0.10	1.03	0.02	0.28
Education	0.44	2.15[a]	−0.23	−1.31	−0.13	−1.06	0.06	0.54
Job	−0.14	−0.79	0.33	1.86	0.06	0.56	−0.12	−1.23
Neighbors	0.12	0.57	0.23	1.23	−0.05	−0.41	−0.07	−0.69
Public safety	−0.06	−0.34	0.18	1.12	0.03	0.30	−0.06	−0.72
The condition of the environment	0.09	0.43	0.001	0.00	−0.03	−0.25	0.004	0.04
Social welfare system	−0.03	−0.14	−0.18	−1.12	0.20	1.77	−0.07	−0.78
The democratic system	−0.13	−0.63	0.26	1.53	−0.25	(−2.02)[a]	0.14	1.36
Family life	−0.10	−0.48	−0.09	−0.44	0.27	1.92	−0.14	−1.25
Leisure	−0.18	−1.11	0.12	0.80	−0.07	−0.70	0.04	0.45
Happiness	0.23	1.15	0.01	0.03	−0.25	(−2.09)[a]	0.14	1.35
(D) Trust in social institution								
Trust generally	−0.24	−0.88	−0.01	−0.04	−0.21	−1.29	0.22	1.64
Trust the central government	−0.02	−0.07	−0.08	−0.34	−0.01	−0.05	0.09	0.70
Trust local governments	0.03	0.12	0.24	1.03	0.33	2.05[a]	−0.32	(−2.35)[a]
Trust the army	−0.19	−0.95	−0.14	−0.74	0.02	0.16	0.06	0.55
Trust the legal system	0.42	1.59	0.06	0.27	−0.06	−0.38	−0.09	−0.66
Trust the police	−0.39	−1.65	−0.16	−0.74	−0.09	−0.61	0.21	1.76

(continued)

(continued)

Logit regression analysis results by country Japan								
Dependent variable	Exit		Broader voice		Bureaucratic voice		Broader loyalty	
Independent variables	Coeff.	z-stat.	Coeff.	z-stat.	Coeff.	z-stat.	Coeff.	z-stat.
(E) Assessment of government performance								
Worry about corruption	−0.87	−1.94	0.20	0.65	0.13	0.61	0.03	0.15
Worry about Economic inequality	−0.26	−0.82	0.22	0.82	−0.14	−0.78	0.12	0.79
Political corruption	−0.20	−0.84	−0.11	−0.55	−0.05	−0.35	0.16	1.32
Duty to vote	−0.07	−0.33	0.15	0.80	0.01	0.09	−0.05	−0.44
Widespread corruption	0.03	0.21	0.16	1.12	0.07	0.86	−0.11	−1.51
No power	−0.06	−0.43	0.16	1.20	−0.20	(−2.33)[a]	0.12	1.57
Complicated	−0.14	−0.93	−0.31	(−2.29)[a]	−0.14	−1.50	0.26	3.25[b]
No matter whether vote	−0.20	−1.16	0.27	2.07[a]	−0.33	(−3.19)[b]	0.17	2.08[a]
Stop thinking	0.21	1.16	0.09	0.53	−0.14	−1.39	0.03	0.36
Pay little attention	0.11	0.63	0.26	1.55	0.02	0.17	−0.12	−1.35
Powerful leader	0.46	2.01[a]	−0.30	−1.54	−0.10	−0.75	0.05	0.47
Experts	−0.47	−1.89	0.09	0.46	0.25	1.76	−0.12	−1.02
Military government	−0.11	−0.27	−0.14	−0.37	−0.13	−0.56	0.19	0.96
Democratic political system	−0.20	−0.73	0.18	0.79	0.13	0.85	−0.10	−0.73
Bribe	0.02	0.27	−0.17	(−2.64)[b]	0.09	1.51	0.01	0.13
(F) Satisfaction with rights								
Right to vote	−0.22	−0.93	−0.23	−1.08	−0.13	−0.88	0.21	1.68
Right to gather and demonstrate	0.02	0.08	0.04	0.16	0.27	1.64	−0.24	−1.73
Right to be informed about government	0.22	1.03	−0.26	−1.45	0.02	0.19	0.05	0.45
Freedom of speech	0.10	0.35	−0.12	−0.49	−0.07	−0.43	0.08	0.57
Right to criticize the government	−0.11	−0.43	0.78	3.13[b]	−0.09	−0.57	−0.19	−1.44
(H) Demographics								
Female	−0.08	−0.26	−0.87	(−3.21)[b]	0.50	2.92[b]	−0.06	−0.39
Age	−0.01	−0.36	−0.02	−1.40	−0.004	−0.43	0.01	1.48
Level of education	0.03	0.13	−0.16	−0.76	0.39	2.59[a]	−0.19	−1.59
Married	−0.41	−1.12	0.00	0.01	0.16	0.72	0.01	0.07
Unemployed	0.60	0.95	0.47	0.80	−0.01	−0.01	−0.41	−1.09
Income	0.04	0.87	0.01	0.18	−0.02	−0.80	0.005	0.24
No religion	0.05	0.16	−0.11	−0.40	−0.03	−0.16	0.05	0.30

(continued)

(continued)

Logit regression analysis results by country Japan								
Dependent variable	Exit		Broader voice		Bureaucratic voice		Broader loyalty	
Independent variables	Coeff.	z-stat.	Coeff.	z-stat.	Coeff.	z-stat.	Coeff.	z-stat.
(I) Region (Base = Kanto)								
Hokkaido/Tohoku	−0.60	−1.19	−0.31	−0.70	−0.34	−1.27	0.49	2.14[a]
Chubu	−0.88	−1.90	0.05	0.15	−0.45	−1.94	0.50	2.53[a]
Kinki	−0.68	−1.50	−0.14	−0.38	0.02	0.10	0.13	0.65
Chugoku/Shikoku	−0.36	−0.68	−0.17	−0.36	−0.29	−0.99	0.40	1.62
Kyushu	0.13	0.29	0.41	0.93	−0.11	−0.38	−0.04	−0.16
(J) City cize								
City cize	0.17	1.19	0.24	1.89	−0.11	−1.40	−0.03	−0.43
(L) Yearly dummy variable (Base = 2004)								
2006	−0.55	−1.39	−0.02	−0.05	−0.53	(−2.24)[a]	0.56	2.77[b]
2008	−0.46	−1.18	−0.36	−1.01	−0.32	−1.40	0.49	2.47[a]
Constant	1.40	0.57	−7.33	(−3.10)[b]	−0.91	−0.61	−0.06	−0.05
n	1282		1282		1282		1282	
Pseudo R squared	0.1446		0.1570		0.1144		0.0994	

Note [a]5% significance level; [b]1% significance level

6.13 Kazakhstan

A quick review of the frequency distribution of options, for Kazakhstan, reveals that those who choose the broader voice option are significant, registering 52.6%, whereas those who choose the broader loyalty option register 32.5%.

The exit option is too small to be statistically significant.

Those who choose the broader voice option are favored by those who do not participate in national elections, are not satisfied with the condition of the environment, negatively assess government performance with regard to corruption, regard government as paying little attention, are not satisfied with the right to criticize government, and have a very poor income level.

Those who choose the bureaucratic voice option are favored by those who are satisfied with family life, do not have a social welfare system, trust the army negatively assess government experts, are highly educated, and are not religious. An educated guess is that this group constitutes a fledgling middle class.

Those who choose the broader loyalty option do not enjoy many public utilities, do not live internationally, are not satisfied with the democratic system or the social welfare system, do not trust social institutions in general, assess government as paying little attention, and are satisfied with the right to criticize government. Demographically, they are female and very poor citizens.

For an overall country summary, the basis of Kazakhstani society features broader loyalty with even a larger number choosing vigorous voice options. Connections and corruptions are not uncommon, it seems. Yet the exit option is not normally encouraged.

Summary statistics of countries Kazakhstan					
	n	Mean	SD	Min	Max
Exit	744	0.05	0.21	0	1
Broader voice	744	0.53	0.50	0	1
Bureaucratic voice	744	0.10	0.30	0	1
Broader loyalty	744	0.33	0.47	0	1
(A) Lifestyles					
Number of public utilities	800	3.48	1.26	1	7
Homeownership	800	0.94	0.23	0	1
Number of family members	800	3.95	1.93	1	13
Pray	780	2.06	1.21	1	5
National elections	784	3.73	1.37	1	5
Proud	772	3.39	0.75	1	4
Relative Standard of Living	794	2.82	0.64	1	5
(B) Exposure to globalization					
Internet	788	1.34	0.87	1	5
Living internationally	800	0.86	0.97	0	6
English ability	796	1.25	0.55	1	4
(C) Satisfaction with aspects of life					
Housing	800	3.80	1.10	1	5
Friendships	789	4.34	0.76	1	5
Household income	794	3.19	1.19	1	5
Health	798	3.47	1.16	1	5
Education	792	3.73	1.01	1	5
Job	726	3.56	1.18	1	5
Neighbors	791	4.12	0.84	1	5
Public safety	776	3.42	1.10	1	5
The condition of the environment	796	2.78	1.22	1	5
Social welfare system	775	2.95	1.14	1	5
The democratic system	752	3.22	1.08	1	5
Family life	761	4.18	0.95	1	5
Leisure	793	3.57	1.14	1	5
Spiritual life	781	3.66	1.03	1	5
Happiness	790	2.94	1.13	1	5
(D) Trust in social institution					
Trust generally	785	0.16	0.37	0	1
Trust the central government	770	2.85	0.79	1	4
Trust local governments	777	2.52	0.84	1	4
Trust the army	755	2.87	0.87	1	4
Trust the legal system	768	2.47	0.86	1	4
Trust the police	780	2.11	0.89	1	4
(E) Assessment of government performance					

(continued)

(continued)

Summary statistics of countries Kazakhstan					
	n	Mean	SD	Min	Max
Worry about corruption	800	0.39	0.49	0	1
Worry about Economic inequality	800	0.17	0.38	0	1
Political corruption	740	1.96	0.71	1	4
Duty to vote	793	4.12	0.93	1	5
Widespread corruption	738	4.17	0.75	1	5
No power	778	3.96	0.98	1	5
Complicated	780	3.75	1.04	1	5
No matter whether vote	771	3.25	1.20	1	5
Pay little attention	766	4.07	0.84	1	5
Powerful leader	714	1.74	0.77	1	3
Experts	686	1.79	0.63	1	3
Military government	719	1.21	0.49	1	3
Democratic political system	719	2.05	0.69	1	3
Bribe	781	8.57	2.14	1	10
(F) Satisfaction with rights					
Right to vote	781	3.25	0.70	1	4
Right to participate in any organizations	749	3.12	0.69	1	4
Right to gather and demonstrate	750	2.89	0.81	1	4
Right to be informed about government	759	2.75	0.88	1	4
Right to criticize the government	747	2.64	0.91	1	4
(H) Demographics					
Female	800	0.53	0.50	0	1
Age	800	40.39	13.46	20	69
Level of education	800	2.5	0.6	1	3
Married	800	0.69	0.46	0	1
Unemployed	800	0.10	0.30	0	1
Income	753	6.60	4.53	1	20
No religion	779	0.23	0.42	0	1
(I) Region (Base = North)					
Almaty	800	0.09	0.28	0	1
Centre	800	0.19	0.39	0	1
East	800	0.21	0.40	0	1
South	800	0.23	0.42	0	1
West	800	0.13	0.34	0	1
(K) Rural					
Rural	800	0.17	0.37	0	1

Frequency Distribution of 7 Responses and Partially Aggregated 4 Responses

Kazakhstan

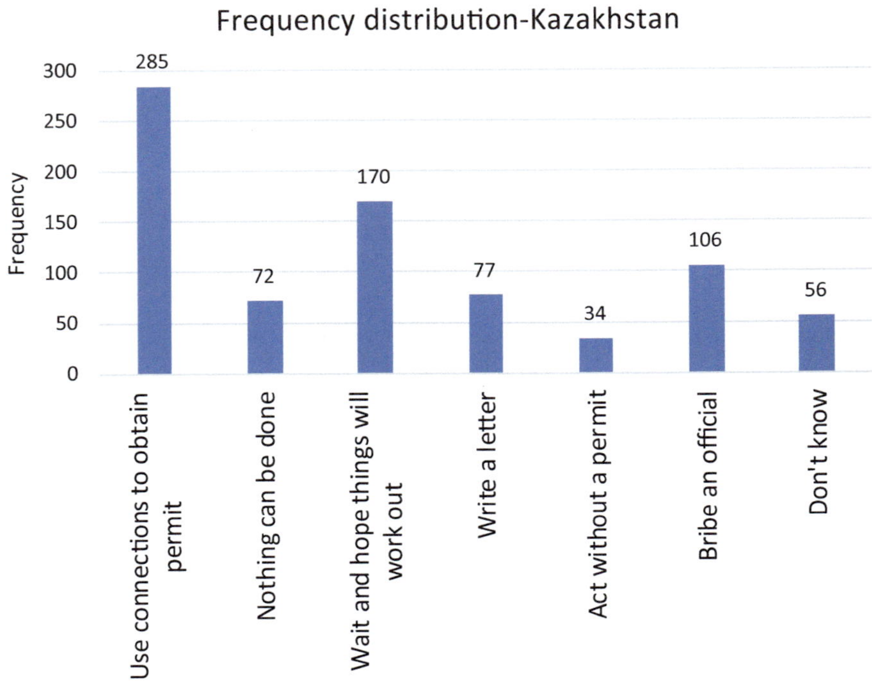

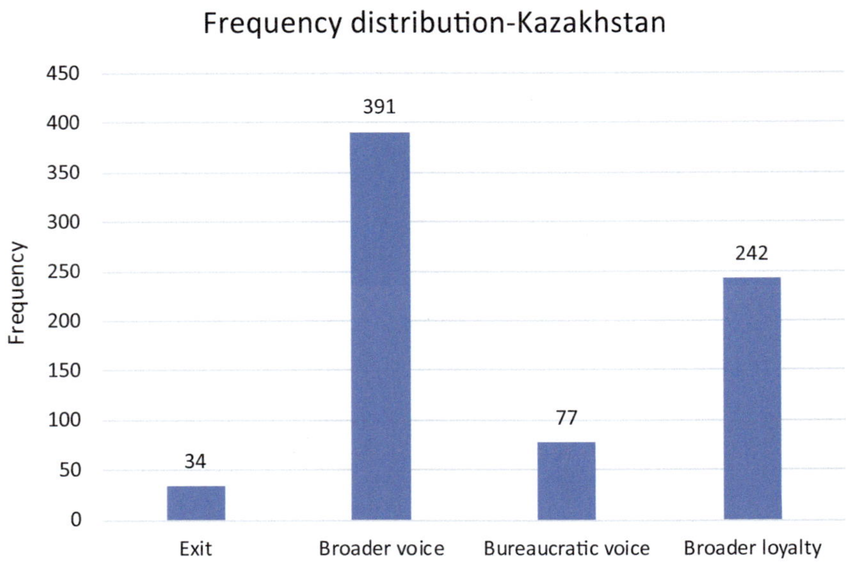

Logit regression analysis results by country Kazakhstan								
Dependent variable	Exit		Broader voice		Bureaucratic voice		Broader loyalty	
Independent variables	Coeff.	z-stat.	Coeff.	z-stat.	Coeff.	z-stat.	Coeff.	z-stat.
(A) Lifestyles								
Number of public utilities	–	–	−0.21	−1.36	0.20	0.68	0.37	2.12[a]
Homeownership	–	–	−0.87	−1.18	2.14	1.24	0.83	0.88
Number of family members	–	–	0.02	0.23	0.02	0.14	0.06	0.58
Pray	–	–	0.03	0.22	−0.51	−1.61	0.11	0.70
National elections	–	–	−0.39	(−2.65)[b]	0.56	1.71	0.19	1.12
Proud	–	–	0.54	2.22[a]	0.39	0.85	−0.47	−1.81
Relative Standard of Living	–	–	0.08	0.30	−0.94	−1.85	0.25	0.80
(B) Exposure to globalization								
Internet	–	–	−0.47	(−2.26)[a]	0.03	0.08	0.37	1.63
Living internationally	–	–	0.25	1.35	0.04	0.13	−0.49	(−2.34)[a]
English ability	–	–	0.20	0.63	0.14	0.23	−0.29	−0.80
(C) Satisfaction with aspects of life								
Housing	–	–	−0.10	−0.62	−0.11	−0.36	0.35	1.83
Friendships	–	–	0.20	0.86	−0.88	−1.77	−0.02	−0.08
Household incom e	–	–	0.26	1.36	−0.05	−0.14	−0.38	−1.82
Health	–	–	0.05	0.26	−0.21	−0.63	0.15	0.75
Education	–	–	−0.01	−0.08	0.50	1.35	−0.16	−0.83
Job	–	–	0.06	0.37	−0.41	−1.34	0.01	0.04
Neighbors	–	–	0.29	1.27	0.16	0.37	−0.46	−1.73
Public safety	–	–	0.21	1.18	−0.31	−0.91	0.06	0.29
The condition of the environment	–	–	−0.46	(−2.52)[a]	0.58	1.56	0.40	1.99[a]
Social welfare system	–	–	0.14	0.72	−0.87	(−2.10)[a]	0.13	0.62
The democratic system	–	–	0.20	0.95	0.49	1.06	−0.62	(−2.62)[b]
Family life	–	–	0.13	0.76	1.16	2.74[b]	−0.59	(−3.02)[b]

(continued)

(continued)

Logit regression analysis results by country Kazakhstan								
Dependent variable	Exit		Broader voice		Bureaucratic voice		Broader loyalty	
Independent variables	Coeff.	z-stat.	Coeff.	z-stat.	Coeff.	z-stat.	Coeff.	z-stat.
Leisure	–	–	−0.31	−1.61	0.00	−0.01	0.20	0.87
Spiritual life	–	–	−0.23	−1.14	0.86	2.30[a]	0.09	0.40
Happiness	–	–	−0.07	−0.41	−0.10	−0.28	0.18	0.98
(D) Trust in social institution								
Trust generally	–	–	−0.62	−1.73	−0.83	−1.06	0.84	2.07[a]
Trust the central government	–	–	−0.30	−1.22	−0.31	−0.66	0.29	1.06
Trust local governm ents	–	–	0.32	1.20	0.92	1.80	−0.34	−1.17
Trust the army	–	–	−0.02	−0.11	0.80	1.99[a]	−0.44	−1.89
Trust the legal system	–	–	−0.11	−0.44	−0.30	−0.70	−0.13	−0.47
Trust the police	–	–	−0.003	−0.01	−0.30	−0.77	0.44	1.79
(E) Assessment of government performance								
Worry about corruption	–	–	0.69	2.26[a]	−1.02	−1.70	−0.48	−1.40
Worry about Economic inequality	–	–	0.05	0.12	−0.50	−0.59	−0.24	−0.52
Political corruption	–	–	−0.39	−1.69	0.31	0.78	0.32	1.22
Duty to vote	–	–	0.00	0.00	0.17	0.45	−0.02	−0.07
Widespread corruption	–	–	0.04	0.15	−0.07	−0.17	−0.18	−0.72
No power	–	–	0.02	0.10	−0.45	−1.44	0.29	1.41
Complicated	–	–	−0.23	−1.20	0.05	0.15	0.09	0.41
No matter whether vote	–	–	0.12	0.83	0.05	0.19	−0.13	−0.82
Pay little attention	–	–	0.56	2.45[a]	−0.66	−1.70	−0.57	(−2.40)[a]
Powerful leader	–	–	−0.16	−0.73	0.30	0.72	0.02	0.07
Experts	–	–	0.11	0.44	−1.29	(−1.98)[a]	0.68	2.32[a]

(continued)

(continued)

Logit regression analysis results by country Kazakhstan								
Dependent variable	Exit		Broader voice		Bureaucratic voice		Broader loyalty	
Independent variables	Coeff.	z-stat.	Coeff.	z-stat.	Coeff.	z-stat.	Coeff.	z-stat.
Military government	–	–	−0.09	−0.27	0.91	1.49	−0.29	−0.87
Democratic political system	–	–	0.32	1.34	0.24	0.55	−0.05	−0.21
Bribe	–	–	−0.02	−0.26	−0.11	−0.80	0.05	0.62
(F) Satisfaction with rights								
Right to vote	–	–	−0.36	−1.06	0.62	0.93	0.45	1.18
Right to participate in any organizations	–	–	−0.39	−1.16	0.14	0.22	0.13	0.34
Right to gather and demonstrate	–	–	0.14	0.48	−0.68	−1.27	0.21	0.65
Right to be informed about government	–	–	0.34	1.29	−0.71	−1.42	−0.42	−1.46
Right to criticize the government	–	–	−0.80	(−3.31)[b]	0.08	0.15	1.00	3.51[b]
(H) Demographics								
Female	–	–	−0.46	−1.52	−0.28	−0.47	0.72	2.11[a]
Age	–	–	−0.01	−0.68	0.01	0.33	0.01	0.77
Level of education	–	–	−0.20	−0.73	1.35	2.12[a]	−0.19	−0.61
Married	–	–	0.28	0.71	−1.37	−1.85	0.34	0.77
Unemployed	–	–	0.53	0.96	−1.30	−1.11	−0.71	−1.14
Income	–	–	0.11	2.69[b]	0.002	0.02	−0.18	(−3.47)[b]
No religion	–	–	−0.82	−1.86	1.87	2.20[a]	0.16	0.32
(I) Region (Base = North)								
Almaty	–	–	1.61	2.09[a]	−0.35	−0.21	−0.27	−0.32
Centre	–	–	0.63	1.18	0.43	0.42	−0.05	−0.08
East	–	–	0.95	1.74	−0.83	−0.73	−0.87	−1.36
South	–	–	0.77	1.48	1.02	0.95	−0.84	−1.35
West	–	–	1.11	1.65	−1.80	−1.27	−0.88	−1.19
(K) Rural								
Rural	–	–	0.37	0.87	−1.29	−1.34	−0.37	−0.76
Constant	–	–	0.90	0.36	−9.07	−1.68	−2.12	−0.76

(continued)

(continued)

Logit regression analysis results by country Kazakhstan								
Dependent variable	Exit		Broader voice		Bureaucratic voice		Broader loyalty	
Independent variables	Coeff.	z-stat.	Coeff.	z-stat.	Coeff.	z-stat.	Coeff.	z-stat.
n	–		367		367		367	
Pseudo R squared	–		0.2713		0.3905		0.2800	

Note [a]5% significance level; [b]1% significance level

6.14 Kyrgyzstan

A quick snapshot of the frequency distribution of options, for Kyrgyzstan, reveals that those who choose the broader voice option account for 44.6% of the respondents. The broader loyalty option choosers represent 35.4% of the survey size. The exit option registers 6.2%. In 2005, Kyrgyzstan experienced the Tulip Revolution, a sign that its citizens' democratic yearning is significant. Political instability is ongoing. As an indication of instability, the Manas International Airport, 25 km from the capital Bishkek, served as a U.S military base from 2005—2014, but after the United States vacated the airport, the Russians tookover the Manas airbase. Most recently, China has acquired the right to use the Manas Airport.

Those who choose the exit option, in Kyrgyzstan, are proficient in English, rate satisfaction with leisure as high, trust the army, negatively assess government performance on political corruption, regard government as not paying attention, negatively assess government on issues of bribery, are satisfied with the right to vote, and have a high-income level. They appear to belong to the middle class and hold a critical view of government.

Those who choose the broader voice option are satisfied with housing and friendships, are not satisfied with leisure, are not happy, assess government as paying little attention, negatively assess government performance on the issue of the right to vote, and have a low-income level. Regionally, those farther from the capital Bishkek, located in the northern part of the country, such as Osh, Jalalabad, and Isyk-Kul, are regions that select the broader voice option.

Those who choose the bureaucratic voice option do not enjoy public utilities, are not satisfied with housing, are not satisfied with the social welfare system, trust the army, negatively assess government on issues of corruption and paying too little attention, are not satisfied with the rights of citizens toward the government. Demographically, this group tends to be those with low income and no religion. Regionally, they tend to be those far from Bishkek.

Those who choose the broader loyalty option suffer from the lack of public utilities and housing, are not satisfied with the social welfare system, negatively assess government corruption, assess government as paying too little attention, are satisfied with the right to vote, do not like government experts. Regionally, those far from the capital, Bishek, do not choose the loyalty option.

Summary statistics of countries Kyrgyzstan					
	n	Mean	SD	Min	Max
Exit	759	0.06	0.24	0	1
Broader voice	759	0.45	0.50	0	1
Bureaucratic voice	759	0.14	0.35	0	1
Broader loyalty	759	0.35	0.48	0	1
(A) Lifestyles					
Number of public utilities	800	2.51	1.38	0	7
Homeownership	798	0.93	0.25	0	1
Number of family members	800	4.67	2.23	1	13
Pray	797	2.43	1.63	1	5
National elections	778	4.31	1.00	1	5
Proud	794	3.42	0.72	1	4
Relative Standard of Living	797	2.86	0.74	1	5
(B) Exposure to globalization					
Internet	798	1.26	0.79	1	5
Living internationally	800	0.86	0.92	0	5
English ability	800	1.28	0.56	1	4
(C) Satisfaction with aspects of life					
Housing	796	3.60	1.25	1	5
Friendships	789	4.30	0.85	1	5
Household income	780	3.08	1.27	1	5
Health	800	3.57	1.27	1	5
Education	785	3.60	1.13	1	5
Job	743	3.09	1.42	1	5
Neighbors	796	4.28	0.82	1	5
Public safety	739	2.96	1.18	1	5
The condition of the environment	778	3.12	1.20	1	5
Social welfare system	750	2.45	1.25	1	5
The democratic system	730	2.88	1.27	1	5
Family life	767	4.17	0.96	1	5
Leisure	784	3.55	1.21	1	5
Happiness	791	3.21	1.25	1	5
(D) Trust in social institution					
Trust generally	794	0.19	0.39	0	1
Trust the central government	788	2.47	0.88	1	4
Trust local governments	781	2.37	0.86	1	4
Trust the army	776	2.78	0.92	1	4
Trust the legal system	755	2.33	0.88	1	4
(E) Assessment of government performance					
Worry about corruption	800	0.50	0.50	0	1

(continued)

(continued)

Summary statistics of countries Kyrgyzstan					
	n	Mean	SD	Min	Max
Worry about Economic inequality	800	0.11	0.31	0	1
Political corruption	772	1.68	0.76	1	4
Duty to vote	796	4.53	0.65	1	5
Widespread corruption	783	4.23	0.88	1	5
No power	780	3.87	1.04	1	5
Complicated	778	3.84	0.99	1	5
No matter whether vote	787	2.82	1.25	1	5
Stop thinking	786	4.24	0.90	1	5
Pay little attention	765	4.17	0.86	1	5
Powerful leader	696	1.81	0.76	1	3
Experts	675	1.98	0.67	1	3
Military government	729	1.50	0.71	1	3
Democratic political system	706	2.13	0.68	1	3
Bribe	785	8.02	2.42	1	10
(F) Satisfaction with rights					
Right to vote	791	3.17	0.83	1	4
Right to participate in any organizations	696	2.89	0.76	1	4
Right to gather and demonstrate	718	2.70	0.86	1	4
Right to be informed about government	739	2.66	0.90	1	4
Right to criticize the government	748	2.71	0.95	1	4
(H) Demographics					
Female	800	0.56	0.50	0	1
Age	800	39.78	13.41	20	69
Level of education	800	2.39	0.65	1	3
Married	800	0.7	0.5	0	1
Unemployed	800	0.10	0.31	0	1
Income	714	17.10	5.16	1	20
No religion	788	0.06	0.24	0	1
(I) Region (Base = Bishkek)					
Isyk-Kul oblast	800	0.09	0.28	0	1
Naryn oblast	800	0.06	0.24	0	1
Chui oblast	800	0.18	0.38	0	1
Talass oblast	800	0.06	0.24	0	1
Batken oblast	800	0.08	0.26	0	1
Jalalabad Oblast	800	0.16	0.37	0	1
Osh Oblast	800	0.23	0.42	0	1

Frequency Distribution of 7 Responses and Partially Aggregated 4 Responses Kyrgyzstan

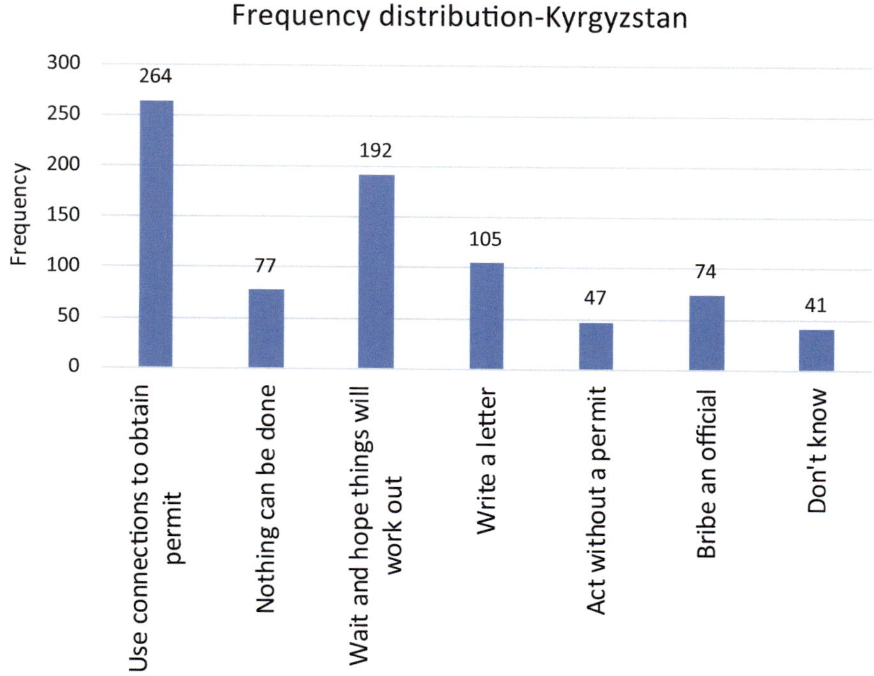

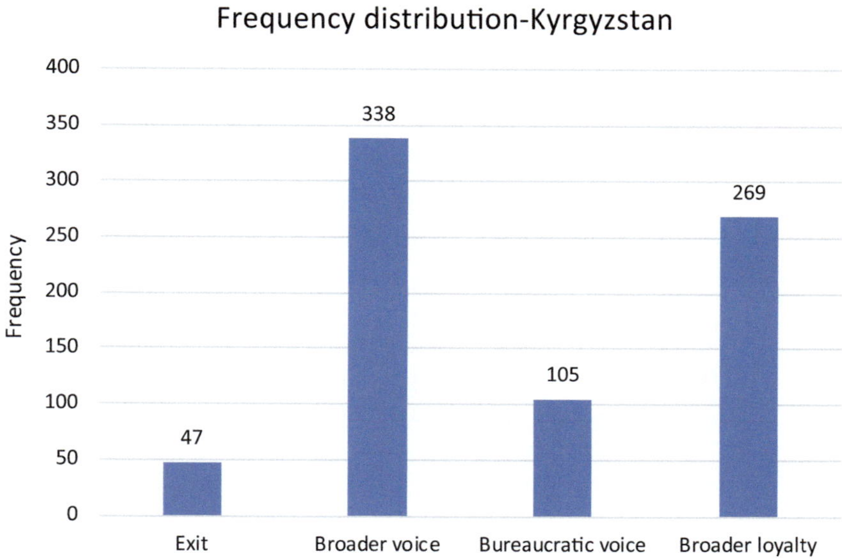

Logit regression analysis results by country Kyrgyzstan								
Dependent variable	Exit		Broader voice		Bureaucratic voice		Broader loyalty	
Independent variables	Coeff.	z-stat.	Coeff.	z-stat.	Coeff.	z-stat.	Coeff.	z-stat.
(A) Lifestyles								
Number of public utilities	−0.34	−1.00	0.06	0.39	−0.85	(−2.38)[a]	0.09	0.52
Homeownership	−2.39	−1.35	−1.15	−1.37	2.18	1.03	2.67	2.07[a]
Number of family members	0.20	1.06	0.06	0.86	−0.41	(−2.14)[a]	−0.10	−1.30
Pray	0.26	1.00	−0.08	−0.82	0.26	1.04	0.01	0.11
National elections	−0.87	−1.73	−0.22	−1.05	1.65	2.65[b]	0.13	0.56
Proud	−0.55	−0.87	−0.06	−0.21	−0.24	−0.39	0.12	0.41
Relative Standard of Living	0.26	0.43	0.50	1.89	0.47	0.93	−0.62	(−2.24)[a]
(B) Exposure to globalization								
Internet	0.02	0.02	0.30	1.22	0.99	1.91	−0.29	−0.99
Living internationally	−0.03	−0.06	−0.15	−0.70	−0.90	−1.69	0.19	0.84
English ability	1.85	2.55[a]	0.06	0.22	−0.45	−0.63	−0.26	−0.77
(C) Satisfaction with aspects of life								
Housing	−0.76	−1.77	0.33	2.09[a]	−0.91	(−2.16)[a]	−0.16	−0.94
Friendships	−0.76	−1.30	0.41	2.00[a]	−0.49	−1.12	−0.44	(−2.03)[a]
Household income	0.04	0.11	0.09	0.61	0.46	1.23	−0.13	−0.78
Health	0.75	1.84	0.05	0.35	−0.27	−0.84	−0.11	−0.64
Education	0.34	0.80	−0.10	−0.58	0.29	0.73	−0.19	−0.99
Job	−0.24	−0.69	−0.09	−0.63	0.08	0.27	0.03	0.22
Neighbors	0.89	1.52	−0.26	−1.24	−0.22	−0.45	0.27	1.23
Public safety	−0.007	−0.02	−0.04	−0.27	−0.62	−1.7	0.32	1.78
The condition of the environment	0.69	1.66	0.001	0.01	0.02	0.05	−0.06	−0.36
Social welfare system	−0.75	−1.65	0.31	1.98[a]	−0.71	(−2.13)[a]	0.05	0.32
The democratic system	−0.05	−0.12	−0.06	−0.38	0.99	2.25[a]	−0.14	−0.78
Family life	−0.94	−1.75	0.04	0.19	−0.57	−1.26	0.38	1.77
Leisure	1.67	2.83[b]	−0.52	(−3.10)[b]	0.62	1.59	0.17	1.01
Happiness	−0.13	−0.31	−0.54	(−3.24)[b]	0.48	1.25	0.50	2.74[b]

(continued)

(continued)

Logit regression analysis results by country Kyrgyzstan								
Dependent variable	Exit		Broader voice		Bureaucratic voice		Broader loyalty	
Independent variables	Coeff.	z-stat.	Coeff.	z-stat.	Coeff.	z-stat.	Coeff.	z-stat.
(D) Trust in social institution								
Trust generally	0.17	0.17	−1.00	(−2.25)[a]	0.33	0.32	1.19	2.47[a]
Trust the central government	−1.29	(−2.06)[a]	0.36	1.46	−0.23	−0.42	−0.10	−0.38
Trust local governments	−1.05	−1.65	−0.14	−0.55	−0.90	−1.41	0.67	2.47[a]
Trust the army	2.27	3.06[b]	−0.40	−1.90	1.35	2.47[a]	−0.18	−0.79
Trust the legal system	–	–	0.42	1.72	−0.11	−0.2	−0.88	(−3.23)[b]
Trust the police	0.16	0.37	−0.001	0.00	−0.0002	0.00	−0.11	−0.52
(E) Assessment of government performance								
Worry about corruption	0.57	0.64	0.74	2.25[a]	−2.72	(−3.04)[b]	0.01	0.03
Worry about Economic inequality	1.33	1.17	−0.66	−1.34	1.97	2.02[a]	0.24	0.44
Political corruption	1.91	3.00[b]	−0.24	−1.07	−1.09	−1.89	0.49	1.99[a]
Duty to vote	−2.01	(−2.26)[a]	0.31	1.07	−0.91	−1.24	0.23	0.70
Widespread corruption	−0.95	−1.89	0.20	1.02	−0.04	−0.09	−0.35	−1.72
No power	−1.28	(−2.91)[b]	0.12	0.64	0.16	0.38	0.07	0.34
Complicated	–	–	−0.37	−1.89	−0.35	−0.85	0.61	2.70[b]
No matter whether vote	−0.46	−1.17	0.16	1.08	0.10	0.35	−0.21	−1.33
Stop thinking	−0.43	−0.93	0.32	1.57	−0.02	−0.05	−0.24	−1.15
Pay little attention	1.89	2.81[b]	−0.52	(−2.23)[a]	1.25	2.34[a]	−0.11	−0.45
Powerful leader	0.10	0.19	0.12	0.52	−0.02	−0.03	−0.18	−0.73
Experts	−0.77	−1.10	0.28	1.10	0.43	0.75	−0.17	−0.63
Military government	0.65	1.27	−0.21	−0.85	0.05	0.1	−0.13	−0.49
Democratic political system	1.53	2.07[a]	0.15	0.65	−0.10	−0.2	−0.62	(−2.47)[a]
Bribe	−0.57	(−2.73)[b]	0.05	0.63	−0.31	−1.81	0.14	1.65

(continued)

(continued)

Logit regression analysis results by country Kyrgyzstan								
Dependent variable	Exit		Broader voice		Bureaucratic voice		Broader loyalty	
Independent variables	Coeff.	z-stat.	Coeff.	z-stat.	Coeff.	z-stat.	Coeff.	z-stat.
(F) Satisfaction with rights								
Right to vote	2.16	2.46[a]	−0.67	(−2.81)[b]	−0.30	−0.47	0.69	2.67[b]
Right to participate in any organizations	−1.54	(−2.26)[a]	0.60	2.28[a]	0.86	1.35	−0.37	−1.47
Right to gather and demonstrate	0.74	1.18	0.02	0.10	−0.39	−0.75	−0.09	−0.39
Right to be informed about government	−1.08	−1.95	−0.07	−0.31	0.67	1.22	−0.09	−0.36
Right to criticize the government	1.05	1.82	0.49	2.50[a]	−1.58	(−3.06)[b]	−0.32	−1.54
(H) Demographics								
Female	1.14	1.37	0.13	0.42	0.60	0.92	−0.56	−1.60
Age	0.05	1.29	0.02	1.16	−0.02	−0.68	−0.01	−0.33
Level of education	0.07	0.10	−0.06	−0.22	−0.61	−1.02	0.15	0.50
Married	−0.64	−0.58	0.42	1.15	1.17	1.28	−0.54	−1.31
Unemployed	2.38	1.67	−0.50	−1.00	1.02	0.81	−0.20	−0.37
Income	0.35	2.26[a]	−0.07	(−2.00)[a]	0.35	2.91[b]	0.002	0.04
No religion	−1.64	−0.59	0.08	0.11	5.92	3.20[b]	−1.79	−1.84
(I) Region (Base = Bishkek)								
Isyk-Kul oblast	0.40	0.20	−2.65	(−3.07)[b]	8.09	3.16[b]	1.31	1.29
Naryn oblast	0.72	0.32	−2.20	−1.94	7.47	3.16[b]	−1.21	−0.85
Chui oblast	−1.50	−1.04	−1.13	−1.70	−0.50	−0.25	1.58	2.03[a]
Talass oblast	−0.84	−0.28	−1.17	−0.99	–	–	3.38	2.47[a]
Batken oblast	–	–	−2.31	(−2.66)[b]	6.24	2.65[b]	2.39	2.38[a]
Jalalabad Oblast	−1.76	−1.15	−3.24	(−4.15)[b]	6.85	3.05[b]	2.72	3.06[b]
Osh Oblast	−0.38	−0.25	−1.59	(−2.22)[a]	4.33	2.08[a]	1.56	1.91
Constant	−7.33	−0.93	0.35	0.14	−10.9	−1.53	−3.02	−0.99
n	289		310		303		310	
Pseudo R squared	0.4339		0.2435		0.4686		0.2478	

Note [a]5% significance level; [b]1% significance level

6.15 Laos

A glance at the frequency distribution of options reveals that, in Laos, one cannot be too vocal with criticisms. This does not mean that the broader voice options are not used. Of the respondents, 25% answer that they use their connections or bribe officials to resolve issues.

Those who choose the exit option are too small for explanatory variables to be statistically significant.

Those who choose the broader voice option negatively assess government performance on issues of bribery.

Those who choose the bureaucratic voice option are not satisfied with the condition of the environment and are not satisfied with leisure. Demographically, they tend not to be married and are employed. Regionally, Savannakhet, adjacent to northeastern Thailand, does not choose the bureaucratic voice very much, whereas Luang Prabang, adjacent to mountainous Vietnam, does choose the bureaucratic voice option frequently.

Summary statistics of countries Laos					
	n	Mean	SD	Min	Max
Exit	995	0.01	0.07	0	1
Broader voice	995	0.25	0.44	0	1
Bureaucratic voice	995	0.31	0.46	0	1
Broader loyalty	995	0.43	0.50	0	1
(A) Lifestyles					
Number of public utilities	1000	3.01	1.29	0	7
Homeownership	1000	0.90	0.31	0	1
Number of family members	1000	4.91	2.16	1	15
Pray	1000	3.38	1.18	1	5
National elections	979	4.75	0.82	1	5
Local elections	986	4.67	0.85	1	5
Proud	1000	3.99	0.11	2	4
Relative Standard of Living	1000	2.97	0.69	1	5
(B) Exposure to globalization					
Internet	843	1.31	0.80	1	5
Living internationally	1000	1.69	0.89	0	6
English ability	995	1.42	0.60	1	4
(C) Satisfaction with aspects of life					
Housing	1000	4.11	1.03	1	5
Friendships	1000	3.96	0.75	1	5
Household income	996	3.27	1.07	1	5

(continued)

(continued)

Summary statistics of countries Laos					
	n	Mean	SD	Min	Max
Health	1000	4.04	1.07	1	5
Education	1000	3.46	1.10	1	5
Job	972	3.62	1.03	1	5
Neighbors	998	3.97	0.73	2	5
Public safety	994	3.66	0.95	1	5
The condition of the environment	997	3.69	0.89	1	5
Social welfare system	813	3.57	0.89	1	5
Family life	992	4.26	0.81	1	5
Leisure	1000	3.90	0.88	1	5
Spiritual life	998	4.21	0.74	2	5
Happiness	1000	3.83	0.89	1	5
(D) Trust in social institution					
Trust generally	993	0.22	0.41	0	1
(E) Assessment of government performance					
Worry about Economic inequality	1000	0.25	0.44	0	1
Duty to vote	1000	4.77	0.47	2	5
No power	987	3.17	1.11	1	5
Complicated	959	2.77	1.02	1	5
No matter whether vote	997	1.97	0.78	1	5
Stop thinking	969	2.35	0.88	1	5
Pay little attention	974	2.49	0.95	1	5
Bribe	998	8.86	2.04	1	10
(H) Demographics					
Female	1000	0.60	0.49	0	1
Age	1000	37.89	12.26	20	69
Level of education	998	1.75	0.86	1	3
Married	1000	0.71	0.45	0	1
Unemployed	1000	0.05	0.22	0	1
Income	996	11.97	6.02	1	20
(I) City (Base = Vientiane)					
Savannakhet	1000	0.25	0.43	0	1
Luang Prabang	1000	0.25	0.43	0	1

Frequency Distribution of 7 Responses and Partially Aggregated 4 Responses Laos

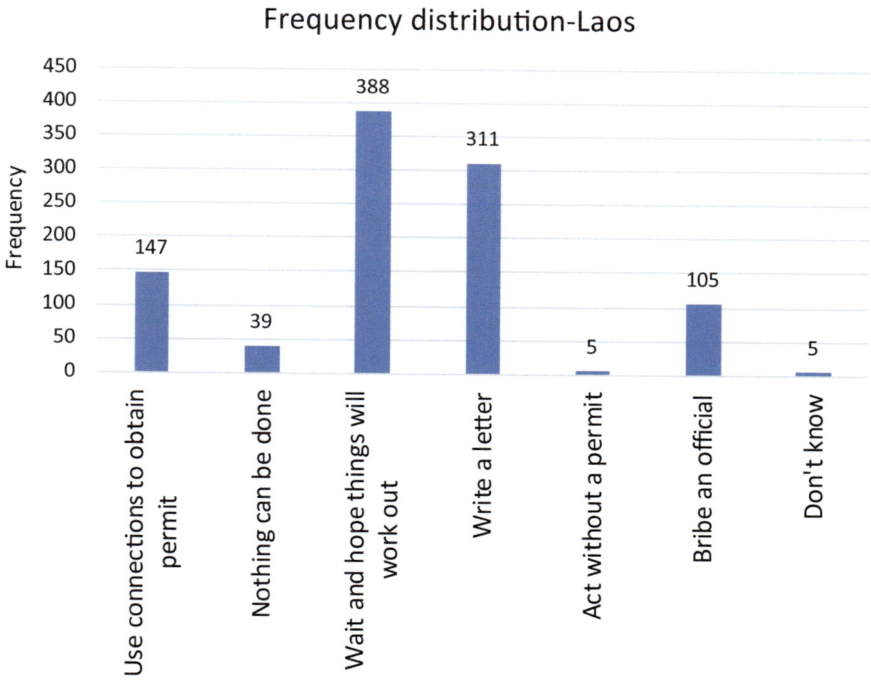

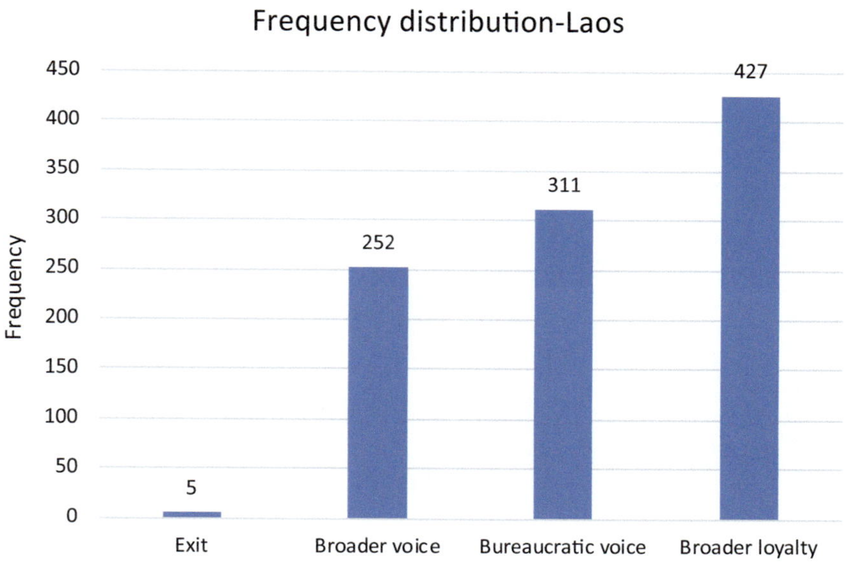

Logit regression analysis results by country Laos								
Dependent variable	Exit		Broader voice		Bureaucratic voice		Broader loyalty	
Independent variables	Coeff.	z-stat.	Coeff.	z-stat.	Coeff.	z-stat.	Coeff.	z-stat.
(A) Lifestyles								
Number of public utilities	–	–	0.17	1.62	0.07	0.72	−0.22	(−2.35)[a]
Homeownership	–	–	−0.45	−1.33	0.50	1.27	0.13	0.38
Number of family members	–	–	−0.04	−0.84	0.05	0.92	0.002	0.05
Pray	–	–	0.003	0.03	0.16	1.76	−0.15	−1.76
National elections	–	–	−0.06	−0.42	−0.04	−0.27	0.09	0.69
Local elections	–	–	0.11	0.80	0.03	0.25	−0.16	−1.22
Proud	–	–	−0.04	−0.06	1.04	0.91	−0.65	−0.77
Relative Standard of Living	–	–	−0.11	−0.61	−0.04	−0.23	0.12	0.73
(B) Exposure to globalization								
Internet	–	–	−0.06	−0.39	0.05	0.31	0.02	0.17
Living internationally	–	–	−0.02	−0.12	0.13	0.96	−0.14	−1.14
English ability	–	–	0.03	0.16	0.23	1.16	−0.26	−1.37
(C) Satisfaction with aspects of life								
Housing	–	–	0.03	0.27	−0.13	−1.08	0.06	0.62
Friendships	–	–	0.24	1.62	0.09	0.60	−0.25	−1.84
Household income	–	–	0.13	1.13	0.09	0.75	−0.15	−1.46
Health	–	–	−0.05	−0.47	−0.06	−0.49	0.11	1.08
Education	–	–	0.07	0.60	−0.06	−0.49	0.004	0.04
Job	–	–	−0.02	−0.17	−0.01	−0.05	−0.02	−0.14
Neighbors	–	–	0.07	0.43	0.21	1.30	−0.19	−1.33
Public safety	–	–	−0.03	−0.26	0.27	1.99	−0.18	−1.58
The condition of the environment	–	–	0.16	1.12	−0.31	(−2.30)[a]	0.09	0.75
Social welfare system	–	–	−0.03	−0.22	−0.07	−0.57	0.09	0.78
The democratic system	–	–	–	–	–	–	–	–
Family life	–	–	−0.06	−0.41	0.31	1.98[a]	−0.18	−1.28
Leisure	–	–	−0.03	−0.23	−0.28	(−2.17)[a]	0.24	1.96
Spiritual life	–	–	−0.01	−0.06	0.10	0.59	−0.05	−0.32
Happiness	–	–	−0.11	−0.90	−0.03	−0.20	0.11	0.96
(D) Trust in social institution								
Trust generally	–	–	−0.24	−0.90	0.19	0.74	0.09	0.37
(E) Assessment of government performance								
Worry about Economic inequality	–	–	−0.17	−0.73	−0.45	−1.83	0.39	1.81
Duty to vote	–	–	0.02	0.07	−0.19	−0.76	0.08	0.35
No power	–	–	−0.04	−0.37	−0.0002	0.00	0.01	0.09

(continued)

(continued)

Logit regression analysis results by country Laos								
Dependent variable	Exit		Broader voice		Bureaucratic voice		Broader loyalty	
Independent variables	Coeff.	z-stat.	Coeff.	z-stat.	Coeff.	z-stat.	Coeff.	z-stat.
Complicated	–	–	0.03	0.30	0.06	0.49	−0.04	−0.34
No matter whether vote	–	–	0.03	0.24	−0.01	−0.07	−0.05	−0.44
Stop thinking	–	–	−0.23	−1.71	−0.06	−0.38	0.25	2.10[a]
Pay little attention	–	–	0.10	0.78	−0.17	−1.25	0.03	0.24
Bribe	–	–	−0.15	(−2.99)[b]	−0.001	−0.02	0.14	2.76[b]
(H) Demographics								
Female	–	–	0.07	0.30	−0.25	−1.11	0.20	0.97
Age	–	–	−0.01	−0.99	−0.01	−0.55	0.01	1.43
Level of education	–	–	−0.15	−1.02	0.14	0.95	0.01	0.09
Married	–	–	0.24	0.99	−0.66	(−2.67)[b]	0.30	1.31
Unemployed	–	–	0.003	0.01	−1.86	(−2.34)[a]	0.96	2.14[a]
Income	–	–	−0.02	−0.77	−0.02	−0.98	0.04	1.92
(I) City (Base = Vientiane)								
Savannakhet	–	–	−0.42	−1.52	−1.01	(−3.15)[b]	1.00	3.98[b]
Luang Prabang	–	–	−0.77	−2.45	1.60	5.64[b]	−1.02	(−3.68)[b]
Constant	–	–	0.49	0.14	−5.55	−1.14	1.43	0.39
n	–		626		626		626	
Pseudo R squared	–		0.0716		0.1843		0.1368	

Note [a]5% significance level; [b]1% significance level

6.16 Malaysia

A quick look at the frequency distribution of options reveals that loyalty dominates the majority of respondents in Malaysia, registering 68%. Those who select the exit option are too small to be statistically significant. Between the voice options, bureaucratic voice options are more frequently chosen than broader voice options.

Those who choose the broader voice option do not enjoy home ownership, do not have family members, do not pray, are satisfied with health and public safety, do not trust in general, negatively assess government on corruption and the democratic political system, and have a high-income level. Regionally, Eastern Malaysia (Sabah, Sarawak, and Labuan) and Central Malaysia (Kuala Lumpur and Putrajaya) do not register the broader voice option.

Those who choose the bureaucratic voice option are more exposed internationally, are not satisfied with health, are happy, do not trust generally, positively assess government on issues surrounding the democratic political system, are male, are highly educated, are married, do not have a high income, and are not from the central region. Demographically, they tend to be female, not so young, are married, are unemployed, and are from Central and Eastern Malaysia.

Summary statistics of countries Malaysia

	n	Mean	SD	Min	Max
Exit	1716	0.01	0.09	0	1
Broader voice	1716	0.14	0.35	0	1
Bureaucratic voice	1716	0.16	0.37	0	1
Broader loyalty	1716	0.68	0.47	0	1
(A) Lifestyles					
LPG	1800	0.47	0.50	0	1
Homeownership	1789	0.70	0.46	0	1
Number of family members	1800	5.23	2.22	1	20
Pray	1788	4.48	1.09	1	5
National elections	1564	4.22	1.34	1	5
Proud	1788	3.57	0.68	1	4
Relative Standard of Living	1795	3.10	0.64	1	5
(B) Exposure to globalization					
Living internationally	1800	1.18	0.95	0	6
(C) Satisfaction with aspects of life					
Housing	1791	3.96	0.88	1	5
Friendships	1794	4.26	0.60	1	5
Household income	1791	3.81	0.85	1	5
Health	1796	4.20	0.76	1	5
Education	1785	3.97	0.85	1	5
Neighbors	1781	4.18	0.70	1	5
Public safety	1793	3.69	1.00	1	5
The condition of the environment	1794	3.79	0.85	1	5
The democratic system	1719	3.86	0.75	1	5
Family life	1792	4.27	0.62	1	5
Leisure	1786	4.07	0.65	1	5
Happiness	1798	4.13	0.72	1	5
(D) Trust in social institution					
Trust generally	1770	0.16	0.36	0	1
Trust the central government	1743	3.19	0.66	1	4
Trust local governments	1756	3.19	0.67	1	4
Trust the army	1724	3.20	0.69	1	4
Trust the legal system	1726	3.08	0.67	1	4
Trust the police	1769	2.91	0.82	1	4
(E) Assessment of government performance					
Worry about corruption	1800	0.43	0.50	0	1
Worry about Economic inequality	1800	0.36	0.48	0	1

(continued)

(continued)

Summary statistics of countries Malaysia					
	n	Mean	SD	Min	Max
Political corruption	1710	2.35	0.76	1	4
Duty to vote	1775	4.52	0.60	1	5
Widespread corruption	1698	3.86	0.89	1	5
No power	1743	3.76	0.97	1	5
Complicated	1734	3.84	0.91	1	5
No matter whether vote	1750	2.29	1.10	1	5
Pay little attention	1731	3.68	0.94	1	5
Powerful leader	1587	1.31	0.54	1	3
Experts	1550	1.68	0.66	1	3
Military government	1576	1.32	0.56	1	3
Democratic political system	1626	2.53	0.57	1	3
Bribe	1744	9.35	1.43	1	10
(F) Satisfaction with rights					
Right to vote	1728	3.39	0.58	1	4
Right to participate in any organizations	1659	3.15	0.61	1	4
Right to gather and demonstrate	1475	2.54	0.79	1	4
Right to be informed about government	1567	2.74	0.75	1	4
Freedom of Speech	1633	2.77	0.76	1	4
Right to criticize the government	1569	2.55	0.78	1	4
(H) Demographics					
Female	1800	0.51	0.50	0	1
Age	1800	37.15	11.97	20	69
Level of education	1800	1.73	0.69	1	3
Married	1800	0.69	0.46	0	1
Unemployed	1795	0.05	0.21	0	1
Income	1672	4.11	1.88	1	10
No religion	1800	0.01	0.08	0	1
(I) Region (Base = Northern)					
Southern	1800	0.17	0.37	0	1
Eastern	1800	0.15	0.36	0	1
Central	1800	0.33	0.47	0	1
East Malaysia	1800	0.10	0.30	0	1
(K) Urban/Rural					
Rural	1800	0.33	0.47	0	1
(L) Yearly dummy variable					
2007	1800	0.56	0.50	0	1

Frequency Distribution of 7 Responses and Partially Aggregated 4 Responses

Malaysia

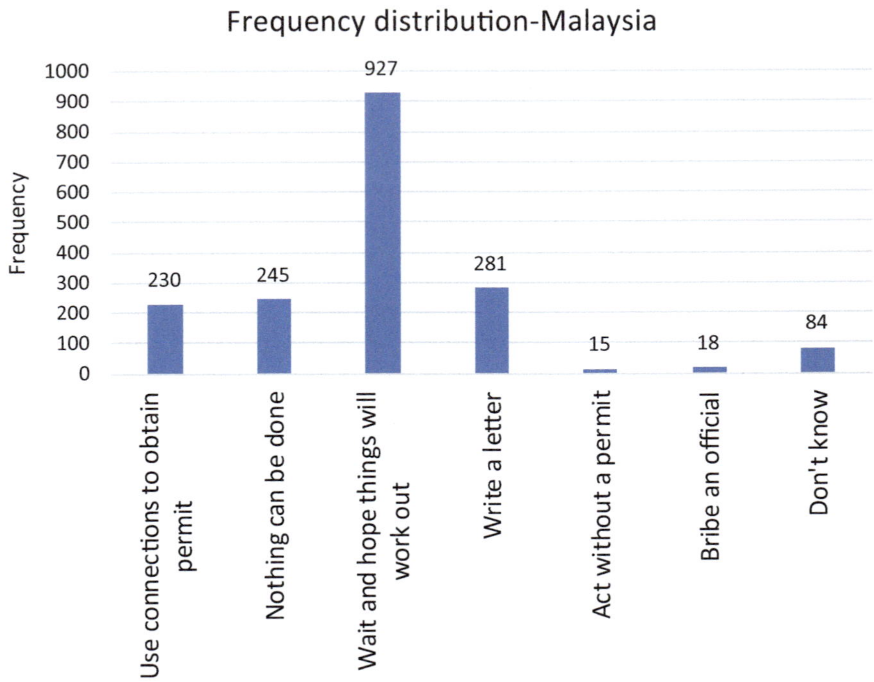

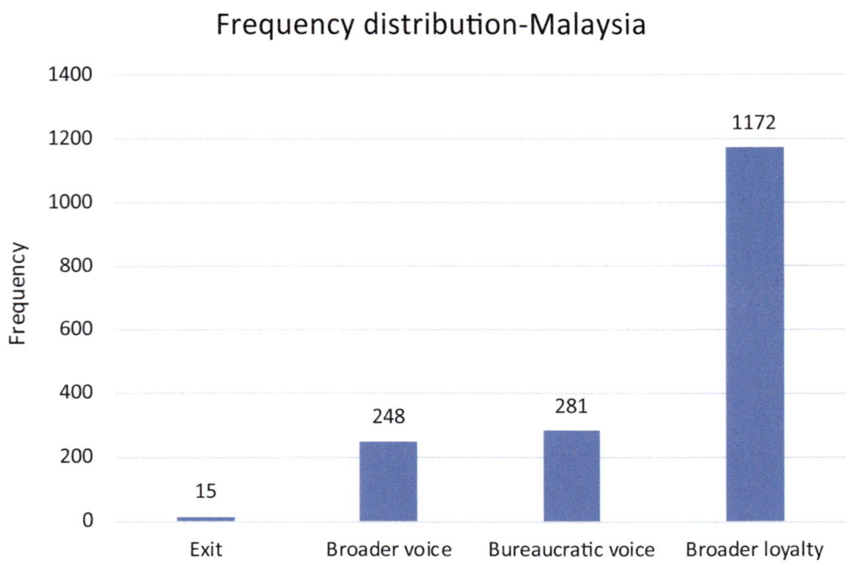

Logit regression analysis results by country Malaysia								
Dependent variable	Exit		Broader voice		Bureaucratic voice		Broader loyalty	
Independent variables	Coeff.	z-stat.	Coeff.	z-stat.	Coeff.	z-stat.	Coeff.	z-stat.
(A) Lifestyles								
Public water supply	–	–	–	–	–	–	–	–
Electricity	–	–	–	–	–	–	–	–
LPG	–	–	−0.42	−1.11	−0.70	−1.87	0.51	1.70
Homeownership	–	–	0.29	1.20	−0.17	−0.74	−0.04	−0.20
Number of family members	–	–	−0.13	(−2.46)[a]	0.07	1.52	0.02	0.51
Pray	–	–	−0.22	(−2.21)[a]	−0.05	−0.50	0.17	2.02[a]
National elections	–	–	−0.21	(−2.72)[b]	0.10	1.13	0.08	1.22
Proud	–	–	0.05	0.28	−0.16	−0.86	−0.004	−0.03
Relative Standard of Living	–	–	0.19	1.13	0.18	1.02	−0.21	−1.48
(B) Exposure to globalization								
Living internationally	–	–	0.18	1.81	0.22	2.19[a]	−0.30	(−3.53)[b]
(C) Satisfaction with aspects of life								
Housing	–	–	0.10	0.76	0.18	1.43	−0.16	−1.59
Friendships	–	–	−0.36	−1.80	0.03	0.14	0.18	1.12
Household income	–	–	−0.26	−1.82	−0.11	−0.80	0.25	2.19[a]
Health	–	–	0.40	2.38[a]	−0.37	(−2.48)[a]	−0.04	−0.36
Education	–	–	−0.01	−0.09	0.04	0.25	−0.03	−0.28
Neighbors	–	–	0.36	1.88	−0.005	−0.03	−0.15	−1.07
Public safety	–	–	0.35	2.64[b]	−0.23	−1.94	−0.04	−0.42
The condition of the environment	–	–	−0.08	−0.56	−0.16	−1.15	0.15	1.34
The democratic system	–	–	−0.05	−0.32	0.04	0.23	0.01	0.09
Family life	–	–	0.23	1.13	−0.22	−1.07	−0.07	−0.46
Leisure	–	–	−0.30	−1.64	−0.09	−0.45	0.28	1.82
Happiness	–	–	−0.17	−1.07	0.50	3.14[b]	−0.24	−1.90
(D) Trust in social institution								
Trust generally	–	–	−0.90	(−2.69)[b]	−0.70	(−2.19)[a]	0.96	3.89[b]
Trust the central government	–	–	0.20	0.80	0.02	0.07	−0.11	−0.57
Trust local governments	–	–	0.09	0.34	−0.17	−0.67	−0.05	−0.26
Trust the army	–	–	0.30	1.50	0.12	0.58	−0.17	−1.08

(continued)

(continued)

Logit regression analysis results by country Malaysia								
Dependent variable	Exit		Broader voice		Bureaucratic voice		Broader loyalty	
Independent variables	Coeff.	z-stat.	Coeff.	z-stat.	Coeff.	z-stat.	Coeff.	z-stat.
Trust the legal system	–	–	−0.21	−1.08	−0.01	−0.04	0.19	1.24
Trust the police	–	–	−0.16	−0.99	−0.05	−0.30	0.21	1.66
(E) Assessment of government performance								
Worry about corruption	–	–	−0.11	−0.54	−0.04	−0.20	0.08	0.48
Worry about Economic inequality	–	–	−0.01	−0.03	0.03	0.12	−0.02	−0.10
Political corruption	–	–	−0.36	(−2.32)[a]	0.19	1.31	0.06	0.51
Duty to vote	–	–	0.05	0.25	0.02	0.08	−0.06	−0.36
Widespread corruption	–	–	0.01	0.10	0.08	0.64	−0.06	−0.64
No power	–	–	−0.19	−1.67	−0.14	−1.24	0.16	1.69
Complicated	–	–	0.12	0.90	0.01	0.06	−0.09	−0.88
No matter whether vote	–	–	0.03	0.26	−0.09	−0.78	−0.02	−0.22
Pay little attention	–	–	0.06	0.44	−0.07	−0.55	0.03	0.32
Powerful leader	–	–	0.23	1.09	−0.25	−1.02	−0.10	−0.55
Experts	–	–	−0.06	−0.34	0.23	1.31	−0.02	−0.12
Military government	–	–	0.33	1.57	−0.44	−1.89	0.05	0.27
Democratic political system	–	–	−0.43	(−2.36)[a]	0.49	2.37[a]	0.07	0.43
Bribe	–	–	−0.02	−0.35	0.10	1.25	−0.03	−0.59
(F) Satisfaction with rights								
Right to vote	–	–	0.02	0.11	0.02	0.10	0.03	0.18
Right to participate in any organizations	–	–	−0.22	−1.12	0.14	0.76	0.02	0.16
Right to gather and demonstrate	–	–	0.05	0.34	−0.24	−1.55	0.06	0.45
Right to be informed about government	–	–	−0.06	−0.33	0.20	1.05	0.01	0.05
Freedom of Speech	–	–	−0.05	−0.27	−0.01	−0.03	0.04	0.27
Right to criticize the government	–	–	0.08	0.39	−0.09	−0.47	0.02	0.10
(H) Demographics								
Female	–	–	−0.08	−0.38	−0.47	(−2.38)[a]	0.47	2.95[b]
Age	–	–	0.01	1.20	−0.01	−0.67	−0.004	−0.41

(continued)

(continued)

Logit regression analysis results by country Malaysia								
Dependent variable	Exit		Broader voice		Bureaucratic voice		Broader loyalty	
Independent variables	Coeff.	z-stat.	Coeff.	z-stat.	Coeff.	z-stat.	Coeff.	z-stat.
Level of education	–	–	0.32	1.89	0.49	2.92[b]	−0.52	(−3.80)[b]
Married	–	–	0.07	0.27	0.66	2.23[a]	−0.37	−1.68
Unemployed	–	–	−1.13	−1.42	−0.60	−0.94	1.19	2.17[a]
Income	–	–	0.13	2.07[a]	−0.13	(−2.19)[a]	0.03	0.52
No religion	–	–	−1.14	−0.87	−0.32	−0.26	1.02	1.05
(I) City (Base = Northern)								
Southern	–	–	−0.62	−1.78	0.10	0.31	0.43	1.60
Eastern	–	–	−0.13	−0.38	−0.17	−0.49	0.25	0.90
Central	–	–	−0.76	(−2.55)[a]	−0.95	(−3.09)[b]	1.17	4.79[b]
East Malaysia	–	–	−1.35	(−2.77)[b]	0.61	1.30	0.80	2.24[a]
(K) Urban/Rural								
Rural	–	–	−0.51	(−2.07)[a]	0.13	0.59	0.25	1.35
(L) Yearly dummy variable								
2007	–	–	0.46	1.23	−0.71	(−2.06)[a]	0.31	1.06
Constant	–	–	−1.20	−0.71	−1.65	−0.90	−0.53	−0.38
n	–		941		941		941	
Pseudo R squared	–		0.1506		0.1911		0.1473	

Note [a]5% significance level; [b]1% significance level

6.17 Mongolia

In brief, the frequency distribution of options, in Mongolia, enables us to say that the exit option and the bureaucratic voice option are so small to be statistically insignificant. So, we have a large response for the broader voice option and the broader loyalty option. Of the former, the "use connections" option is seven times as large as the "bribe an official" option. Of the latter, the "wait and hope things will work out" option is five times larger than the "write a letter" option.

Those who choose the broader voice option suffer from a lack of public utilities, do not trust in general, do not trust the local government, do not trust the legal system, negatively assess government as not thinking, negatively assess government on issues of bribery, and are young.

Those who choose the broader bureaucratic voice option negatively assess government on bribery.

Summary statistics of countries Mongolia					
	n	Mean	SD	Min	Max
Exit	767	0.03	0.17	0	1
Broader voice	767	0.42	0.49	0	1
Bureaucratic voice	767	0.07	0.26	0	1
Broader loyalty	767	0.48	0.50	0	1
(A) Lifestyles					
Number of public utilities	800	2.84	1.26	0	7
Homeownership	799	0.52	0.50	0	1
Number of family members	800	4.46	1.63	1	11
Pray	793	2.17	1.04	1	5
National elections	792	4.74	0.67	1	5
Proud	795	3.80	0.53	1	4
Relative Standard of Living	795	2.83	0.65	1	5
(B) Exposure to globalization					
Internet	775	1.44	0.90	1	5
Living internationally	800	0.77	1.05	0	6
English ability	767	1.46	0.71	1	4
(C) Satisfaction with aspects of life					
Housing	794	3.70	1.17	1	5
Friendships	785	4.31	0.85	1	5
Household income	798	2.78	1.03	1	5
Health	793	3.42	1.09	1	5
Education	793	3.36	1.07	1	5
Job	746	3.07	1.38	1	5
Neighbors	737	3.87	1.01	1	5
Public safety	773	2.55	1.14	1	5
The condition of the environment	781	2.75	1.18	1	5
Social welfare system	723	2.48	1.09	1	5
The democratic system	750	3.05	1.13	1	5
Family life	796	3.97	0.91	1	5
Leisure	767	3.39	1.09	1	5
Spiritual life	745	3.58	0.97	1	5
Happiness	798	3.55	0.74	1	5
(D) Trust in social institution					
Trust generally	790	0.22	0.42	0	1
Trust the central government	779	2.64	0.81	1	4
Trust local governments	774	2.54	0.84	1	4
Trust the army	743	2.79	0.79	1	4
Trust the legal system	757	2.38	0.86	1	4
Trust the police	782	2.42	0.88	1	4

(continued)

(continued)

Summary statistics of countries Mongolia					
	n	Mean	SD	Min	Max
(E) Assessment of government performance					
Worry about corruption	800	0.61	0.49	0	1
Worry about Economic inequality	800	0.46	0.50	0	1
Political corruption	755	1.70	0.77	1	4
Duty to vote	798	4.67	0.55	2	5
Widespread corruption	765	4.26	1.00	1	5
No power	761	3.79	1.12	1	5
Complicated	751	3.40	1.13	1	5
No matter whether vote	772	2.54	1.21	1	5
Stop thinking	785	4.15	0.96	1	5
Pay little attention	769	4.09	0.99	1	5
Powerful leader	671	2.13	0.85	1	3
Experts	615	1.86	0.79	1	3
Military government	651	1.40	0.65	1	3
Democratic political system	719	2.39	0.63	1	3
Bribe	771	9.48	1.39	1	10
(F) Satisfaction with rights					
Right to vote	786	3.47	0.73	1	4
Right to gather and demonstrate	682	2.69	0.92	1	4
Right to be informed about government	717	2.50	0.91	1	4
Freedom of speech	708	2.68	0.96	1	4
Right to criticize the government	696	2.46	0.98	1	4
(H) Demographics					
Female	800	0.53	0.50	0	1
Age	800	38.26	12.54	20	69
Level of education	800	2.0	0.7	1	3
Married	800	0.73	0.45	0	1
Unemployed	798	0.18	0.38	0	1
Income	799	3.21	1.22	1	7
No religion	794	0.19	0.39	0	1
(I) Region (Base = Ulaanbaatar)					
Sukhbaatar	800	0.08	0.27	0	1
Khuvsgul	800	0.22	0.41	0	1
Khovd	800	0.16	0.37	0	1
Dundgobi	800	0.17	0.38	0	1
(K) Urban/Rural					
Rural	800	0.33	0.47	0	1

Frequency Distribution of 7 Responses and Partially Aggregated 4 Responses
Mongolia

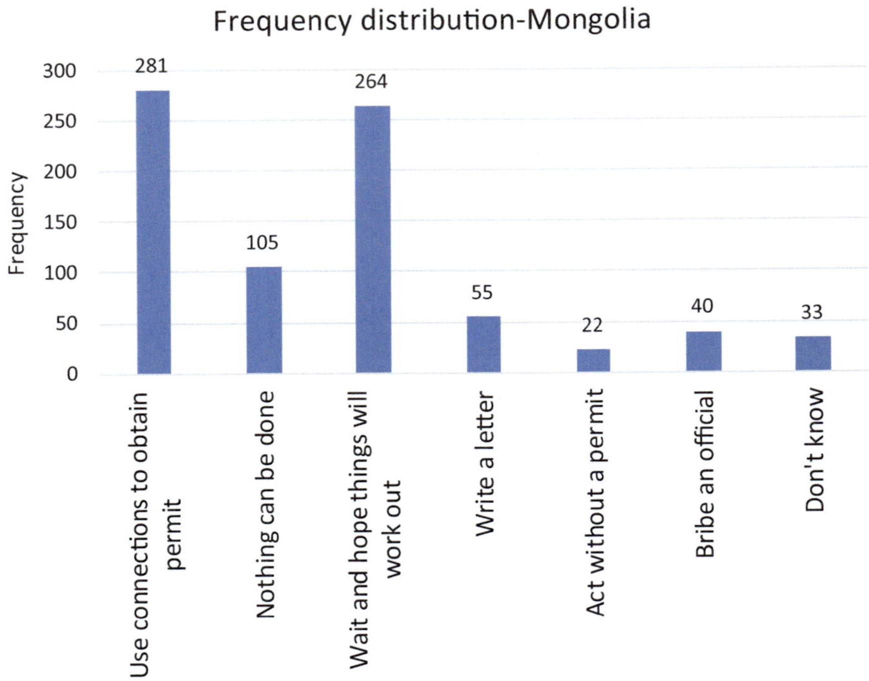

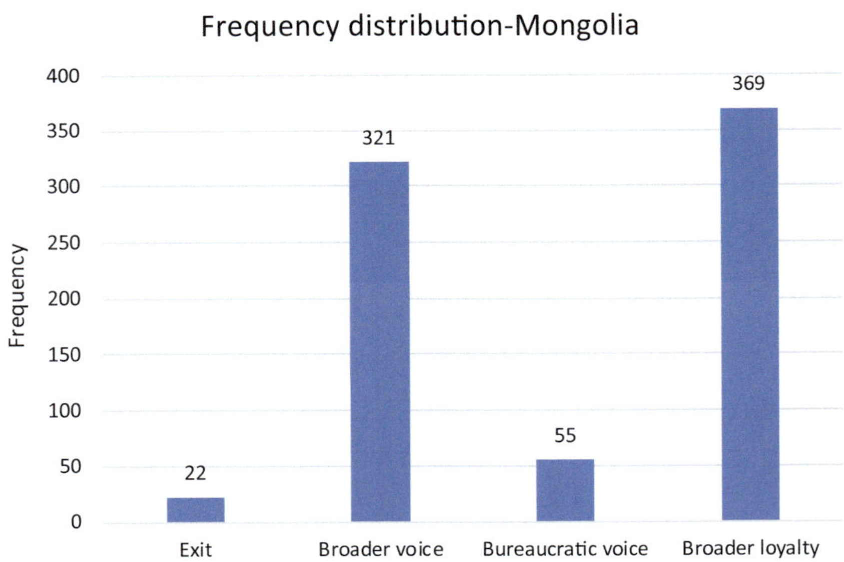

Logit regression analysis results by country Mongolia								
Dependent variable	Exit		Broader voice		Bureaucratic voice		Broader loyalty	
Independent variables	Coeff.	z-stat.	Coeff.	z-stat.	Coeff.	z-stat.	Coeff.	z-stat.
(A) Lifestyles								
Number of public utilities	–	–	0.48	2.22[a]	–	–	−0.10	−0.52
Homeownership	–	–	−0.48	−1.17	–	–	0.28	0.74
Number of family members	–	–	−0.12	−1.08	–	–	0.02	0.23
Pray	–	–	−0.06	−0.33	–	–	−0.02	−0.14
National elections	–	–	0.44	1.37	–	–	−0.48	−1.52
Proud	–	–	−0.59	−1.35	–	–	0.27	0.67
Relative Standard of Living	–	–	0.19	0.65	–	–	0.14	0.52
(B) Exposure to globalization								
Internet	–	–	−0.37	−1.35	–	–	0.06	0.21
Living internationally	–	–	0.14	0.67	–	–	−0.07	−0.35
English ability	–	–	−0.18	−0.67	–	–	−0.02	−0.09
(C) Satisfaction with aspects of life								
Housing	–	–	0.05	0.30	–	–	0.06	0.38
Friendships	–	–	0.03	0.13	–	–	−0.22	−0.89
Household income	–	–	0.21	0.87	–	–	−0.37	−1.64
Health	–	–	−0.19	−0.85	–	–	0.27	1.30
Education	–	–	−0.02	−0.10	–	–	0.04	0.23
Job	–	–	−0.23	−1.37	–	–	0.17	1.05
Neighbors	–	–	−0.13	−0.64	–	–	0.11	0.59
Public safety	–	–	−0.21	−0.97	–	–	0.22	1.08
The condition of the environment	–	–	0.10	0.45	–	–	−0.08	−0.37
Social welfare system	–	–	0.11	0.48	–	–	−0.07	−0.33
The democratic system	–	–	0.09	0.45	–	–	−0.06	−0.32
Family life	–	–	0.02	0.11	–	–	−0.04	−0.19
Leisure	–	–	0.12	0.60	–	–	−0.003	−0.01
Spiritual life	–	–	−0.05	−0.20	–	–	0.20	0.78
Happiness	–	–	0.07	0.25	–	–	−0.19	−0.72
(D) Trust in social institution								
Trust generally	–	–	−1.00	(−2.11)[a]	–	–	0.54	1.24
Trust the central government	–	–	0.26	0.96	–	–	0.08	0.30
Trust local governments	–	–	−0.75	(−2.52)[a]	–	–	0.50	1.76

(continued)

(continued)

Logit regression analysis results by country Mongolia								
Dependent variable	Exit		Broader voice		Bureaucratic voice		Broader loyalty	
Independent variables	Coeff.	z-stat.	Coeff.	z-stat.	Coeff.	z-stat.	Coeff.	z-stat.
Trust the army	–	–	−0.01	−0.03	–	–	0.005	0.02
Trust the legal system	–	–	−0.83	(−2.64)[b]	–	–	0.96	3.09[b]
Trust the police	–	–	0.47	1.51	–	–	−0.53	−1.79
(E) Assessment of government performance								
Worry about corruption	–	–	0.20	0.51	–	–	0.02	0.07
Worry about Economic inequality	–	–	0.04	0.12	–	–	−0.07	−0.21
Political corruption	–	–	0.24	0.97	–	–	−0.39	−1.68
Duty to vote	–	–	−0.03	−0.07	–	–	0.18	0.50
Widespread corruption	–	–	−0.09	−0.40	–	–	0.17	0.83
No power	–	–	0.02	0.10	–	–	0.06	0.34
Complicated	–	–	0.08	0.44	–	–	0.01	0.06
No matter whether vote	–	–	0.08	0.51	–	–	−0.07	−0.48
Stop thinking	–	–	−0.82	(−3.02)[b]	–	–	0.51	2.08[a]
Pay little attention	–	–	0.15	0.63	–	–	−0.12	−0.55
Powerful leader	–	–	−0.17	−0.77	–	–	0.30	1.51
Experts	–	–	−0.22	−0.93	–	–	−0.14	−0.60
Military government	–	–	0.45	1.55	–	–	−0.22	−0.82
Democratic political system	–	–	0.02	0.08	–	–	−0.10	−0.39
Bribe	–	–	−0.48	(−3.24)[b]	–	–	0.40	2.72[b]
(F) Satisfaction with rights								
Right to vote	–	–	0.49	1.68	–	–	−0.15	−0.57
Right to gather and demonstrate	–	–	−0.37	−1.38	–	–	−0.05	−0.21
Right to be informed about government	–	–	−0.21	−0.81	–	–	−0.01	−0.05
Freedom of speech	–	–	0.52	1.54	–	–	−0.14	−0.43
Right to criticize the government	–	–	0.11	0.38	–	–	−0.03	−0.10
(H) Demographics								
Female	–	–	−0.12	−0.34	–	–	0.13	0.39
Age	–	–	−0.04	(−2.26)[a]	–	–	−0.001	−0.04
Level of education	–	–	0.46	1.44	–	–	−0.49	−1.61
Married	–	–	−0.08	−0.19	–	–	0.34	0.84
Unemployed	–	–	−0.15	−0.29	–	–	−0.27	−0.55

(continued)

(continued)

Logit regression analysis results by country Mongolia								
Dependent variable	Exit		Broader voice		Bureaucratic voice		Broader loyalty	
Independent variables	Coeff.	z-stat.	Coeff.	z-stat.	Coeff.	z-stat.	Coeff.	z-stat.
Income	–	–	0.17	1.10	–	–	−0.09	−0.60
No religion	–	–	−0.85	−1.63	–	–	0.71	1.41
(I) Region (Base = Ulaanbaatar)								
Sukhbaatar	–	–	1.00	1.08	–	–	−1.15	−1.14
Khuvsgul	–	–	−0.47	−0.63	–	–	−0.61	−0.91
Khovd	–	–	−1.47	−1.95	–	–	1.12	1.63
Dundgobi	–	–	−0.38	−0.63	–	–	−0.06	−0.11
(K) Urban/Rural								
Rural	–	–	0.41	0.76	–	–	−0.31	−0.63
Constant	–	–	7.69	2.09[a]	–	–	−6.25	−1.74
n	–		268		–		268	
Pseudo R squared	–		0.2420		–		0.1867	

Note [a]5% significance level; [b]1% significance level

6.18 Nepal

For Nepal, the frequency distribution of options shows that voicing choices are vigorously pursued. Both the broader voice option and the bureaucratic voice option are similar in the frequency that they are chosen, with the former taking 45.2% and the latter taking 37.2%. The broader loyalty option accounts for 16.7%. The exit option represents 0.09%.

Those who choose the broader voice option do not trust generally, trust the legal system, assess government positively in the area of duty to vote, assess government as yearning for a powerful leader, negatively assess government as the respondents don't believe the government's intention for not seeking a military government, negatively assess government on issues of bribery, and negatively assess government about the right to criticize government.

Those who choose the bureaucratic voice option do not enjoy home ownership, trust in general, do not trust the legal system, do not want government to be led by a powerful leader, want government to become a military government, and positively assess government as maintaining citizens' right to criticize the government.

Those who choose the broader loyalty option do not have good public utilities, are not satisfied with health, are happy, do not want government led by experts, do not want government to be a democratic political system, and are satisfied with the right to be informed about government. Demographically, the unemployed and the rich tend to choose bureaucratic loyalty.

Summary statistics of countries Nepal					
	n	Mean	SD	Min	Max
Exit	796	0.01	0.09	0	1
Broader voice	796	0.45	0.50	0	1
Bureaucratic voice	796	0.37	0.48	0	1
Broader loyalty	796	0.17	0.37	0	1
(A) Lifestyles					
Number of public utilities	800	4.46	1.29	1	7
Homeownership	799	0.43	0.49	0	1
Number of family members	800	4.89	2.44	1	20
Pray	800	3.90	1.41	1	5
National elections	758	3.63	1.50	1	5
Proud	800	3.75	0.56	1	4
Relative Standard of Living	798	2.81	0.71	1	5
(B) Exposure to globalization					
Living internationally	800	1.48	1.27	0	6
English ability	800	2.40	0.99	1	4
(C) Satisfaction with aspects of life					
Housing	800	3.79	0.87	1	5
Friendships	798	4.04	0.57	1	5
Household income	800	3.59	0.91	1	5
Health	799	3.81	0.78	1	5
Education	799	3.51	1.04	1	5
Job	777	3.62	0.91	1	5
Neighbors	787	3.84	0.65	1	5
Public safety	776	2.98	1.04	1	5
The condition of the environment	786	2.53	1.05	1	5
Social welfare system	615	2.47	0.99	1	5
The democratic system	666	2.56	1.09	1	5
Family life	795	4.05	0.62	1	5
Leisure	790	3.54	0.87	1	5
Spiritual life	785	3.94	0.53	1	5
Happiness	799	3.45	1.08	1	5
(D) Trust in social institution					
Trust generally	788	0.27	0.44	0	1
Trust the central government	743	2.32	0.83	1	4
Trust the legal system	731	2.63	0.86	1	4

(continued)

(continued)

Summary statistics of countries Nepal					
	n	Mean	SD	Min	Max
Trust the police	759	2.31	0.79	1	4
(E) Assessment of government performance					
Worry about corruption	800	0.96	0.20	0	1
Worry about Economic inequality	800	0.82	0.38	0	1
Political corruption	760	1.62	0.77	1	4
Duty to vote	796	4.48	0.71	1	5
Widespread corruption	790	4.60	0.57	1	5
No power	746	3.09	1.33	1	5
Complicated	733	3.98	1.09	1	5
No matter whether vote	791	2.10	1.14	1	5
Stop thinking	796	4.67	0.62	1	5
Pay little attention	790	4.41	0.66	1	5
Powerful leader	705	1.68	0.68	1	3
Experts	671	1.90	0.57	1	3
Military government	649	1.36	0.59	1	3
Democratic political system	736	2.26	0.72	1	3
Bribe	791	9.13	1.93	1	10
(F) Satisfaction with rights					
Right to vote	758	3.02	0.61	1	4
Right to participate in any organizations	725	2.79	0.71	1	4
Right to gather and demonstrate	729	2.39	0.74	1	4
Right to be informed about government	722	2.42	0.80	1	4
Right to criticize the government	724	2.42	0.85	1	4
(H) Demographics					
Female	800	0.50	0.50	0	1
Age	800	35.75	11.43	20	69
Level of education	758	1.98	0.90	1	3
Married	800	0.76	0.43	0	1
Unemployed	800	0.21	0.41	0	1
Income	781	4.9	2.7	1	11

Frequency Distribution of 7 Responses and Partially Aggregated 4 Responses
Nepal

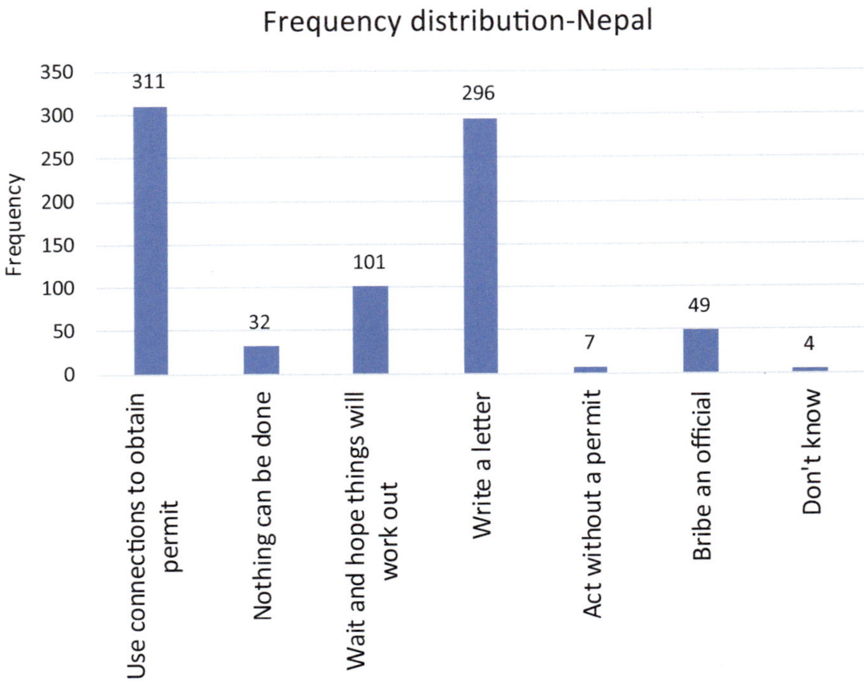

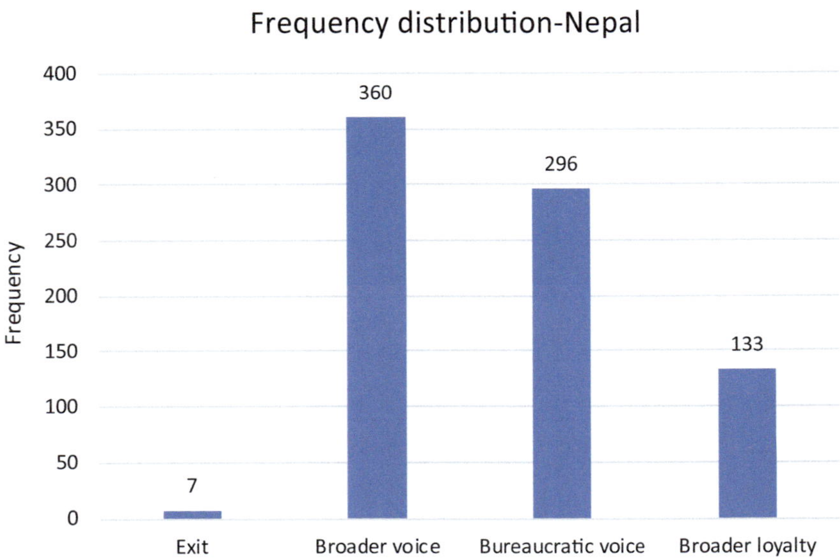

Logit regression analysis results by country Nepal								
Dependent variable	Exit		Broader voice		Bureaucratic voice		Broader loyalty	
Independent variables	Coeff.	z-stat.	Coeff.	z-stat.	Coeff.	z-stat.	Coeff.	z-stat.
(A) Lifestyles								
Number of public utilities	–	–	0.29	1.65	0.11	0.64	−1.23	(−3.31)[b]
Homeownership	–	–	0.60	1.71	−0.75	(−2.04)[a]	1.22	1.81
Number of family members	–	–	−0.04	−0.71	0.08	1.3	−0.14	−1.02
Pray	–	–	0.04	0.30	0.06	0.48	−0.29	−1.34
National elections	–	–	−0.05	−0.40	0.01	0.11	0.05	0.23
Proud	–	–	0.07	0.20	0.12	0.36	−0.29	−0.48
Relative Standard of Living	–	–	−0.05	−0.20	0.22	0.85	−0.74	−1.63
(B) Exposure to globalization								
Living internationally	–	–	−0.01	−0.05	0.15	0.92	−0.34	−1.05
English ability	–	–	−0.14	−0.53	0.34	1.25	−0.23	−0.48
(C) Satisfaction with aspects of life								
Housing	–	–	−0.19	−0.80	0.20	0.89	−0.39	−0.99
Friendships	–	–	0.07	0.22	−0.10	−0.33	0.29	0.52
Household income	–	–	−0.23	−1.09	0.12	0.55	0.52	1.47
Health	–	–	−0.05	−0.23	0.43	1.82	−1.21	(−2.79)[b]
Education	–	–	0.07	0.40	−0.08	−0.43	−0.22	−0.65
Job	–	–	0.39	1.93	−0.21	−1.02	−0.59	−1.84
Neighbors	–	–	0.14	0.49	0.10	0.36	0.01	0.02
Public safety	–	–	−0.09	−0.52	0.003	0.02	0.05	0.14
The condition of the environment	–	–	0.17	0.98	−0.16	−0.89	−0.44	−1.22
Social welfare system	–	–	−0.28	−1.44	0.18	0.94	0.24	0.63
The democratic system	–	–	0.13	0.79	−0.11	−0.67	−0.001	0.00
Family life	–	–	−0.14	−0.55	0.12	0.45	−0.25	−0.54
Leisure	–	–	0.05	0.27	0.05	0.29	−0.24	−0.70
Spiritual life	–	–	−0.10	−0.39	−0.17	−0.62	0.83	1.40
Happiness	–	–	0.02	0.11	−0.24	−1.19	1.22	2.98[b]
(D) Trust in social institution								
Trust generally	–	–	−0.85	(−2.16)[a]	1.17	2.90[b]	−1.14	−1.54
Trust the central government	–	–	0.29	1.33	−0.35	−1.63	−0.23	−0.57

(continued)

(continued)

Logit regression analysis results by country Nepal								
Dependent variable	Exit		Broader voice		Bureaucratic voice		Broader loyalty	
Independent variables	Coeff.	z-stat.	Coeff.	z-stat.	Coeff.	z-stat.	Coeff.	z-stat.
Trust the legal system	–	–	0.53	2.44[a]	−0.54	(−2.44)[a]	0.06	0.14
Trust the police	–	–	−0.22	−1.01	0.41	1.77	−0.35	−0.90
(E) Assessment of government performance								
Worry about corruption	–	–	1.07	1.40	−0.69	−0.93	−2.56	−1.95
Worry about Economic inequality	–	–	−0.67	−1.33	0.74	1.33	0.09	0.11
Political corruption	–	–	−0.27	−1.35	0.11	0.56	0.36	1.01
Duty to vote	–	–	0.71	2.43[a]	−0.55	−1.92	−0.35	−0.85
Widespread corruption	–	–	−0.22	−0.73	0.08	0.24	0.42	0.85
No power	–	–	−0.03	−0.22	0.03	0.21	0.42	1.43
Complicated	–	–	−0.05	−0.31	0.17	1.01	−0.44	−1.40
No matter whether vote	–	–	−0.10	−0.62	−0.07	−0.46	0.33	1.23
Stop thinking	–	–	−0.32	−1.06	0.19	0.6	0.31	0.49
Pay little attention	–	–	0.40	1.38	−0.28	−0.97	−0.46	−0.75
Powerful leader	–	–	1.00	3.18[b]	−0.83	(−2.60)[b]	−0.78	−1.18
Experts	–	–	−0.02	−0.07	0.34	1.2	−1.46	(−2.37)[a]
Military government	–	–	−0.82	(−2.51)[a]	0.85	2.66[b]	0.47	0.78
Democratic political system	–	–	0.61	2.28[a]	−0.34	−1.3	−1.04	(−2.04)[a]
Bribe	–	–	−0.18	(−2.03)[a]	0.06	0.75	0.36	1.76
(F) Satisfaction with rights								
Right to vote	–	–	−0.21	−0.66	0.12	0.39	0.11	0.18
Right to participate in any organizations	–	–	0.37	1.27	−0.22	−0.72	−1.28	−1.94
Right to gather and demonstrate	–	–	−0.29	−1.07	0.19	0.7	0.24	0.47
Right to be informed about government	–	–	−0.09	−0.30	−0.31	−0.98	1.24	2.40[a]
Right to criticize the government	–	–	−0.60	(−2.05)[a]	0.62	2.06[a]	0.49	0.87

(continued)

(continued)

Logit regression analysis results by country Nepal								
Dependent variable	Exit		Broader voice		Bureaucratic voice		Broader loyalty	
Independent variables	Coeff.	z-stat.	Coeff.	z-stat.	Coeff.	z-stat.	Coeff.	z-stat.
(H) Demographics								
Female	–	–	0.01	0.03	−0.04	−0.09	0.26	0.39
Age	–	–	−0.01	−0.50	0.005	0.28	−0.003	−0.10
Level of education	–	–	0.01	0.03	−0.17	−0.63	−0.12	−0.25
Married	–	–	0.11	0.27	−0.10	−0.22	−0.35	−0.48
Unemployed	–	–	0.16	0.44	−0.63	−1.64	2.05	2.87[b]
Income	–	–	−0.03	−0.51	−0.03	−0.43	0.28	2.07[a]
Constant	–	–	−2.25	−0.69	−2.39	−0.73	10.76	1.82
n	–		319		319		319	
Pseudo R squared	–		0.2580		0.2265		0.4338	

Note [a]5% significance level; [b]1% significance level

6.19 Pakistan

For Pakistan, the frequency distribution of options shows that the broader loyalty option is overwhelmingly selected by 58.7% of respondents. The broader voice option registers 17.7%, whereas the bureaucratic voice option registers 16.7%. The exit option accounts for 6.9%.

Those who choose the exit option are not satisfied with the democratic system, do not trust generally, do not trust the legal system, negatively assess government for widespread corruption, negatively assess government for not thinking, and negatively assess government on aspects of the democratic political system.

Those who choose the broader voice option have a low household income, negatively assess government for bribery, and are young.

Those who choose the bureaucratic voice option are proud of Pakistan, have a relatively high standard of living, negatively assess government for having no power, negatively assess government because voting does not make a difference, negatively assess government for not thinking, negatively assess government on the democratic system, negatively assess government for bribery, and are not satisfied with the right to be informed about government. Regionally, they tend to be from the Northwestern Frontier province.

Those who choose the bureaucratic loyalty option are not proud of Pakistan, are not satisfied with health, are not satisfied with the democratic system, do not trust the police, negatively assess government for having no power, and negatively assess government on issues of bribery. Regionally, they tend to be from the Northwest Frontier Province.

Summary statistics of countries Pakistan

	n	Mean	SD	Min	Max
Exit	970	0.07	0.25	0	1
Broader voice	970	0.18	0.38	0	1
Bureaucratic voice	970	0.17	0.37	0	1
Broader loyalty	970	0.59	0.49	0	1
(A) Lifestyles					
Number of public utilities	1086	3.09	1.49	0	7
Homeownership	1086	0.88	0.33	0	1
Number of family members	1086	7.36	3.51	1	30
Pray	1050	4.27	1.01	1	5
National elections	1000	4.14	1.09	1	5
Proud	1067	3.72	0.61	1	4
Relative Standard of Living	1076	2.92	1.02	1	5
(B) Exposure to globalization					
Internet	949	1.34	0.97	1	5
Living internationally	1086	0.64	1.08	0	6
(C) Satisfaction with aspects of life					
Housing	1081	4.11	0.94	1	5
Friendships	1066	4.06	0.73	1	5
Household income	1082	3.37	1.09	1	5
Health	1075	3.51	1.02	1	5
Education	1059	3.32	1.05	1	5
Neighbors	1050	3.83	0.92	1	5
Public safety	994	2.93	1.10	1	5
The condition of the environment	958	2.98	1.04	1	5
The democratic system	938	2.96	1.10	1	5
Family life	1047	3.73	0.94	1	5
Leisure	1025	3.55	0.96	1	5
Spiritual life	1023	3.84	0.83	1	5
Happiness	1067	3.47	1.01	1	5
(D) Trust in social institution					
Trust generally	1021	0.50	0.50	0	1
Trust the central government	1017	2.84	0.85	1	4
Trust local governments	1014	2.74	0.77	1	4
Trust the army	1055	3.14	0.83	1	4
Trust the legal system	1019	2.54	0.83	1	4
Trust the police	1056	2.02	0.94	1	4

(continued)

(continued)

Summary statistics of countries Pakistan					
	n	Mean	SD	Min	Max
(E) Assessment of government performance					
Worry about corruption	1086	0.66	0.47	0	1
Worry about Economic inequality	1086	0.54	0.50	0	1
Political corruption	949	2.26	0.84	1	4
Duty to vote	1075	4.36	0.78	1	5
Widespread corruption	992	3.95	0.93	1	5
No power	1002	3.83	0.96	1	5
Complicated	973	3.90	0.98	1	5
No matter whether vote	1020	3.12	1.20	1	5
Stop thinking	1016	4.02	0.93	1	5
Pay little attention	999	3.96	0.96	1	5
Powerful leader	939	2.03	0.79	1	3
Experts	917	2.00	0.67	1	3
Military government	981	1.92	0.74	1	3
Democratic political system	893	2.28	0.68	1	3
Bribe	1032	9.26	1.99	1	10
(F) Satisfaction with rights					
Right to vote	1053	3.16	0.77	1	4
Right to participate in any organizations	926	2.54	0.83	1	4
Right to gather and demonstrate	948	2.52	0.93	1	4
Right to be informed about government	958	2.57	0.83	1	4
Freedom of speech	917	2.58	0.86	1	4
Right to criticize the government	874	2.49	0.92	1	4
(H) Demographics					
Female	1086	0.41	0.49	0	1
Age	1086	35.22	10.99	20	65
Level of education	1086	1.43	0.62	1	3
Married	1079	0.8	0.4	0	1
Unemployed	1083	0.02	0.16	0	1
Income	1078	2.74	1.55	1	10
(I) Region (Base = Punjab)					
Sindh	1086	0.26	0.44	0	1
NWFP	1086	0.16	0.37	0	1
Balochistan	1086	0.11	0.31	0	1
(K) Rural					
Rural	1086	0.55	0.50	0	1

Frequency Distribution of 7 Responses and Partially Aggregated 4 Responses

Pakistan

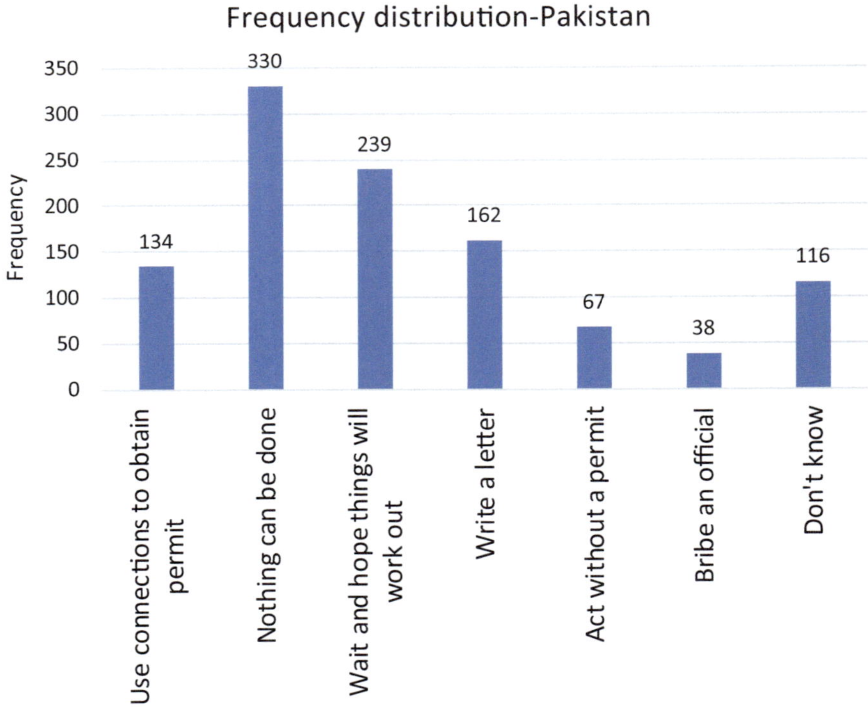

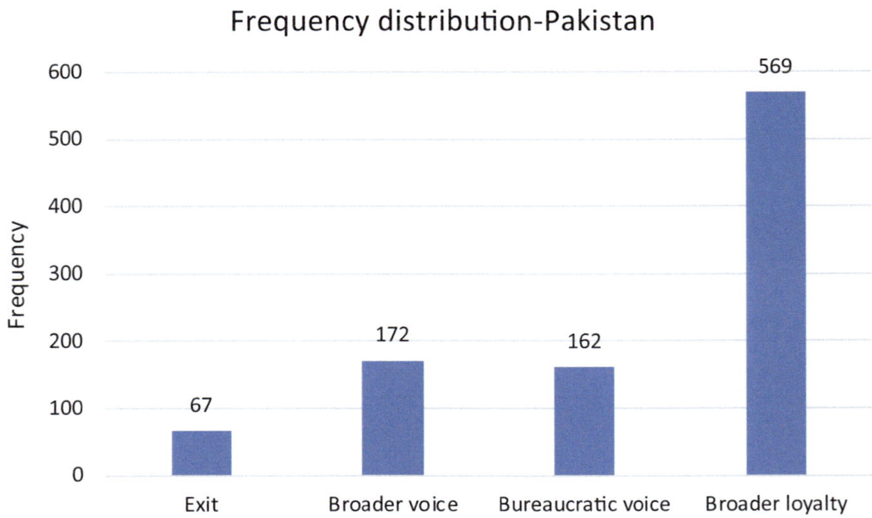

Logit regression analysis results by country Pakistan								
Dependent variable	Exit		Broader voice		Bureaucratic voice		Broader loyalty	
Independent variables	Coeff.	z-stat.	Coeff.	z-stat.	Coeff.	z-stat.	Coeff.	z-stat.
(A) Lifestyles								
Number of public utilities	−0.22	−0.62	−0.09	−0.56	0.20	1.03	−0.01	−0.10
Homeownership	1.69	1.39	−0.39	−0.67	1.29	1.68	−0.24	−0.52
Number of family members	0.10	1.06	−0.003	−0.04	−0.0002	0.00	−0.07	−1.47
Pray	0.54	1.30	0.31	1.28	0.09	0.40	−0.25	−1.52
National elections	0.45	1.46	0.06	0.38	−0.07	−0.34	−0.06	−0.49
Proud	−0.11	−0.24	0.26	0.81	0.85	2.36[a]	−0.46	(−2.10)[a]
Relative Standard of Living	0.37	0.91	−0.32	−1.47	0.66	2.35[a]	0.08	0.47
(B) Exposure to globalization								
Internet	0.20	0.48	0.23	1.34	−0.06	−0.24	−0.21	−1.42
Living internationally	0.32	0.86	0.32	1.74	−0.03	−0.15	−0.20	−1.29
(C) Satisfaction with aspects of life								
Housing	−0.85	−1.94	−0.06	−0.27	−0.24	−0.78	0.25	1.31
Friendships	0.19	0.35	0.11	0.36	−0.26	−0.71	−0.04	−0.17
Household income	0.30	0.87	0.20	0.95	−0.29	−1.18	−0.06	−0.40
Health	0.53	1.48	0.52	2.47[a]	0.25	0.92	−0.67	(−4.07)[b]
Education	0.15	0.40	0.19	0.90	−0.23	−0.98	0.03	0.17
Neighbors	0.22	0.45	−0.32	−1.34	0.33	1.10	0.02	0.10
Public safety	0.15	0.40	−0.07	−0.34	−0.03	−0.10	0.12	0.70
The condition of the environment	0.47	1.00	0.24	0.98	−0.005	−0.02	−0.30	−1.63
The democratic system	−1.22	(−2.44)[a]	−0.32	−1.55	−0.07	−0.29	0.38	2.33[a]
Family life	−0.03	−0.07	−0.02	−0.10	−0.17	−0.63	0.08	0.43
Leisure	−0.27	−0.71	0.01	0.04	−0.25	−0.93	0.16	0.89
Spiritual life	0.86	1.87	−0.26	−1.05	−0.07	−0.23	0.01	0.05
Happiness	0.06	0.18	−0.22	−1.20	0.15	0.72	0.22	1.52
(D) Trust in social institution								
Trust generally	−1.87	(−2.35)[a]	0.28	0.74	−0.01	−0.03	0.19	0.68
Trust the central government	0.43	0.93	−0.07	−0.23	−0.48	−1.47	0.14	0.66
Trust local governments	−0.52	−0.84	0.08	0.25	−0.42	−1.14	0.29	1.19
Trust the army	0.98	1.94	−0.26	−1.09	0.17	0.56	−0.05	−0.28
Trust the legal system	−1.03	(−2.34)[a]	0.41	1.56	−0.21	−0.70	0.19	0.91
Trust the police	−0.16	−0.40	0.01	0.04	0.50	2.03[a]	−0.34	(−2.03)[a]

(continued)

(continued)

Logit regression analysis results by country Pakistan								
Dependent variable	Exit		Broader voice		Bureaucratic voice		Broader loyalty	
Independent variables	Coeff.	z-stat.	Coeff.	z-stat.	Coeff.	z-stat.	Coeff.	z-stat.
(E) Assessment of government performance								
Worry about corruption	0.65	0.70	−0.05	−0.12	0.26	0.60	−0.11	−0.35
Worry about Economic inequality	0.16	0.22	−0.18	−0.48	0.10	0.24	0.23	0.81
Political corruption	−0.10	−0.22	−0.44	−1.62	0.17	0.56	0.13	0.67
Duty to vote	−0.38	−0.94	−0.001	0.00	−0.27	−1.05	0.32	1.61
Widespread corruption	1.55	2.37[a]	−0.12	−0.57	−0.17	−0.74	0.10	0.60
No power	0.15	0.43	0.19	0.89	−0.62	(−2.77)[b]	0.32	2.01[a]
Complicated	−0.59	−1.39	−0.02	−0.11	−0.12	−0.51	0.19	1.16
No matter whether vote	0.26	0.98	0.12	0.77	−0.35	(−2.01)[a]	0.05	0.48
Stop thinking	1.36	2.24[a]	0.40	1.58	−0.66	(−2.55)[a]	−0.17	−0.97
Pay little attention	−0.11	−0.23	−0.02	−0.07	0.33	1.37	−0.27	−1.63
Powerful leader	0.24	0.50	0.27	1.02	−0.44	−1.38	−0.06	−0.27
Experts	0.48	0.89	−0.26	−0.94	−0.65	−1.83	0.27	1.28
Military government	0.41	0.78	0.14	0.54	0.02	0.08	−0.10	−0.51
Democratic political system	1.69	2.84[b]	0.54	1.91	−0.80	(−2.49)[a]	−0.38	−1.78
Bribe	0.15	0.78	0.56	2.83[b]	0.42	2.61[b]	−0.35	(−3.71)[b]
(F) Satisfaction with rights								
Right to vote	0.74	1.32	0.06	0.22	0.10	0.29	−0.39	−1.74
Right to participate in any organizations	0.08	0.14	−0.003	−0.01	−0.58	−1.62	0.23	1.03
Right to gather and demonstrate	−0.58	−1.21	0.16	0.66	0.02	0.07	0.02	0.13
Right to be informed about government	−0.22	−0.37	−0.22	−0.82	0.92	2.62[b]	−0.12	−0.58
Freedom of speech	−0.03	−0.06	0.04	0.14	0.20	0.60	−0.03	−0.15
Right to criticize the government	−0.12	−0.20	0.37	1.32	0.39	1.14	−0.40	−1.80
(H) Demographics								
Female	1.04	1.09	0.43	0.93	−1.06	−1.82	−0.49	−1.35
Age	−0.02	−0.89	0.05	2.83[b]	−0.03	−1.32	−0.01	−0.88
Level of education	−1.02	−1.66	0.23	0.74	0.06	0.18	−0.003	−0.01
Married	−0.09	−0.13	−0.47	−1.15	0.79	1.44	0.09	0.26
Unemployed	–	–	−0.63	−0.63	0.08	0.07	0.95	1.22
Income	0.24	0.76	−0.01	−0.07	0.20	1.45	−0.09	−0.88

(continued)

(continued)

Logit regression analysis results by country Pakistan								
Dependent variable	Exit		Broader voice		Bureaucratic voice		Broader loyalty	
Independent variables	Coeff.	z-stat.	Coeff.	z-stat.	Coeff.	z-stat.	Coeff.	z-stat.
(I) Region (Base = Punjab)								
Sindh	2.00	1.86	0.43	0.82	−1.00	−1.43	−0.96	(−2.04)[a]
NWFP	2.39	1.67	−0.73	−1.28	−2.11	(−2.90)[b]	1.13	2.59[a]
Balochistan	1.58	1.33	−0.73	−0.97	1.49	1.88	−1.16	(−2.02)[a]
(K) Rural								
Rural	0.12	0.11	0.03	0.06	1.07	1.96	−0.63	−1.57
Constant	−29.8	(−3.78)[b]	−14.3	(−3.87)[b]	−0.81	−0.24	7.13	3.03[b]
n	426		426		426		426	
Pseudo R squared	0.4655		0.2424		0.3718		0.2327	

Note [a]5% significance level; [b]1% significance level

6.20 The Philippines

For the Philippines, the frequency distribution of options reveals that the broader voice option is overwhelming. In particular, "use connections" represent close to 50% of responses, compared to the rather underwhelming 2% for "bribe an official." Next to the broader voice option is the broader loyalty option accounting for 29.8%.

Those who choose the exit option are not proud of the Philippines, do not trust local governments, and are young. Regionally, they tend to be from Balance Luzon. Respondents from Visayas are not more exit-prone than those from Manila and Mindanao.

Those who choose the broader voice option are proud of the Philippines, are not satisfied with friendships, do not trust the central government, trust the legal system, and negatively assess government on bribery. Regionally, those from Balance Luzon, adjacent to the National Capital Region, are voice-prone.

Those who choose the bureaucratic voice option have minimum access to public water supply, have a command of English, and positively assess government on duty to vote.

Those who choose the broader loyalty option are satisfied with leisure, trust the central government, do not trust the legal system, are not satisfied with daily life, do not trust the central government, trust the legal system, negatively assess government to respond (irrespective of how one votes), and positively assess government on bribery.

Summary statistics of countries Philippines					
	n	Mean	SD	Min	Max
Exit	1788	0.03	0.18	0	1
Broader voice	1788	0.50	0.50	0	1
Bureaucratic voice	1788	0.17	0.38	0	1
Broader loyalty	1788	0.30	0.46	0	1
(A) Lifestyles					
Public water supply	1800	0.59	0.49	0	1
Electricity	1800	0.96	0.19	0	1
LPG	1800	0.30	0.46	0	1
Homeownership	1800	0.85	0.35	0	1
Number of family members	1800	5.18	2.16	1	20
Pray	1799	4.69	0.69	1	5
National elections	1788	4.52	1.01	1	5
Proud	1800	3.86	0.42	1	4
Relative Standard of Living	1794	2.89	0.62	1	5
(B) Exposure to globalization					
Living internationally	1800	1.31	1.08	0	6
English ability	1799	2.31	0.72	1	4
(C) Satisfaction with aspects of life					
Housing	1799	4.03	1.06	1	5
Friendships	1799	4.41	0.70	1	5
Household income	1799	3.64	1.08	1	5
Health	1800	4.22	0.83	1	5
Education	1798	4.03	0.98	1	5
Job	1794	3.72	1.14	1	5
Neighbors	1799	4.09	0.86	1	5
Public safety	1799	3.98	0.92	1	5
The condition of the environment	1800	3.78	0.98	1	5
Social welfare system	1797	3.51	1.04	1	5
The democratic system	1796	3.35	1.12	1	5
Family life	1797	4.33	0.76	1	5
Leisure	1800	3.99	0.84	1	5
Happiness	1799	4.07	0.90	1	5
(D) Trust in social institution					
Trust generally	1794	0.12	0.32	0	1
Trust the central government	1784	2.79	0.77	1	4
Trust local governments	1789	2.92	0.73	1	4
Trust the army	1790	2.84	0.78	1	4
Trust the legal system	1786	2.73	0.79	1	4
Trust the police	1792	2.82	0.72	1	4

(continued)

(continued)

Summary statistics of countries Philippines					
	n	Mean	SD	Min	Max
(E) Assessment of government performance					
Worry about corruption	1800	0.51	0.50	0	1
Worry about Economic inequality	1800	0.25	0.43	0	1
Political corruption	1789	1.87	0.74	1	4
Duty to vote	1800	4.37	0.73	1	5
Widespread corruption	1796	3.83	1.14	1	5
No power	1789	3.43	1.06	1	5
Complicated	1795	3.63	1.10	1	5
No matter whether vote	1797	2.80	1.20	1	5
Stop thinking	1797	3.73	1.15	1	5
Pay little attention	1797	3.62	1.05	1	5
Powerful leader	1777	1.50	0.61	1	3
Experts	1755	1.67	0.58	1	3
Military government	1774	1.43	0.58	1	3
Democratic political system	1777	1.91	0.66	1	3
Bribe	1798	8.18	2.63	1	10
(F) Satisfaction with rights					
Right to vote	1798	3.23	0.74	1	4
Right to participate in any organizations	1773	2.79	0.79	1	4
Right to gather and demonstrate	1780	2.49	0.84	1	4
Right to be informed about government	1790	2.95	0.77	1	4
Freedom of Speech	1793	3.08	0.74	1	4
Right to criticize the government	1793	2.85	0.83	1	4
(H) Demographics					
Female	1800	0.50	0.50	0	1
Age	1800	38.60	12.43	20	69
Level of education	1797	2.01	0.75	1	3
Married	1800	0.74	0.44	0	1
Unemployed	1797	0.17	0.37	0	1
Income	1508	17.45	3.77	7	21
(I) Region (Base = Metro Manila)					
Balance Luzon	1800	0.25	0.43	0	1
Visayas	1800	0.25	0.43	0	1
Mindanao	1800	0.25	0.43	0	1
(L) Yearly dummy variable (Base = 2004)					
2007	1800	0.56	0.50	0	1

Frequency Distribution of 7 Responses and Partially Aggregated 4 Responses
Philippines

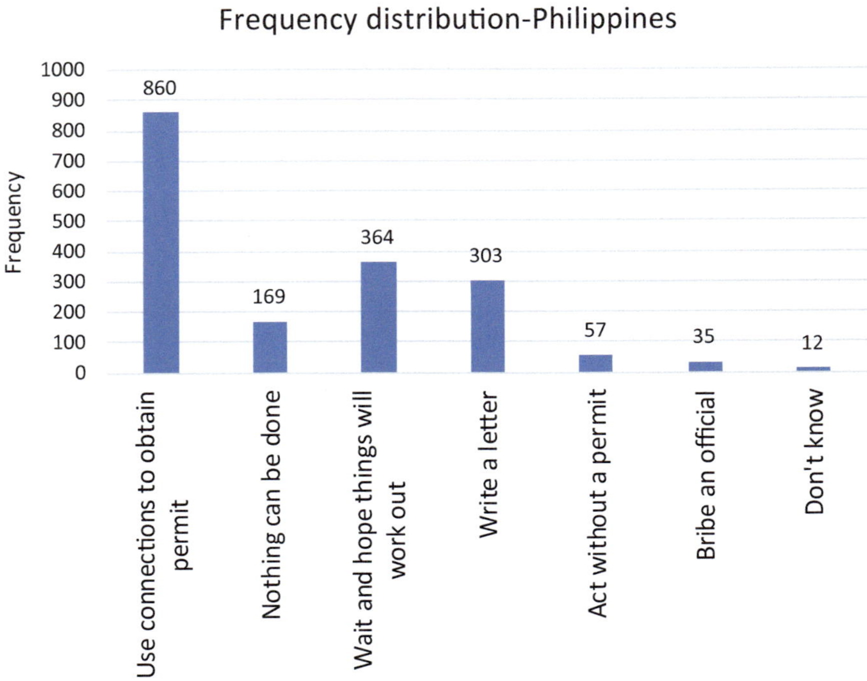

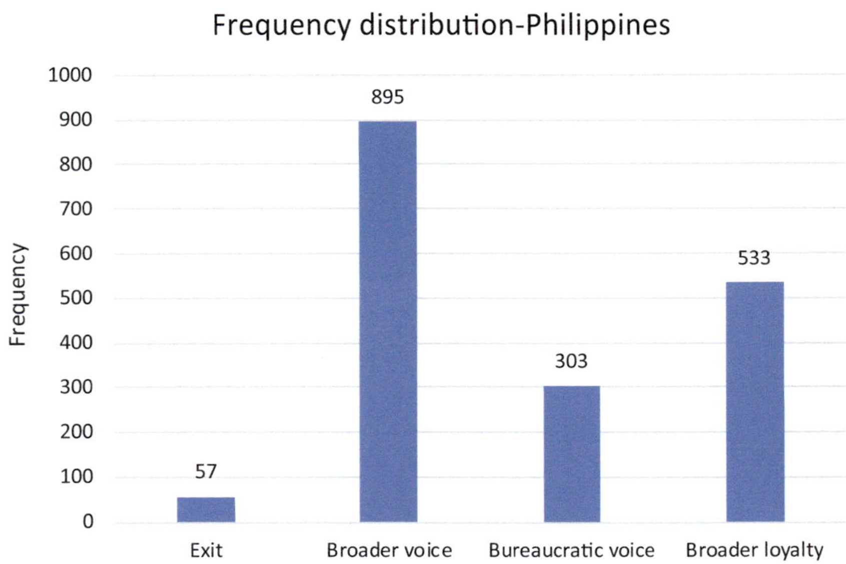

Logit regression analysis results by country Philippines								
Dependent variable	Exit		Broader voice		Bureaucratic voice		Broader loyalty	
Independent variables	Coeff.	z-stat.	Coeff.	z-stat	Coeff.	z-stat.	Coeff.	z-stat.
(A) Lifestyles								
Public water supply	0.14	0.32	0.10	0.69	−0.44	(−2.26)[a]	0.10	0.64
Electricity	−0.33	−0.38	−0.35	−1.03	0.25	0.5	0.37	0.95
LPG	−1.30	−1.91	0.24	1.25	−0.23	−0.86	0.02	0.11
Homeownership	0.33	0.65	−0.01	−0.05	−0.04	−0.16	−0.06	−0.30
Number of family members	0.04	0.55	0.01	0.52	−0.0005	−0.01	−0.02	−0.69
Pray	−0.43	−1.93	0.01	0.11	0.25	1.69	−0.07	−0.74
National elections	0.08	0.44	0.03	0.43	−0.03	−0.37	−0.01	−0.16
Proud	−0.75	(−2.39)[a]	0.38	2.66[b]	−0.20	−1.02	−0.16	−1.07
Relative Standard of Living	−0.27	−0.89	0.05	0.48	0.11	0.73	−0.07	−0.58
(B) Exposure to globalization								
Living internationally	0.11	0.60	−0.01	−0.15	−0.08	−0.89	0.05	0.74
English ability	−0.49	−1.56	−0.19	−1.79	0.53	3.81[b]	−0.09	−0.74
(C) Satisfaction with aspects of life								
Housing	−0.10	−0.55	0.04	0.61	−0.10	−1.18	0.03	0.45
Friendships	0.09	0.37	−0.20	(−2.16[a])	0.21	1.63	0.09	0.89
Household income	−0.08	−0.39	−0.09	−1.26	0.06	0.58	0.10	1.31
Health	−0.13	−0.56	0.14	1.63	−0.14	−1.25	−0.05	−0.54
Education	0.30	1.35	−0.003	−0.04	−0.06	−0.60	−0.003	−0.04
Job	0.52	2.50[a]	0.01	0.10	0.03	0.28	−0.11	−1.62
Neighbors	−0.31	−1.52	−0.01	−0.13	−0.08	−0.81	0.11	1.28
Public safety	0.20	0.85	0.03	0.38	−0.03	−0.26	−0.03	−0.32
The condition of the environment	0.24	1.03	0.05	0.60	−0.10	−0.92	−0.004	−0.05
Social welfare system	−0.02	−0.08	0.08	1.06	−0.06	−0.57	−0.08	−0.94
The democratic system	−0.01	−0.03	−0.04	−0.59	0.02	0.25	0.06	0.81
Family life	0.04	0.16	−0.09	−0.93	0.08	0.66	0.02	0.16
Leisure	−0.27	−1.15	0.15	1.79	0.15	1.24	−0.25	(−2.81)[b]
Happiness	0.03	0.14	0.06	0.84	−0.01	−0.07	−0.06	−0.82
(D) Trust in social institution								
Trust generally	−0.03	−0.06	−0.30	−1.62	−0.01	−0.05	0.27	1.39
Trust the central government	−0.07	−0.25	−0.28	(−2.62[b])	0.05	0.38	0.27	2.31[a]
Trust local governments	−1.06	(−3.48)[b]	0.16	1.48	0.07	0.52	−0.07	−0.57
Trust the army	0.28	1.02	0.005	0.05	−0.20	−1.53	0.08	0.80
Trust the legal system	0.13	0.46	0.39	4.01[b]	−0.11	−0.84	−0.37	(−3.53)[b]
Trust the police	0.52	1.72	−0.08	−0.78	0.04	0.24	0.002	0.02

(continued)

(continued)

Logit regression analysis results by country Philippines								
Dependent variable	Exit		Broader voice		Bureaucratic voice		Broader loyalty	
Independent variables	Coeff.	z-stat.	Coeff.	z-stat	Coeff.	z-stat.	Coeff.	z-stat.
(E) Assessment of government performance								
Worry about corruption	0.31	0.84	−0.17	−1.33	0.09	0.51	0.13	0.99
Worry about Economic inequality	0.18	0.49	−0.01	−0.10	0.31	1.73	−0.29	−1.86
Political corruption	−0.03	−0.12	0.07	0.77	−0.12	−1.00	0.01	0.06
Duty to vote	−0.45	−1.87	−0.16	−1.83	0.43	3.30[b]	0.04	0.43
Widespread corruption	0.12	0.59	−0.02	−0.28	−0.08	−0.92	0.04	0.59
No power	0.36	1.81	0.01	0.13	−0.07	−0.83	−0.03	−0.48
Complicated	0.07	0.33	−0.02	−0.24	0.12	1.36	−0.07	−0.91
No matter whether vote	−0.12	−0.69	−0.05	−0.90	−0.08	−0.99	0.16	2.57[a]
Stop thinking	0.06	0.30	0.06	0.90	−0.12	−1.29	−0.02	−0.23
Pay little attention	−0.18	−0.85	0.01	0.10	−0.04	−0.39	0.04	0.50
Powerful leader	−0.33	−0.97	−0.04	−0.35	0.05	0.30	0.06	0.49
Experts	0.14	0.45	0.11	0.99	−0.23	−1.45	−0.003	−0.02
Military government	−0.21	−0.63	0.02	0.21	0.11	0.74	−0.05	−0.38
Democratic political system	0.20	0.76	−0.09	−0.93	−0.01	−0.10	0.08	0.81
Bribe	0.07	0.89	−0.05	(−2.09)[a]	−0.05	−1.40	0.08	2.99[b]
(F) Satisfaction with rights								
Right to vote	−0.04	−0.16	0.15	1.71	−0.05	−0.37	−0.14	−1.46
Right to participate in any organizations	−0.23	−0.92	0.01	0.08	0.10	0.80	−0.03	−0.32
Right to gather and demonstrate	0.27	1.12	0.03	0.33	−0.02	−0.15	−0.07	−0.71
Right to be informed about government	0.10	0.37	−0.11	−1.13	−0.03	−0.21	0.10	0.96
Freedom of Speech	−0.12	−0.40	−0.08	−0.80	0.21	1.42	−0.01	−0.13
Right to criticize the government	−0.03	−0.12	−0.01	−0.11	0.13	1.13	−0.07	−0.81
(H) Demographics								
Female	0.20	0.56	−0.04	−0.37	−0.004	−0.02	0.02	0.17
Age	0.05	3.00[b]	−0.005	−0.87	0.01	1.26	−0.01	−1.30
Level of education	0.44	1.55	−0.10	−0.94	0.18	1.27	−0.07	−0.64
Married	−0.07	−0.16	−0.14	−0.90	0.18	0.90	0.03	0.16
Unemployed	0.15	0.29	−0.08	−0.49	0.39	1.76	−0.21	−1.10
Income	0.05	0.80	−0.03	−1.61	0.03	1.10	0.01	0.74
(I) Region (Base = Metro Manila)								
Balance Luzon	−1.16	(−2.08)[a]	−0.09	−0.48	0.19	0.74	0.14	0.68
Visayas	−1.84	(−2.87)[b]	0.57	2.62[b]	−0.40	−1.34	−0.23	−1.01
Mindanao	−0.89	−1.66	0.11	0.54	0.28	1.00	−0.24	−1.06

(continued)

(continued)

Logit regression analysis results by country Philippines								
Dependent variable	Exit		Broader voice		Bureaucratic voice		Broader loyalty	
Independent variables	Coeff.	z-stat.	Coeff.	z-stat	Coeff.	z-stat.	Coeff.	z-stat.
(L) Yearly dummy variable (Base = 2004)								
2007	−0.18	−0.32	0.01	0.04	0.06	0.25	0.02	0.10
Constant	−1.24	−0.46	−0.22	−0.20	−5.84	(−3.77)[b]	0.61	0.53
n	1353		1353		1353		1353	
Pseudo R squared	0.2418		0.0720		0.1105		0.0541	

Note [a]5% significance level; [b]1% significance level

6.21 Russia

The frequency distribution, at first glance, gives a surprise. The Russian data pattern is very similar to that of the United States! Russia and the United States resemble each other as far as frequency distribution is concerned: many choose "use connections" in Russia and the United States; "bribe an official" is a small response size for both societies; the combined frequency of "nothing can be done" and "wait and hope things will work out" is significantly large in both societies; and "write a letter" is significant also in both societies.

To return to the specifics of the Russian data, the response of the exit option is too small for regression analysis to be statistically significant. Data on the broader voice option shows this group is neither satisfied with household income nor with education. Another distinguishing feature of the Russian response is that those who trust the central government voice their grievances frequently. Those who are not satisfied with the right to vote are vocal, and those who are satisfied with freedom of speech are also vocal. In contrast, female respondents do not voice their dissatisfaction or opinions very much.

Those respondents in the bureaucratic voice option pray and are satisfied with friendships. It is important to note that those who do not trust the central government tend to choose broadly bureaucratic voice. Also, those who believe that government is run by the military tend to choose the bureaucratic voice option. Those who are satisfied with the right to vote choose the bureaucratic voice option. Female respondents also choose the bureaucratic option.

Those who choose the broader loyalty option participate in national elections, are not satisfied with friendships, are satisfied with leisure, and trust both local governments and the legal system. This option is also favored by those who negatively assess government performance about duty to vote and negatively assess government performance in paying too little attention to the people. Those who regard their political orientation as left on the spectrum choose broader loyalty.

Summary statistics of countries Russia					
	n	Mean	SD	Mn	Max
Exit	916	0.06	0.23	0	1
Broader voice	916	0.46	0.50	0	1
Bureaucratic voice	916	0.21	0.41	0	1
Broader loyalty	916	0.27	0.45	0	1
(A) Lifestyles					
Number of public utilities	1055	4.14	1.12	2	7
Homeownership	1039	0.79	0.40	0	1
Number of family members	1055	2.59	1.25	1	10
Pray	981	2.06	1.30	1	5
National elections	1037	4.10	1.15	1	5
Proud	1021	3.19	0.79	1	4
Relative Standard of Living	1038	2.82	0.77	1	5
(B) Exposure to globalization					
Internet	1026	1.84	1.42	1	5
Living internationally	1055	0.41	0.74	0	5
English ability	1038	1.51	0.73	1	4
(C) Satisfaction with aspects of life					
Housing	1054	3.39	1.08	1	5
Friendships	1030	4.07	0.77	1	5
Household income	1039	2.68	1.01	1	5
Health	1043	3.21	1.08	1	5
Education	1024	3.56	1.00	1	5
Job	881	3.44	1.00	1	5
Neighbors	1027	3.83	0.76	1	5
Public safety	1028	3.46	0.94	1	5
The condition of the environment	1024	3.02	1.05	1	5
Social welfare system	949	2.58	1.02	1	5
The democratic system	898	2.87	1.02	1	5
Family life	987	3.92	0.90	1	5
Leisure	1017	3.46	1.02	1	5
Your life as a whole	1021	3.56	0.85	1	5
(D) Trust in social institution					
Trust generally	1010	0.33	0.47	0	1
Trust the central government	1006	2.58	0.80	1	4
Trust local governments	995	2.34	0.82	1	4

(continued)

(continued)

Summary statistics of countries Russia					
	n	Mean	SD	Mn	Max
Trust the army	995	2.55	0.87	1	4
Trust the legal system	975	2.19	0.80	1	4
Trust the police	1006	2.02	0.82	1	4
(E) Assessment of government performance					
Worry about corruption	1055	0.48	0.50	0	1
Worry about Economic inequality	1055	0.37	0.48	0	1
Political corruption	985	1.95	0.72	1	4
Duty to vote	1034	4.20	0.97	1	5
Widespread corruption	994	3.86	0.98	1	5
No power	1024	3.88	1.09	1	5
Complicated	999	3.63	1.10	1	5
No matter whether vote	1011	3.21	1.24	1	5
Pay little attention	1022	4.11	0.92	1	5
Powerful leader	895	1.80	0.75	1	3
Experts	853	1.91	0.64	1	3
Military government	914	1.16	0.44	1	3
Democratic political system	895	2.23	0.60	1	3
Bribe	1010	8.65	1.98	1	10
(F) Satisfaction with rights					
Right to vote	1016	3.37	0.75	1	4
Right to participate in any organizations	919	3.12	0.74	1	4
Right to gather and demonstrate	886	2.99	0.81	1	4
Right to be informed about government	891	2.57	0.98	1	4
Freedom of speech	958	2.88	0.86	1	4
(G) Political spectrum					
Political spectrum	619	5.72	2.20	1	10
(H) Demographics					
Female	1055	0.54	0.50	0	1
Age	1055	43.23	14.17	20	69
Level of education	1055	2.0	0.8	1	3
Married	1053	0.58	0.49	0	1
Unemployed	1040	0.06	0.23	0	1
Income	911	3.51	2.06	1	10

Frequency Distribution of 7 Responses and Partially Aggregated 4 Responses

Russia

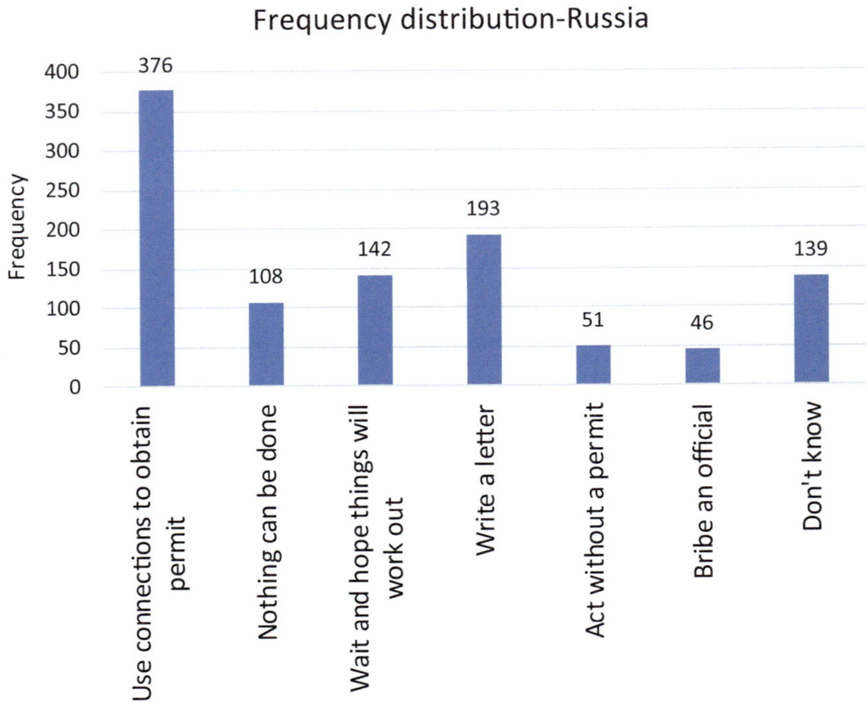

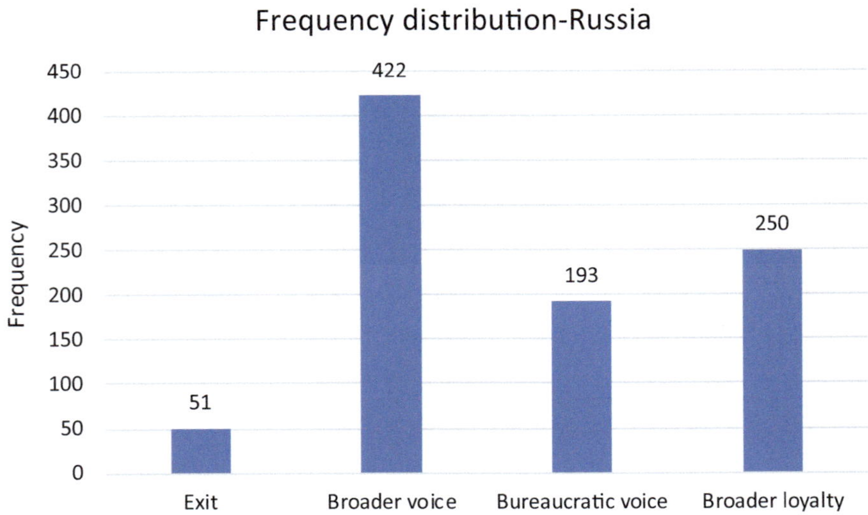

Logit regression analysis results by country Russia								
Dependent variable	Exit		Broader voice		Bureaucratic voice		Broader loyalty	
Independent variables	Coeff.	z-stat.	Coeff.	z-stat.	Coeff.	z-stat.	Coeff.	z-stat.
(A) Lifestyles								
Number of public utilities	–	–	−0.24	−1.07	0.33	0.81	0.65	1.72
Homeownership	–	–	−0.29	−0.59	−0.95	−1.10	0.30	0.37
Number of family members	–	–	0.06	0.31	−0.75	−1.89	0.10	0.31
Pray	–	–	−0.30	−1.79	0.53	2.13[a]	−0.05	−0.21
National elections	–	–	−0.42	−1.67	0.49	1.08	1.20	2.34[a]
Proud	–	–	0.27	0.82	−0.84	−1.43	0.56	1.03
Relative Standard of Living	–	–	−0.002	−0.01	0.41	0.64	−0.13	−0.22
(B) Exposure to globalization								
Internet	–	–	0.13	0.80	−0.03	−0.11	0.29	0.91
Living internationally	–	–	0.03	0.10	−0.30	−0.69	0.03	0.05
English ability	–	–	−0.10	−0.30	−0.35	−0.62	0.38	0.69
(C) Satisfaction with aspects of life								
Housing	–	–	−0.13	−0.54	−0.22	−0.52	−0.38	−0.92
Friendships	–	–	0.04	0.11	2.15	2.72[b]	−2.00	(−2.34)[a]
Household income	–	–	−0.60	(−2.15)[a]	0.84	1.94	0.41	0.83
Health	–	–	0.54	1.91	−0.60	−1.50	−0.86	−1.54
Education	–	–	−0.58	(−2.04)[a]	0.69	1.24	0.90	1.85
Job	–	–	0.56	1.92	−1.08	−1.85	0.63	1.32
Neighbors	–	–	−0.31	−0.78	0.68	1.09	−0.81	−1.15
Public safety	–	–	0.08	0.33	0.54	1.10	−0.86	−1.80
The condition of the environment	–	–	0.39	1.24	−0.27	−0.52	−0.80	−1.51
Social welfare system	–	–	−0.36	−1.19	−0.71	−1.49	1.29	2.46[a]
The democratic system	–	–	0.29	1.03	0.13	0.30	−0.44	−1.02
Family life	–	–	−0.34	−1.12	−0.86	−1.62	2.07	3.24[b]
Leisure	–	–	0.55	1.93	−0.54	−1.20	0.43	0.89
Life as a whole	–	–	−0.46	−1.23	−0.32	−0.48	–	–
(D) Trust in social institution								
Trust generally	–	–	−0.39	−0.90	0.14	0.21	1.22	1.55
Trust the central government	–	–	0.88	(2.17)[a]	−1.57	(−2.40)[a]	−0.42	−0.59

(continued)

(continued)

Logit regression analysis results by country Russia								
Dependent variable	Exit		Broader voice		Bureaucratic voice		Broader loyalty	
Independent variables	Coeff.	z-stat.	Coeff.	z-stat.	Coeff.	z-stat.	Coeff.	z-stat.
Trust local governments	–	–	−0.48	−1.35	0.11	0.22	1.73	2.37[a]
Trust the army	–	–	−0.34	−1.20	0.21	0.45	0.59	1.23
Trust the legal system	–	–	−0.54	−1.61	−0.90	−1.44	1.45	2.33[a]
Trust the police	–	–	0.50	1.25	1.29	1.80	−1.37	−1.90
(E) Assessment of government performance								
Worry about corruption	–	–	0.54	1.19	0.24	0.33	−1.03	−1.30
Worry about Economic inequality	–	–	−0.25	−0.61	−0.74	−1.08	−0.19	−0.28
Political corruption	–	–	−0.34	−1.04	0.35	0.68	0.60	1.01
Duty to vote	–	–	0.44	1.56	0.42	0.85	−1.31	(−2.77)[b]
Widespread corruption	–	–	−0.11	−0.46	−0.07	−0.18	−0.13	−0.31
No power	–	–	0.18	0.91	−0.09	−0.30	0.30	0.87
Complicated	–	–	−0.004	−0.02	0.54	1.56	−0.40	−0.99
No matter whether vote	–	–	−0.09	−0.38	−0.07	−0.18	0.52	1.18
Pay little attention	–	–	−0.35	−1.31	−0.59	−1.43	1.38	2.32[a]
Powerful leader	–	–	0.06	0.20	−1.00	−1.84	0.74	1.41
Experts	–	–	0.04	0.10	−0.55	−0.97	0.58	1.05
Military government	–	–	−0.66	−1.11	1.87	2.05[a]	−1.93	−1.41
Democratic political system	–	–	−0.56	−1.45	0.91	1.53	−0.23	−0.37
Bribe	–	–	0.05	0.41	0.001	0.00	−0.25	−1.22
(F) Satisfaction with rights								
Right to vote	–	–	−0.83	(−2.11)[a]	1.24	2.21[a]	0.50	0.72
Right to participate in any organizations	–	–	−0.02	−0.05	−0.96	−1.51	0.10	0.16
Right to gather and demonstrate	–	–	0.50	1.31	−0.73	−1.22	−1.23	−1.76
Right to be informed about government	–	–	−0.39	−1.27	0.68	1.34	−0.15	−0.32
Freedom of speech	–	–	0.81	2.22[a]	0.02	0.03	−0.53	−0.83
(G) Political spectrum								
Political spectrum	–	–	−0.12	−1.13	−0.13	−0.82	−0.55	3.01[a]

(continued)

(continued)

Logit regression analysis results by country Russia								
Dependent variable	Exit		Broader voice		Bureaucratic voice		Broader loyalty	
Independent variables	Coeff.	z-stat.	Coeff.	z-stat.	Coeff.	z-stat.	Coeff.	z-stat.
(H) Demographics								
Female	–	–	−1.05	(−2.34)[a]	2.84	3.06[b]	0.02	0.03
Age	–	–	−0.03	−1.36	−0.01	−0.17	0.07	1.67
Level of education	–	–	0.53	1.44	0.51	0.84	−1.25	(−1.97)[a]
Married	–	–	−0.54	−1.03	1.65	1.79	−0.23	−0.27
Unemployed	–	–	0.35	0.30	1.58	1.00	1.05	0.50
Income	–	–	0.09	0.66	0.23	0.90	−0.65	(−2.66)[b]
Constant	–	–	6.77	1.98[a]	−9.42	−1.72	−13.18	(−2.18)[a]
n	–		206		206		206	
Pseudo R squared	–		0.2487		0.4493		0.4738	

Note [a]5% significance level; [b]1% significance level

6.22 Singapore

The frequency distribution of Singapore reveals that respondents of this city-state have some difficulties in selecting the two responses: "bribe an official" and "act without a permit." The former registered a response of zero out of 1702 respondents. The latter registered four out of 1702 respondents. Thus, the exit option is statistical insignificant and cannot be analyzed further.

Those who favor the broader voice option do not enjoy homeownership and do not pray, but are proud of Singapore. Those who choose this option do not trust the central government, assess government performance as negative (government has no power and government business is complicated), assess government performance positively without specifying the areas of government performance although they do not pay much attention; and believe that government should be led by powerful persons. Singaporeans who prefer this option are not satisfied with their right to participate in any organization. Demographically, those who select this option are low income and have no religion.

For those that favor the bureaucratic voice option, they have large families (many children), are not satisfied with leisure, negatively assess government (government has no power), are satisfied with the right to participate in organizations, and are not satisfied with the right to criticize the government.

The cluster of traits for those who choose the broader loyalty option include do not have a command of English, are not satisfied with the democratic system, are satisfied with leisure, assess government as complicated, and believe that government should be a democratic political system. Those in this grouping are satisfied with the right to criticize the government.

Summary statistics of countries Singapore					
	n	Mean	SD	Min	Max
Exit	1702	0.002	0.05	0	1
Broader voice	1702	0.104	0.31	0	1
Bureaucratic voice	1702	0.484	0.50	0	1
Broader loyalty	1702	0.410	0.49	0	1
(A) Lifestyles					
LPG	1838	0.78	0.41	0	1
Homeownership	1835	0.93	0.25	0	1
Number of family members	1838	4.01	1.50	1	13
Pray	1820	3.45	1.67	1	5
National elections	1600	3.61	1.48	1	5
Local elections	–	–	–	–	–
Proud	1770	3.43	0.70	1	4
Relative standard of living	1837	3.25	0.72	1	5
(B) Exposure to globalization					
Living internationally	1838	2.70	1.73	0	6
English ability	1836	3.32	0.88	1	4
(C) Satisfaction with aspects of life					
Housing	1837	4.12	0.75	1	5
Friendships	1833	4.20	0.66	1	5
Household income	1826	3.66	0.93	1	5
Health	1835	4.06	0.75	1	5
Education	1828	3.88	0.84	1	5
Job	1623	3.76	0.91	1	5
Neighbors	1828	3.96	0.75	1	5
Public safety	1829	4.10	0.70	1	5
The condition of the environment	1826	4.00	0.72	1	5
Social welfare system	–	–	–	–	–
The democratic system	1739	3.69	0.82	1	5
Family life	1833	4.29	0.68	1	5
Leisure	1828	4.03	0.72	1	5
Happiness	1837	4.00	0.85	1	5
(D) Trust in social institution					
Trust generally	1696	0.34	0.47	0	1
Trust the central government	1703	3.19	0.59	1	4
Trust the legal system	1727	3.17	0.61	1	4
Trust the police	1774	3.22	0.63	1	4

(continued)

(continued)

Summary statistics of countries Singapore					
	n	Mean	SD	Min	Max
(E) Assessment of government performance					
Worry about corruption	1838	0.26	0.44	0	1
Worry about Economic inequality	1838	0.23	0.42	0	1
Political corruption	1720	3.31	0.60	1	4
Duty to vote	1821	4.42	0.58	2	5
Widespread corruption	1650	2.51	0.91	1	5
No power	1758	3.45	0.97	1	5
Complicated	1762	3.28	0.97	1	5
No matter whether vote	1764	2.42	0.98	1	5
Stop thinking	–	–	–	–	–
Pay little attention	1743	3.08	0.95	1	5
Powerful leader	1583	1.28	0.52	1	3
Experts	1544	1.69	0.63	1	3
Military government	1592	1.31	0.54	1	3
Democratic political system	1635	2.27	0.59	1	3
Bribe	1786	9.25	1.55	1	10
(F) Satisfaction with rights					
Right to vote	1762	3.42	0.61	1	4
Right to participate in any organizations	1664	3.08	0.62	1	4
Right to gather and demonstrate	1513	2.50	0.80	1	4
Right to be informed about government	–	–	–	–	–
Freedom of speech	1607	2.62	0.79	1	4
Right to criticize the government	1528	2.26	0.85	1	4
(H) Demographics					
Female	1838	0.55	0.50	0	1
Age	1838	39.98	11.40	20	69
Level of education	1838	1.86	0.82	1	3
Married	1838	0.69	0.46	0	1
Unemployed	1831	0.04	0.21	0	1
Income	1732	4.08	2.56	0	11
No religion	1837	0.13	0.34	0	1
(L) Yearly dummy variable (Base = 2004)					
2006	1838	0.56	0.50	0	1

Frequency Distribution of 7 Responses and Partially Aggregated 4 Responses Singapore

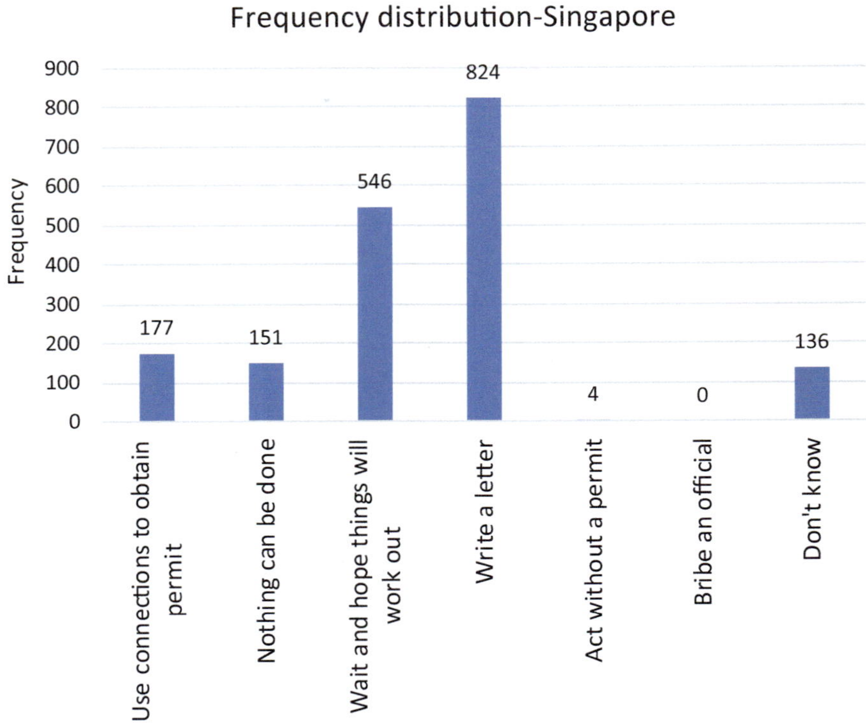

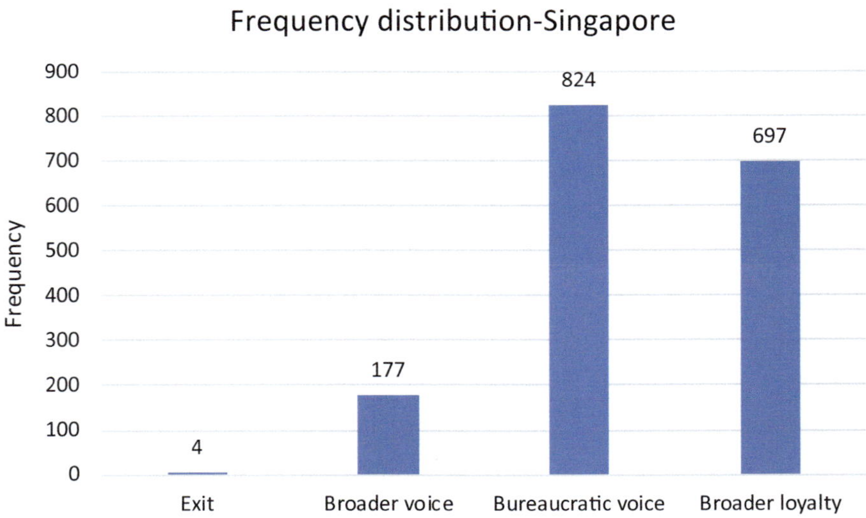

Logit regression analysis results by country Singapore								
Dependent variable	Exit		Broader voice		Bureaucratic voice		Broader loyalty	
Independent variables	Coeff.	z-stat	Coeff.	z-stat	Coeff.	z-stat	Coeff.	z-stat
(A) Lifestyles								
LPG	–	–	1.15	1.76	0.06	0.25	−0.30	−1.16
Homeownership	–	–	−1.74	(−2.12)[a]	0.93	1.99	−0.67	−1.45
Number of family members	–	–	0.22	1.55	0.02	0.30	−0.07	−1.10
Pray	–	–	−0.42	(−3.53)[b]	0.25	4.11[b]	−0.04	−0.64
National elections	–	–	0.26	1.80	−0.11	−1.68	0.04	0.52
Local elections	–	–	–	–	–	–	–	–
Proud	–	–	0.77	2.33[a]	−0.20	−1.31	−0.17	−1.08
Relative standard of living	–	–	−0.43	−1.56	0.18	1.36	−0.01	−0.06
(B) Exposure to globalization								
Living internationally	–	–	−0.03	−0.22	0.05	0.79	−0.09	−1.49
English ability	–	–	0.44	1.46	0.21	1.48	−0.34	(−2.39)[a]
(C) Satisfaction with aspects of life								
Housing	–	–	−0.45	−1.66	−0.07	−0.51	0.29	1.90
Friendships	–	–	0.22	0.64	0.17	1.01	−0.21	−1.24
Household income	–	–	−0.09	−0.39	0.13	1.05	0.02	0.13
Health	–	–	−0.01	−0.02	−0.04	−0.24	0.09	0.56
Education	–	–	−0.19	−0.62	−0.10	−0.65	0.10	0.67
Job	–	–	0.08	0.30	0.13	0.99	−0.15	−1.06
Neighbors	–	–	0.05	0.17	0.04	0.28	0.02	0.12
Public safety	–	–	−0.001	0.00	−0.07	−0.42	0.03	0.16
The condition of the environment	–	–	−0.177	−0.60	0.19	1.25	−0.24	−1.56
Social welfare system	–	–	–	–	–	–	–	–
The democratic system	–	–	−0.04	−0.15	0.31	2.30[a]	−0.30	(−2.19)[a]
Family life	–	–	−0.24	−0.66	0.24	1.29	−0.25	−1.28
Leisure	–	–	0.33	0.92	−0.49	(−2.93)[b]	0.40	2.28[a]
Happiness	–	–	−0.07	−0.26	−0.05	−0.41	0.04	0.28

(continued)

(continued)

Logit regression analysis results by country Singapore								
Dependent variable	Exit		Broader voice		Bureaucratic voice		Broader loyalty	
Independent variables	Coeff.	z-stat	Coeff.	z-stat	Coeff.	z-stat	Coeff.	z-stat
(D) Trust in social institution								
Trust generally	–	–	−0.12	−0.29	0.06	0.31	0.16	0.82
Trust the central government	–	–	−1.36	(−3.33)[b]	0.42	2.13[a]	−0.11	−0.53
Trust local governments	–	–	–	–	–	–	–	–
Trust the army	–	–	–	–	–	–	–	–
Trust the legal system	–	–	0.18	0.42	0.05	0.26	−0.10	−0.46
Trust the police	–	–	−0.16	−0.37	−0.14	−0.65	0.29	1.33
(E) Assessment of government performance								
Worry about corruption	–	–	−0.15	−0.32	0.39	1.83	−0.25	−1.15
Worry about Economic inequality	–	–	0.02	0.05	0.21	1.02	−0.16	−0.73
Political corruption	–	–	−0.08	−0.22	−0.12	−0.78	0.17	1.07
Duty to vote	–	–	0.61	1.51	−0.11	−0.64	−0.07	−0.39
Widespread corruption	–		0.12	0.51	−0.01	−0.08	0.03	0.28
No power	–	–	−0.63	(−2.62)[b]	0.41	3.41[b]	−0.24	−1.91
Complicated	–	–	−1.00	(−3.76)[b]	−0.11	−0.94	0.42	3.26[a]
No matter whether vote	–	–	−0.30	−1.10	−0.18	−1.55	0.23	1.88
Stop thinking	–	–	–	–	–	–	–	–
Pay little attention	–	–	0.79	2.85[b]	−0.22	−1.87	−0.04	−0.31
Powerful leader	–	–	1.31	3.27[b]	−0.35	−1.69	−0.02	−0.07
Experts	–	–	−0.43	−1.14	0.20	1.20	0.002	0.01
Military government	–	–	0.14	0.35	0.29	1.48	−0.39	−1.88
Democratic political system	–	–	−0.21	−0.62	−0.26	−1.66	0.38	2.33[a]
Bribe	–	–	−0.03	−0.25	−0.11	−1.81	0.09	1.53

(continued)

(continued)

Logit regression analysis results by country Singapore								
Dependent variable	Exit		Broader voice		Bureaucratic voice		Broader loyalty	
Independent variables	Coeff.	z-stat	Coeff.	z-stat	Coeff.	z-stat	Coeff.	z-stat
(F) Satisfaction with rights								
Right to vote	–	–	0.45	1.14	−0.16	−0.87	−0.08	−0.46
Right to participate in any organizations	–	–	−1.26	(−3.14)[b]	0.62	3.34[b]	−0.21	−1.11
Right to gather and demonstrate	–	–	−0.25	−0.80	0.12	0.83	0.03	0.18
Right to be informed about government	–	–	–	–	–	–	–	–
Freedom of speech	–	–	0.81	2.62[b]	−0.04	−0.25	−0.41	(−2.32)”
Right to criticize the government	–	–	0.17	0.59	−0.68	(−4.62)[b]	0.81	4.88[b]
(H) Demographics								
Female	–	–	−0.33	−0.93	−0.02	−0.14	0.19	1.02
Age	–	–	−0.03	−1.31	0.01	0.82	0.003	0.27
Level of education	–	–	0.29	0.85	0.22	1.37	−0.24	−1.42
Married	–	–	0.40	0.92	−0.26	−1.22	0.12	0.54
Unemployed	–	–	−0.04	−0.04	0.29	0.50	−0.62	−0.97
Income	–	–	−0.31	(−2.91)[b]	0.08	1.71	−0.01	−0.16
No religion	–	–	−1.58	(−2.60)[b]	0.47	1.64	0.36	1.24
(L) Yearly dummy variable (Base = 2004)								
2006	–	–	0.46	0.97	−0.07	−0.28	−0.19	−0.77
Constant	–	–	3.12	0.90	−3.41	(−2.10)[a]	0.75	0.45
n	–		741		741		741	
Pseudo R squared	–		0.4620		0.1843		0.1736	

Note [a]5% significance level; [b]1% significance level

6.23 South Korea

In the case of South Korea, the frequency distribution of options reveals that the broader loyalty option accounts for 70.8%, whereas the broader voice option accounts for 21.2%. Those who select the broader loyalty option, they are proud of South Korea, are worried about economic inequality, positively assess government performance, and have a low level of education. In contrast, those who select the broader voice option are not proud of South Korea, have a high household income, are not worried about economic inequality, and assess negatively government performance on issues of bribery. Those who identify with the broader bureaucratic voice option give a lukewarm assessment of government performance, have a high level of education, and reside in the middle region (i.e., Kyunsang Bukdo, Chungchongdo).

Summary statistics of countries South Korea

	n	Mean	SD	Min	Max
Exit	1719	0.017	0.13	0	1
Broader voice	1719	0.212	0.41	0	1
Bureaucratic voice	1719	0.062	0.24	0	1
Broader loyalty	1719	0.709	0.45	0	1
(A) Lifestyles					
Public water supply	1842	0.95	0.22	0	1
LPG	1842	0.86	0.35	0	1
Homeownership	1841	0.78	0.41	0	1
Number of family members	1842	3.70	1.22	1	10
Pray	1814	2.40	1.54	1	5
National elections	1798	4.41	1.04	1	5
Proud	1827	2.95	0.70	1	4
(B) Exposure to globalization					
Living internationally	1842	0.71	0.93	0	6
(C) Satisfaction with aspects of life					
Housing	1840	3.39	0.91	1	5
Friendships	1836	3.76	0.75	1	5
Household income	1838	2.99	0.88	1	5
Health	1839	3.50	0.93	1	5
Education	1821	3.22	0.85	1	5
Job	1778	3.15	0.94	1	5
Neighbors	1828	3.57	0.76	1	5
Public safety	1803	3.12	0.91	1	5
The condition of the environment	1834	3.23	0.85	1	5
Social welfare system	1795	2.61	0.92	1	5
Family life	1840	3.63	0.79	1	5
Leisure	1829	3.07	0.94	1	5
Happiness	1835	3.47	0.90	1	5
(D) Trust in social institution					
Trust generally	1755	0.71	0.45	0	1

(continued)

(continued)

Summary statistics of countries South Korea					
	n	Mean	SD	Min	Max
Trust the central government	1756	1.94	0.71	1	4
Trust local governments	1769	2.00	0.69	1	4
Trust the army	1776	2.40	0.75	1	4
Trust the legal system	1757	2.20	0.72	1	4
Trust the police	1802	2.24	0.73	1	4
(E) Assessment of government performance					
Worry about corruption	1842	0.20	0.40	0	1
Worry about Economic inequality	1842	0.34	0.48	0	1
Political corruption	1822	1.58	0.63	1	4
Duty to vote	1837	4.42	0.62	1	5
Widespread corruption	1820	4.24	0.72	1	5
No power	1813	3.92	0.92	1	5
Complicated	1811	3.99	0.80	1	5
No matter whether vote	1823	2.59	1.14	1	5
Pay little attention	1828	4.04	0.85	1	5
Powerful leader	1709	1.68	0.69	1	3
Experts	1695	1.94	0.63	1	3
Military government	1683	1.33	0.54	1	3
Democratic political system	1736	2.20	0.65	1	3
Bribe	1826	9.03	1.70	1	10
(F) Satisfaction with rights					
Right to vote	1808	3.09	0.58	1	4
Right to participate in any organizations	1775	2.90	0.61	1	4
Right to gather and demonstrate	1719	2.60	0.70	1	4
Right to be informed about government	1728	2.50	0.75	1	4
Freedom of speech	1772	2.64	0.71	1	4
Right to criticize the government	1752	2.61	0.74	1	4
(H) Demographics					
Female	1842	0.49	0.50	0	1
Age	1842	40.02	12.20	20	69
Level of education	1841	2.22	0.69	1	3
Married	1842	0.74	0.44	0	1
Unemployed	1841	0.05	0.22	0	1
Income	1780	3.03	2.17	1	20
No religion	1835	0.45	0.50	0	1
(I) Region (Base = Seoul metropolitan area)					
Middle area	1842	0.13	0.34	0	1
South-west area	1842	0.11	0.31	0	1
South-east area	1842	0.27	0.44	0	1
(L) Yearly dummy variable (Base = 2004)					
2006	1842	0.56	0.50	0	1

Frequency Distribution of 7 Responses and Partially Aggregated 4 Responses

South Korea

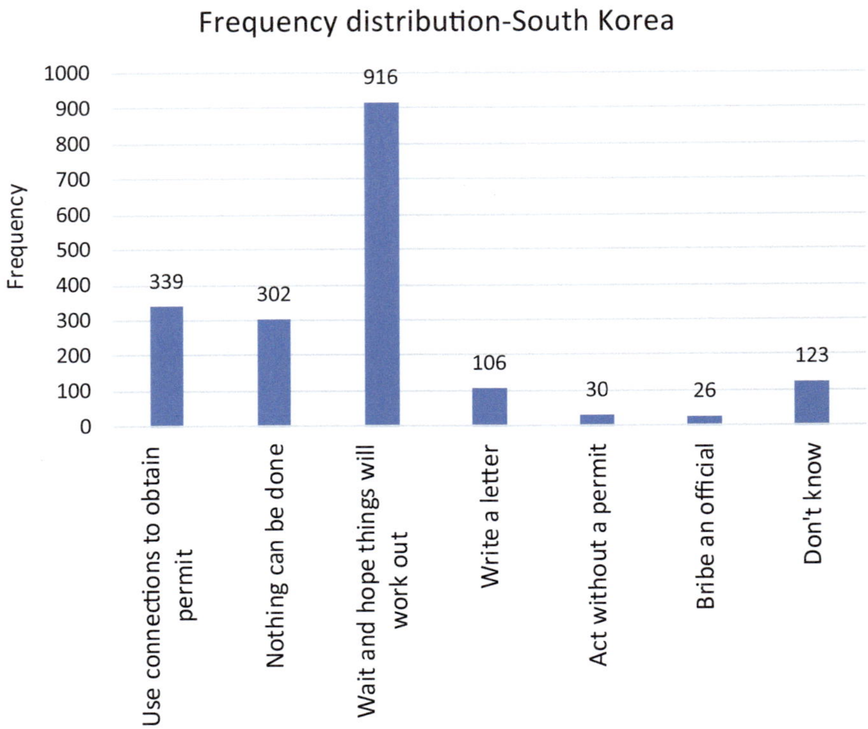

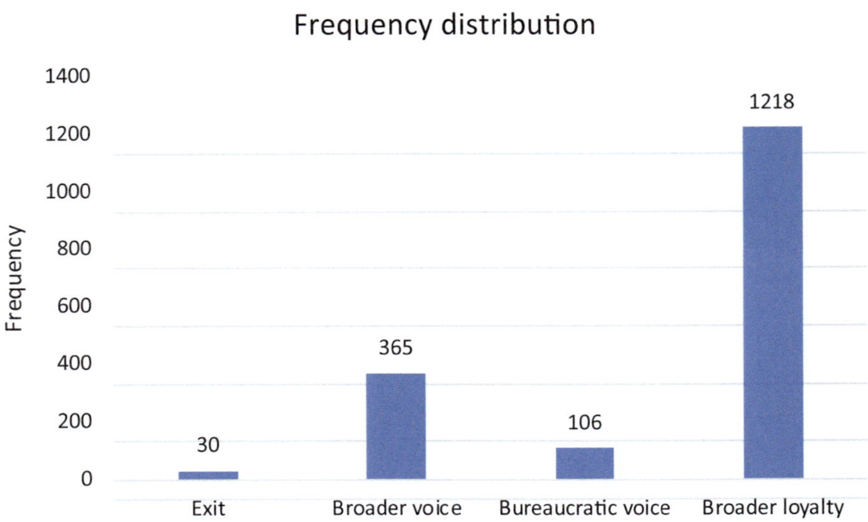

Logit regression analysis results by country South Korea								
Dependent variable	Exit		Broader voice		Bureaucratic voice		Broader loyalty	
Independent variables	Coeff.	z-stat.	Coeff.	z-stat.	Coeff.	z-stat.	Coeff.	z-stat.
(A) Lifestyles								
Public water supply	–	–	−0.47	−1.38	0.76	0.93	0.12	0.36
LPG	0.66	0.74	0.05	0.16	−0.02	−0.03	−0.03	−0.12
Homeownership	0.02	0.02	−0.38	−1.96	0.47	1.26	0.24	1.34
Number of family members	0.42	1.81	0.09	1.23	−0.01	−0.10	−0.09	−1.46
Pray	0.16	0.57	0.003	0.05	0.13	1.17	−0.04	−0.75
National elections	0.18	0.50	0.11	1.16	0.17	0.90	−0.13	−1.53
Proud	−0.63	−1.49	−0.25	(−2.13)[a]	−0.29	−1.32	0.31	2.86[b]
(B) Exposure to globalization								
Living internationally	0.13	0.39	−0.02	−0.23	−0.32	−1.96	0.08	1.06
(C) Satisfaction with aspects of life								
Housing	−0.26	−0.71	−0.19	−1.82	0.13	0.70	0.15	1.50
Friendships	0.51	1.21	0.08	0.66	−0.09	−0.41	−0.12	−1.07
Household income	−0.42	−0.98	0.26	2.08[a]	−0.12	−0.55	−0.16	−1.40
Health	0.16	0.49	−0.12	−1.22	0.01	0.04	0.10	1.12
Education	0.06	0.16	0.01	0.08	−0.12	−0.57	0.03	0.30
Job	0.10	0.26	−0.01	−0.06	0.002	0.01	0.02	0.18
Neighbors	−0.70	−1.67	0.001	0.01	−0.23	−1.13	0.09	0.78
Public safety	0.20	0.54	−0.05	−0.45	0.06	0.35	0.01	0.10
The condition of the environment	0.24	0.57	0.10	0.81	−0.06	−0.30	−0.07	−0.69
Social welfare system	−0.79	−1.93	0.12	1.15	0.06	0.34	−0.06	−0.69
Family life	−0.17	−0.35	0.19	1.39	−0.02	−0.10	−0.17	−1.36
Leisure	−0.07	−0.20	−0.11	−1.05	−0.15	−0.86	0.15	1.64
Happiness	0.13	0.32	−0.11	−1.01	0.36	1.79	0.00002	0.00
(D) Trust in social institution								
Trust generally	−0.79	−1.22	−0.002	−0.01	0.23	0.69	0.03	0.17
Trust the central government	0.27	0.49	−0.16	−1.05	0.03	0.13	0.11	0.80
Trust local governments	0.94	1.66	−0.10	−0.67	−0.01	−0.04	0.06	0.44
Trust the army	−0.90	−1.88	0.12	0.91	−0.14	−0.60	−0.02	−0.18
Trust the legal system	0.24	0.49	−0.05	−0.36	−0.08	−0.32	0.04	0.33

(continued)

(continued)

Logit regression analysis results by country South Korea								
Dependent variable	Exit		Broader voice		Bureaucratic voice		Broader loyalty	
Independent variables	Coeff.	z-stat.	Coeff.	z-stat.	Coeff.	z-stat.	Coeff.	z-stat.
Trust the police	−0.52	−1.13	−0.12	−0.89	0.29	1.24	0.05	0.40
(E) Assessment of government performance								
Worry about corruption	−1.42	−1.60	0.11	0.55	0.49	1.46	−0.12	−0.69
Worry about Economic inequality	−1.30	−1.82	−0.38	(−2.22)[a]	−0.09	−0.32	0.43	2.79[b]
Political corruption	−0.31	−0.55	−0.08	−0.61	0.46	2.12[a]	−0.01	−0.12
Duty to vote	−0.28	−0.50	0.10	0.68	0.50	1.66	−0.24	−1.84
Widespread corruption	0.85	1.42	0.08	0.61	0.11	0.50	−0.12	−1.08
No power	−0.28	−0.77	−0.05	−0.49	−0.19	−1.30	0.13	1.52
Complicated	0.16	0.38	−0.10	−0.95	0.25	1.26	0.01	0.14
No matter whether vote	0.22	0.88	−0.06	−0.78	−0.22	−1.60	0.08	1.22
Pay little attention	0.45	0.90	0.26	2.31[a]	−0.14	−0.83	−0.20	(−2.01)[a]
Powerful leader	−0.36	−0.82	0.30	2.48[a]	−0.37	−1.60	−0.13	−1.21
Experts	0.74	1.46	−0.09	−0.67	−0.12	−0.50	0.06	0.50
Military government	0.19	0.34	−0.05	−0.33	0.31	1.19	−0.04	−0.31
Democratic political system	−0.26	−0.59	0.13	0.97	0.01	0.02	−0.12	−1.00
Bribe	−0.34	(−2.09)[a]	−0.18	(−4.08)[b]	0.21	1.93	0.13	3.02[b]
(F) Satisfaction with rights								
Right to vote	0.67	1.28	−0.29	(−2.01)[a]	0.17	0.70	0.15	1.13
Right to participate in any organizations	−0.57	−1.11	0.31	1.90	−0.03	−0.11	−0.18	−1.27
Right to gather and demonstrate	−1.07	(−2.12)[a]	0.002	0.01	−0.06	−0.27	0.06	0.49
Right to be informed about government	0.27	0.49	0.02	0.15	−0.41	−1.60	0.08	0.66
Freedom of speech	−0.14	−0.25	−0.13	−0.84	0.48	1.78	−0.06	−0.42
Right to criticize the government	0.59	1.02	0.04	0.26	−0.17	−0.67	0.003	0.02

(continued)

(continued)

Logit regression analysis results by country South Korea								
Dependent variable	Exit		Broader voice		Bureaucratic voice		Broader loyalty	
Independent variables	Coeff.	z-stat.	Coeff.	z-stat.	Coeff.	z-stat.	Coeff.	z-stat.
(H) Demographics								
Female	−1.38	−1.93	−0.30	−1.70	0.34	1.12	0.26	1.63
Age	−0.004	−0.11	−0.01	−1.05	−0.02	−1.04	0.01	1.22
Level of education	−0.57	−0.96	0.33	2.24[a]	0.56	2.05[a]	−0.41	(−3.02)[b]
Married	−0.39	−0.44	0.37	1.51	0.31	0.69	−0.33	−1.52
Unemployed	–	–	0.27	0.75	0.23	0.33	−0.15	−0.44
Income	0.10	0.82	−0.04	−1.01	0.03	0.39	0.01	0.38
No religion	0.62	0.80	0.20	1.05	−0.10	−0.28	−0.15	−0.86
(I) Region (Base = Seoul metropolitan area)								
Middle area	0.05	0.05	0.08	0.31	0.92	2.17[a]	−0.30	−1.33
South-west area	−0.21	−0.19	0.08	0.29	0.83	1.90	−0.36	−1.44
South-east area	0.63	0.89	0.14	0.67	0.55	1.44	−0.28	−1.49
(L) Yearly dummy variable (Base = 2004)								
2006	−0.88	−1.20	0.09	0.45	−0.25	−0.74	0.04	0.24
Constant	−2.02	−0.39	−0.66	−0.47	−9.28	(−3.51)[b]	1.71	1.34
n	1110		1110		1110		1110	
Pseudo R squared	0.2900		0.0875		0.1713		0.0760	

Note [a]5% significance level; [b]1% significance level

6.24 Sri Lanka

For Sri Lanka, a glance at the frequency distribution of the options reveals that the broader voice option and the broader loyalty option compete respectively with 43.6% and 41.2%. As the bureaucratic voice option represents 15.8% of the respondents, more active voices occupy larger percentages. These figures make sense given the unstable politics in the 2000s and into the 2010s that created a momentum of moving toward civil war and then back to peace.

Those in the broader voice option are equipped with LPG, do not have a high standard of living, do not have a command of English, are satisfied with family life, trust the army, assess government performance as suffering from widespread corruption, assess politics as meaningless (no matter how one votes), and are male.

Those who choose the broader loyalty option are equipped with LPG, do not participate in national elections, assess government performance as negative, are female, and have a low income level.

Summary statistics of countries Sri Lanka					
	n	Mean	SD	Min	Max
Exit	1574	0.019	0.14	0	1
Broader voice	1574	0.425	0.49	0	1
Bureaucratic voice	1574	0.154	0.36	0	1
Broader loyalty	1574	0.402	0.49	0	1
(A) Lifestyles					
Public water supply	1613	0.85	0.35	0	1
Electricity	1613	0.98	0.13	0	1
LPG	1613	0.60	0.49	0	1
Homeownership	1590	0.87	0.34	0	1
Number of family members	1613	4.91	2.20	1	22
National elections	1586	4.64	0.82	1	5
Proud	1607	3.75	0.59	1	4
Relative Standard of Living	1607	3.37	0.74	1	5
(B) Exposure to globalization					
Living internationally	1613	1.04	1.08	0	6
English ability	1578	2.46	0.93	1	4
(C) Satisfaction with aspects of life					
Housing	1611	4.22	0.99	1	5
Friendships	1600	4.16	0.81	1	5
Household income	1609	3.72	1.03	1	5
Health	1611	4.13	0.86	1	5
Education	1607	4.08	0.88	1	5
Neighbors	1597	3.99	0.82	1	5
Public safety	1598	3.76	0.98	1	5
The condition of the environment	1599	3.60	1.04	1	5
Social welfare system	1566	3.36	1.05	1	5
The democratic system	1556	3.26	1.10	1	5
Family life	1564	4.44	0.74	1	5
Leisure	1609	3.99	0.95	1	5
Happiness	1611	4.01	0.81	1	5
(D) Trust in social institution					
Trust generally	1587	0.18	0.38	0	1
Trust the central government	1580	2.36	0.93	1	4

(continued)

(continued)

Summary statistics of countries Sri Lanka					
	n	Mean	SD	Min	Max
Trust the army	1586	3.01	0.93	1	4
Trust the legal system	1590	2.62	0.94	1	4
Trust the police	1581	2.35	0.98	1	4
(E) Assessment of government performance					
Worry about corruption	1613	0.52	0.50	0	1
Worry about Economic inequality	1613	0.23	0.42	0	1
Political corruption	1588	1.85	0.79	1	4
Duty to vote	1608	4.56	0.64	1	5
Widespread corruption	1602	4.33	0.81	1	5
No power	1577	3.57	1.12	1	5
Complicated	1558	3.88	0.96	1	5
No matter whether vote	1579	2.69	1.27	1	5
Stop thinking	1604	4.36	0.80	1	5
Pay little attention	1580	4.17	0.83	1	5
Powerful leader	1560	1.40	0.68	1	3
Experts	1549	2.08	0.72	1	3
Military government	1526	1.52	0.72	1	3
Democratic political system	1583	2.57	0.63	1	3
(F) Satisfaction with rights					
Right to vote	1598	3.13	0.78	1	4
Right to participate in any organizations	1579	2.91	0.72	1	4
Right to be informed about government	1573	2.46	0.83	1	4
Right to criticize the government	1567	2.50	0.89	1	4
(H) Demographics					
Female	1613	0.49	0.50	0	1
Age	1613	38.28	12.02	20	69
Level of education	1554	2.21	0.55	1	3
Married	1610	0.74	0.44	0	1
Unemployed	1609	0.31	0.46	0	1
Income	1487	2.93	1.22	1	5
(L) Yearly dummy variable (Base = 2003)					
2005	1613	0.50	0.50	0	1

Frequency Distribution of 7 Responses and Partially Aggregated 4 Responses
Sri Lanka

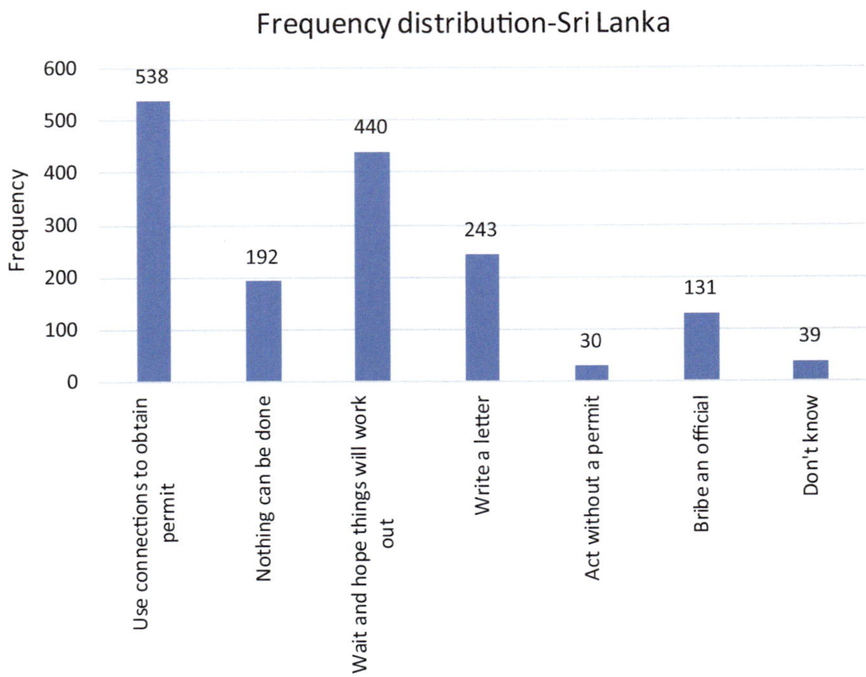

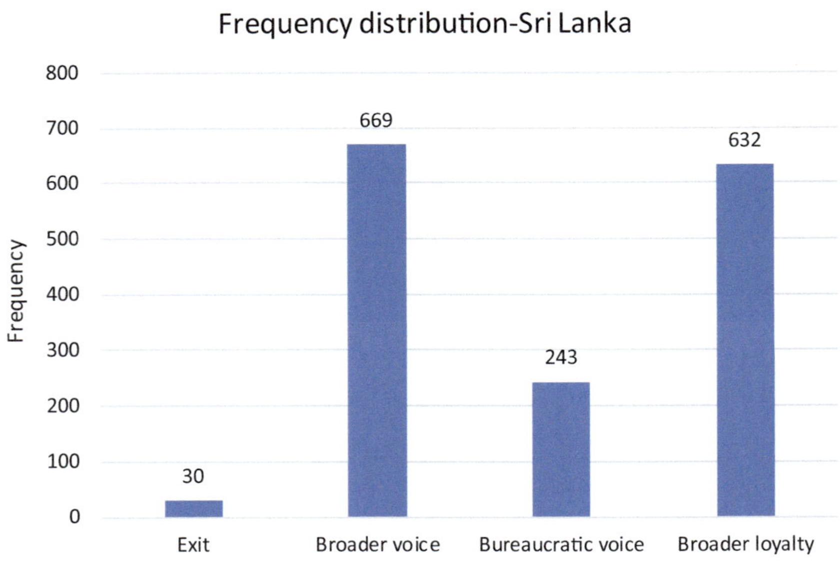

Logit regression analysis results by country Sri Lanka								
Dependent variable	Exit		Broader voice		Bureaucratic voice		Broader loyalty	
Independent variables	Coeff.	z-stat.	Coeff.	z-stat.	Coeff.	z-stat.	Coeff.	z-stat.
(A) Lifestyles								
Public water supply	−1.68	(−2.15)[a]	0.38	1.55	0.62	1.66	−0.41	−1.76
Electricity	–	–	1.04	1.44	−1.31	−1.66	−0.25	−0.39
LPG	0.77	1.00	0.61	3.68[b]	−0.54	(−2.37)[a]	−0.33	(−2.05)[a]
Homeownership	0.31	0.31	0.09	0.42	−0.05	−0.15	−0.08	−0.34
Number of family members	0.24	1.53	−0.03	−1.04	0.01	0.32	0.02	0.62
National elections	0.55	0.86	0.22	2.25[a]	−0.05	−0.39	−0.20	(−2.14)[a]
Proud	−0.17	−0.38	−0.01	−0.07	0.33	1.58	−0.10	−0.72
Relative Standard of Living	−0.35	−0.68	−0.28	(−2.49)[a]	0.16	1.11	0.22	1.95
(B) Exposure to globalization								
Living internationally	−0.37	−1.10	−0.09	−1.12	0.04	0.36	0.06	0.78
English ability	0.66	1.49	−0.22	(−2.22)[a]	0.28	2.04[a]	0.06	0.60
(C) Satisfaction with aspects of life								
Housing	0.57	1.34	−0.05	−0.51	−0.14	−1.16	0.11	1.22
Friendships	−0.24	−0.58	0.01	0.12	−0.17	−1.25	0.10	0.94
Household income	−0.42	−1.09	0.01	0.16	0.07	0.52	−0.04	−0.48
Health	−0.33	−0.90	0.06	0.57	0.16	1.09	−0.13	−1.25
Education	−0.12	−0.31	0.07	0.64	−0.12	−0.84	0.01	0.07
Neighbors	0.56	1.14	−0.02	−0.16	−0.08	−0.50	−0.01	−0.08
Public safety	0.33	0.83	0.05	0.55	0.09	0.66	−0.08	−0.87
The condition of the environment	−0.58	−1.50	−0.08	−0.87	0.07	0.53	0.06	0.65
Social welfare system	0.39	1.09	−0.05	−0.59	−0.04	−0.31	0.06	0.62
The democratic system	0.19	0.60	0.10	1.33	−0.16	−1.45	−0.05	−0.60
Family life	−0.10	−0.22	0.30	2.60[b]	−0.09	−0.61	−0.18	−1.64
Leisure	−0.64	−1.91	−0.10	−1.21	0.33	2.45[a]	−0.03	−0.35
Happiness	−0.30	−0.72	0.12	1.13	−0.20	−1.44	0.01	0.09
(D) Trust in social institution								
Trust generally	−0.02	−0.03	−0.19	−0.94	−0.02	−0.08	0.16	0.83
Trust the central government	0.49	1.25	0.06	0.68	−0.11	−0.87	−0.03	−0.30
Trust the army	−0.47	−1.11	0.22	2.14[a]	−0.18	−1.28	−0.10	−0.94
Trust the legal system	−0.56	−1.30	−0.07	−0.69	0.20	1.40	−0.02	−0.21
Trust the police	0.02	0.05	−0.04	−0.49	−0.07	−0.55	0.09	1.04

(continued)

(continued)

Logit regression analysis results by country Sri Lanka								
Dependent variable	Exit		Broader voice		Bureaucratic voice		Broader loyalty	
Independent variables	Coeff.	z-stat.	Coeff.	z-stat.	Coeff.	z-stat.	Coeff.	z-stat.
(E) Assessment of government performance								
Worry about corruption	−1.60	(−2.31)[a]	−0.08	−0.53	0.07	0.33	0.14	0.94
Worry about Economic inequality	0.19	0.25	0.11	0.64	−0.34	−1.29	0.03	0.20
Political corruption	0.24	0.58	0.21	2.02[a]	0.05	0.34	−0.25	(−2.35)[a]
Duty to vote	−0.37	−0.62	−0.15	−1.21	0.17	0.95	0.03	0.26
Widespread corruption	1.00	1.71	0.27	2.55[a]	−0.11	−0.74	−0.25	(−2.43)[a]
No power	0.31	0.98	−0.07	−0.92	0.28	2.44[a]	−0.09	−1.12
Complicated	0.06	0.19	0.11	1.30	−0.16	−1.30	−0.02	−0.23
No matter whether vote	−0.76	(−2.40)[a]	0.22	3.46[b]	−0.11	−1.17	−0.13	−1.93
Stop thinking	−0.25	−0.46	−0.15	−1.34	−0.05	−0.30	0.17	1.47
Pay little attention	1.00	1.68	−0.06	−0.53	0.04	0.26	−0.05	−0.41
Powerful leader	0.36	0.78	−0.06	−0.53	0.26	1.68	−0.12	−1.03
Experts	−0.74	−1.45	0.05	0.45	0.08	0.55	−0.05	−0.52
Military government	0.74	1.65	0.18	1.68	−0.36	(−2.21)[a]	−0.06	−0.58
Democratic political system	−0.63	−1.39	−0.16	−1.30	0.08	0.49	0.15	1.27
(F) Satisfaction with rights								
Right to vote	−0.65	−1.26	0.02	0.20	−0.20	−1.20	0.09	0.77
Right to participate in any organizations	−0.08	−0.17	0.24	1.85	−0.06	−0.32	−0.22	−1.73
Right to be informed about government	0.42	0.90	−0.05	−0.46	0.28	1.75	−0.08	−0.72
Right to criticize the government	0.82	1.85	−0.14	−1.36	−0.15	−1.06	0.15	1.50
(H) Demographics								
Female	−1.17	−1.65	−0.34	(−2.27)[a]	0.03	0.12	0.38	2.54[a]
Age	0.05	1.36	−0.004	−0.54	0.002	0.19	0.001	0.14
Level of education	0.39	0.57	0.01	0.08	0.29	1.30	−0.22	−1.33
Married	−0.09	−0.10	0.004	0.02	0.09	0.34	−0.09	−0.45
Unemployed	−2.15	(−1.98)[a]	0.21	1.32	0.24	1.07	−0.30	−1.82

(continued)

(continued)

Logit regression analysis results by country Sri Lanka								
Dependent variable	Exit		Broader voice		Bureaucratic voice		Broader loyalty	
Independent variables	Coeff.	z-stat.	Coeff.	z-stat.	Coeff.	z-stat.	Coeff.	z-stat.
Income	−0.16	−0.49	0.09	1.22	0.13	1.28	−0.17	(−2.33)[a]
(L) Yearly dummy variable								
2005	0.40	0.48	−1.03	(−5.30)[b]	1.06	3.86[b]	0.46	2.41[a]
Constant	−9.89	−1.65	−4.16	(−2.93)[b]	−3.54	−1.91	3.97	2.89[b]
n	994		994		994		994	
Pseudo R squared	0.3717		0.1027		0.1057		0.0838	

Note [a]5% significance level; [b]1% significance level

6.25 Taiwan

The frequency distribution of options, in Taiwan, reveal that the broader loyalty option is overwhelming strong, registering 57.8%, whereas the broader voice option registers 19.7% among respondents. Those that support the broader loyalty option own a home, do not pray, live internationally, are not satisfied with friendships, are satisfied with education, are satisfied with the social welfare system, do not trust others in general, do not prefer military governments nor governments led by experts, do not have a high level of education, reside in the Western region (Taizhong) as opposed to Northern (Taibei) and Southern (Tainan) regions, and reside in cities that are not large.

Those who prefer the broader voice option live internationally, are satisfied with education, negatively assess government performance, are positive about military government, and are satisfied with the right to participate in organizations.

For those Taiwanese who pursue the bureaucratic voice option, they do not own home, trust others in general, do not prefer government by a powerful leader, are moderately positive in their assessment of government bribery, are not satisfied with right to participate in organizations, have a high level of education, and reside in large cities.

The exit option is contributed to by those who are not proud of Taiwan, are not satisfied with education, are not satisfied with leisure, are satisfied with public safety, do not trust others in general, do not trust the police, and assess government performance negatively (choosing the response “no matter whether one votes or not”).

Summary statistics of countries Taiwan					
	n	Mean	SD	Min	Max
Exit	977	0.05	0.22	0	1
Broader voice	977	0.20	0.40	0	1
Bureaucratic voice	977	0.18	0.38	0	1
Broader loyalty	977	0.58	0.49	0	1
(A) Lifestyles					
Number of public utilities	1006	6.13	0.64	3	7
Homeownership	1006	0.88	0.32	0	1
Number of family members	1006	4.41	1.64	1	13
Pray	1001	1.99	1.15	1	5
National elections	983	4.22	1.07	1	5
Proud	975	2.84	0.86	1	4
Relative Standard of Living	1003	3.01	0.44	1	5
(B) Exposure to globalization					
Internet	1005	2.69	1.74	1	5
Living internationally	1006	0.89	1.01	0	6
(C) Satisfaction with aspects of life					
Housing	1005	3.63	0.84	1	5
Friendships	1006	3.89	0.72	1	5
Household income	1006	3.27	0.77	1	5
Health	1006	3.62	0.84	1	5
Education	1004	3.34	0.77	1	5
Job	951	3.21	0.84	1	5
Neighbors	1001	3.66	0.75	1	5
Public safety	1005	2.55	0.96	1	5
The condition of the environment	1006	3.21	0.79	1	5
Social welfare system	999	2.78	0.88	1	5
The democratic system	996	3.11	0.84	1	5
Family life	1006	3.74	0.69	2	5
Leisure	1006	3.49	0.74	1	5
Spiritual life	1006	3.52	0.73	1	5
Happiness	1003	3.55	0.92	1	5
(D) Trust in social institution					
Trust generally	996	0.40	0.49	0	1
Trust the central government	966	2.13	0.82	1	4
Trust the army	931	2.51	0.78	1	4
Trust the legal system	952	2.11	0.82	1	4
Trust the police	986	2.36	0.76	1	4
(E) Assessment of government performance					
Worry about corruption	1006	0.28	0.45	0	1
Worry about Economic inequality	1006	0.31	0.46	0	1

(continued)

(continued)

Summary statistics of countries Taiwan					
	n	Mean	SD	Min	Max
Political corruption	996	1.70	0.68	1	4
Duty to vote	1006	4.17	0.79	1	5
Widespread corruption	1002	3.95	0.86	1	5
No power	1002	3.87	0.92	1	5
Complicated	994	3.83	0.86	1	5
No matter whether vote	1004	2.23	0.96	1	5
Stop thinking	1002	3.69	0.99	1	5
Pay little attention	996	3.78	0.88	1	5
Powerful leader	953	1.24	0.51	1	3
Experts	951	2.14	0.64	1	3
Military government	946	1.30	0.55	1	3
Democratic political system	978	2.29	0.57	1	3
Bribe	1006	9.30	1.29	1	10
(F) Satisfaction with rights					
Right to vote	995	3.07	0.71	1	4
Right to participate in any organizations	977	2.84	0.73	1	4
Right to gather and demonstrate	979	2.66	0.79	1	4
Right to be informed about government	956	2.40	0.77	1	4
Freedom of speech	994	2.90	0.76	1	4
Right to criticize the government	980	2.75	0.81	1	4
(H) Demographics					
Female	1006	0.49	0.50	0	1
Age	1006	40.56	12.32	20	69
Level of education	1006	1.96	0.78	1	3
Married	1006	0.70	0.46	0	1
Income	984	7.76	4.63	1	19
No religion	1003	0.24	0.43	0	1
(I) Region					
Northern	1006	0.47	0.50	0	1
Western	1006	0.24	0.43	0	1
Southern	1006	0.29	0.45	0	1
(J) City cize					
City cize	1006	1.53	0.50	1	2
(K) Rural					
Rural	1006	0.28	0.45	0	1

Frequency Distribution of 7 Responses and Partially Aggregated 4 Responses

Taiwan

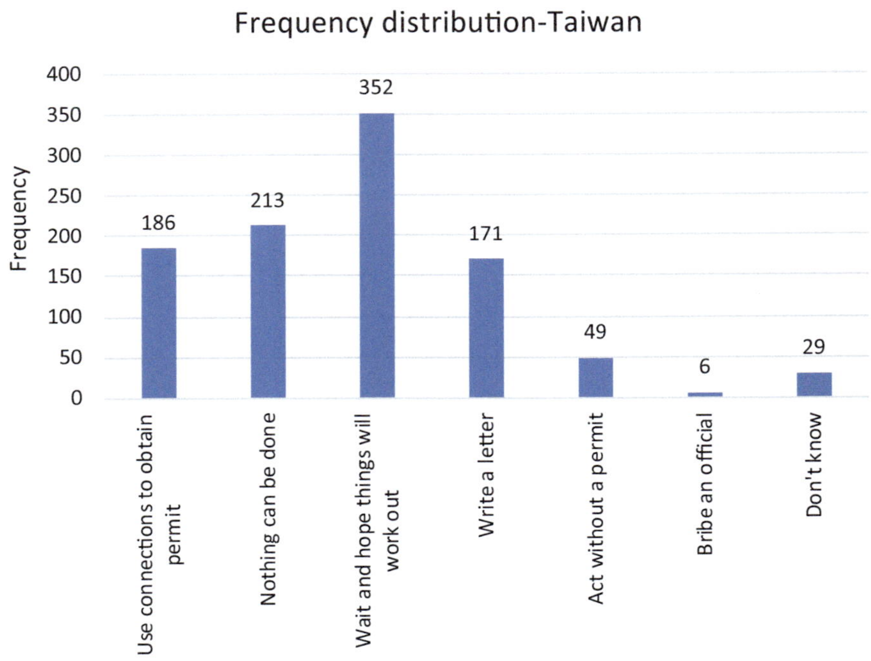

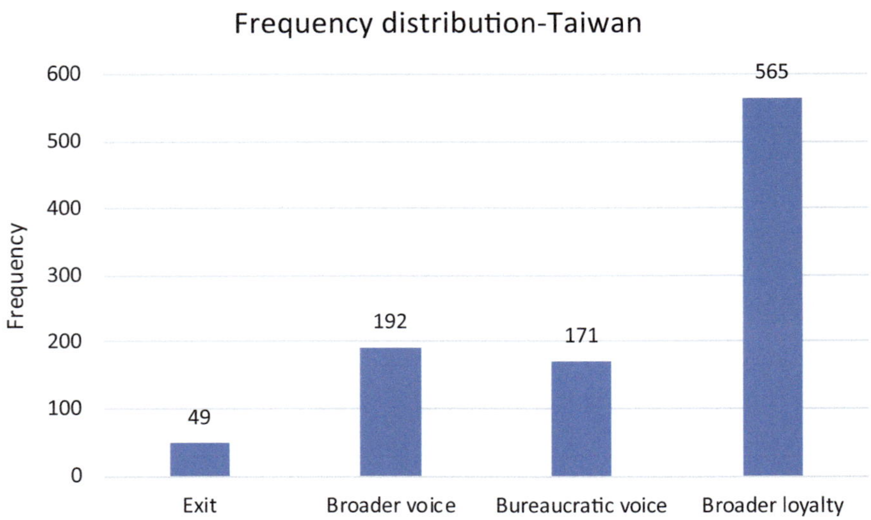

Logit regression analysis results by country Taiwan								
Dependent variable	Exit		Broader voice		Bureaucratic voice		Broader loyalty	
Independent variables	Coeff.	z-stat.	Coeff.	z-stat.	Coeff.	z-stat.	Coeff.	z-stat.
(A) Lifestyles								
Number of public utilities	−0.30	−0.73	0.24	1.19	−0.42	−1.82	0.05	0.28
Homeownership	−0.26	−0.35	−0.07	−0.20	−0.97	(−2.41)[a]	0.76	2.34[a]
Number of family members	0.07	0.46	0.04	0.49	0.11	1.18	−0.06	−0.97
Pray	0.27	1.18	0.18	1.77	0.09	0.69	−0.26	(−2.75)[b]
National elections	0.26	0.64	−0.13	−0.81	0.17	0.87	0.003	0.02
Proud	−0.71	(−2.10)[a]	0.02	0.17	0.24	1.41	0.04	0.32
Relative Standard of Living	1.43	1.93	−0.29	−0.85	0.38	0.95	−0.46	−1.61
(B) Exposure to globalization								
Internet	0.09	0.49	0.10	1.11	−0.20	−1.89	0.05	0.59
Living internationally	0.29	1.11	−0.51	(−3.47)[b]	0.07	0.52	0.25	2.36[a]
(C) Satisfaction with aspects of life								
Housing	0.19	0.49	0.01	0.05	0.11	0.55	−0.09	−0.62
Friendships	0.41	0.98	0.28	1.43	0.40	1.68	−0.53	(−3.10)[b]
Household income	−0.04	−0.08	0.29	1.41	0.20	0.87	−0.26	−1.52
Health	−0.03	−0.07	0.10	0.64	−0.36	−1.93	0.08	0.56
Education	−0.75	(−2.05)[a]	−0.39	(−2.06)[a]	0.11	0.50	0.37	2.27[a]
Job	0.24	0.54	−0.08	−0.46	−0.20	−0.94	0.19	1.18
Neighbors	−0.27	−0.73	−0.08	−0.42	0.24	1.16	−0.13	−0.84
Public safety	0.85	2.28[a]	0.02	0.15	−0.16	−0.90	0.04	0.28
The condition of the environment	−0.67	−1.66	0.17	0.93	0.18	0.82	−0.17	−1.05
Social welfare system	−0.21	−0.51	−0.12	−0.67	−0.27	−1.31	0.32	2.06[a]
The democratic system	−0.07	−0.18	0.01	0.03	−0.23	−1.26	0.11	0.78
Family life	0.50	1.17	−0.09	−0.48	0.02	0.10	0.14	0.80
Leisure	−0.94	(−2.06)[a]	0.10	0.49	0.06	0.23	−0.05	−0.26
Spiritual life	0.28	0.68	−0.04	−0.19	0.45	1.81	−0.33	−1.83
Happiness	0.55	1.78	−0.04	−0.32	−0.11	−0.67	0.04	0.37
(D) Trust in social institution								
Trust generally	−1.51	(−2.47)[a]	0.23	0.94	0.80	2.83[b]	−0.51	(−2.45)[a]
Trust the central government	0.34	0.87	−0.32	−1.80	0.42	2.10[a]	−0.07	−0.47
Trust the army	0.13	0.35	0.06	0.31	−0.29	−1.42	0.06	0.41
Trust the legal system	−0.37	−1.03	0.28	1.67	0.01	0.07	−0.23	−1.59

(continued)

(continued)

Logit regression analysis results by country Taiwan								
Dependent variable	Exit		Broader voice		Bureaucratic voice		Broader loyalty	
Independent variables	Coeff.	z-stat.	Coeff.	z-stat.	Coeff.	z-stat.	Coeff.	z-stat.
Trust the police	−1.15	(−3.02)[b]	−0.31	−1.79	0.38	1.91	0.22	1.51
(E) Assessment of government performance								
Worry about corruption	0.16	0.29	0.001	0.00	−0.01	−0.03	0.02	0.08
Worry about Economic inequality	−0.04	−0.07	−0.03	−0.13	−0.12	−0.41	−0.04	−0.19
Political corruption	0.74	1.90	−0.60	(−3.03)[b]	−0.03	−0.14	0.20	1.16
Duty to vote	0.93	1.91	−0.06	−0.34	0.26	1.25	−0.24	−1.53
Widespread corruption	0.35	0.98	0.05	0.30	−0.01	−0.05	−0.04	−0.26
No power	0.42	1.36	0.15	0.93	−0.14	−0.81	−0.11	−0.82
Complicated	−0.90	(−2.69)[b]	−0.09	−0.57	0.31	1.81	0.04	0.27
No matter whether vote	−0.03	−0.07	−0.07	−0.36	0.33	1.55	−0.20	−1.22
Stop thinking	−0.81	(−2.81)[b]	0.01	0.06	0.11	0.69	0.03	0.27
Pay little attention	−0.23	−0.69	−0.09	−0.50	−0.28	−1.48	0.32	2.13[a]
Powerful leader	−0.12	−0.23	0.19	0.84	−0.90	(−2.52)[a]	0.19	0.93
Experts	−0.15	−0.37	0.22	1.16	0.56	2.51[a]	−0.49	(−2.93)[b]
Military government	−0.08	−0.16	0.45	2.00[a]	0.30	1.06	−0.50	(−2.40)[a]
Democratic political system	−0.45	−0.97	−0.24	−1.11	0.21	0.81	0.04	0.23
Bribe	0.25	1.07	−0.09	−1.11	0.34	2.74[b]	−0.09	−1.22
(F) Satisfaction with rights								
Right to vote	0.16	0.37	−0.02	−0.10	0.07	0.30	0.05	0.27
Right to participate in any organizations	−0.50	−1.14	0.44	2.18[a]	−0.65	(−2.71)[b]	0.15	0.87
Right to gather and demonstrate	0.13	0.32	0.22	1.29	−0.22	−1.09	−0.01	−0.09
Right to be informed about government	−0.05	−0.14	0.00	−0.02	−0.08	−0.39	0.03	0.22
Freedom of speech	0.01	0.02	0.06	0.29	0.27	1.22	−0.21	−1.26
Right to criticize the government	0.04	0.10	−0.22	−1.27	0.05	0.28	0.08	0.53
(H) Demographics								
Female	−0.35	−0.64	0.05	0.21	−0.67	(−2.40)[a]	0.46	2.32[a]
Age	0.04	1.20	−0.001	−0.08	−0.03	−1.86	0.01	0.94
Level of education	0.53	1.18	−0.10	−0.52	0.78	3.29[b]	−0.52	(−2.99)[b]

(continued)

(continued)

Logit regression analysis results by country Taiwan								
Dependent variable	Exit		Broader voice		Bureaucratic voice		Broader loyalty	
Independent variables	Coeff.	z-stat.	Coeff.	z-stat.	Coeff.	z-stat.	Coeff.	z-stat.
Married	−0.15	−0.21	−0.23	−0.75	0.85	2.25[a]	−0.13	−0.47
Income	−0.10	−1.45	0.02	0.58	−0.02	−0.50	0.01	0.27
No religion	0.11	0.16	0.09	0.29	0.18	0.55	−0.02	−0.08
(I) Region (Base = Southern)								
Northern	–	–	–	–	–	–	−0.62	−1.87
Western	–	–	–	–	–	–	−1.16	(−3.79)[b]
(J) City cize								
City cize	0.07	0.14	0.51	1.86	0.96	3.01[b]	−0.98	(−3.66)[b]
(K) Rural								
Rural	–	–	–	–	–	–	−0.16	−0.61
Constant	−7.03	−1.15	−2.59	−1.05	−11.3	(−3.75)[b]	7.46	3.38[b]
n	640		640		640		640	
Pseudo R squared	0.3640		0.1313		0.2465		0.1857	

Note [a]5% significance level; [b]1% significance level

6.26 Tajikistan

In the case of Tajikistan, the frequency distribution reveals that the broader voice option is predominant, registering 63%, whereas the broader loyalty option registers 26.2%. Contributing to the broader voice option are those who are proud of Tajikistan, have a good standard of living, are Internet-users (who regard Tajikistan negatively), do not trust the police, and are not satisfied with the right to vote. Contributing to the broader loyalty option are those who are proud of Tajikistan, have a relatively high standard of living, are not satisfied with housing, are satisfied with the social welfare system, trust the police, and are satisfied with the right to vote. Looking at regional differences in terms of the broader loyalty option choosers, it is clear that the Sogd region and the Khalton region, which are relatively rich in water and commerce and closer to foreign neighbors, such as Kyrgizstan and Uzbekistan, register more negative loyalty. In comparison, the Region of Republican Subordination where the capital, Dushanbe, is located and the autonomous province of Gorno-Badakhshan, which are demographically sparse with the exception of Dushanbe, register less negative loyalty to the regime.

Summary statistics of countries Tajikistan					
	n	Mean	SD	Min	Max
Exit	749	0.02	0.13	0	1
Broader voice	749	0.63	0.48	0	1
Bureaucratic voice	749	0.09	0.29	0	1
Broader loyalty	749	0.26	0.44	0	1
(A) Lifestyles					
Homeownership	799	0.96	0.20	0	1
Number of family members	800	6.94	2.92	1	19
Pray	794	2.96	1.62	1	5
National elections	798	3.66	1.29	1	5
Proud	785	3.21	0.87	1	4
Relative Standard of Living	800	2.70	0.79	1	5
(B) Exposure to globalization					
Internet	768	1.27	0.74	1	5
Living internationally	800	0.98	0.93	0	5
English ability	794	1.25	0.50	1	4
(C) Satisfaction with aspects of life					
Housing	800	3.82	1.12	1	5
Friendships	798	4.27	0.81	1	5
Household income	797	3.14	1.12	1	5
Health	797	3.85	1.04	1	5
Education	684	3.32	1.16	1	5
Job	674	3.14	1.17	1	5
Neighbors	794	4.26	0.86	1	5
Public safety	740	3.50	0.93	1	5
The condition of the environment	778	3.19	0.94	1	5
Social welfare system	757	2.61	1.04	1	5
The democratic system	728	2.93	1.11	1	5
Family life	778	4.18	0.89	1	5
Leisure	784	2.89	1.16	1	5
Spiritual life	759	2.93	1.11	1	5
Happiness	798	2.93	1.00	1	5
(D) Trust in social institution					
Trust generally	795	0.31	0.46	0	1
Trust the central government	768	2.90	0.71	1	4
Trust local governments	766	2.44	0.78	1	4
Trust the army	761	2.59	0.89	1	4
Trust the legal system	751	2.70	0.85	1	4
Trust the police	772	2.08	0.84	1	4

(continued)

(continued)

Summary statistics of countries Tajikistan					
	n	Mean	SD	Min	Max
(E) Assessment of government performance					
Worry about corruption	800	0.54	0.50	0	1
Worry about Economic inequality	800	0.21	0.41	0	1
Political corruption	781	1.65	0.70	1	4
Duty to vote	786	4.14	0.95	1	5
Widespread corruption	785	4.14	0.94	1	5
No power	791	3.64	1.07	1	5
Complicated	762	3.56	1.08	1	5
No matter whether vote	767	3.14	1.19	1	5
Stop thinking	771	4.06	1.07	1	5
Pay little attention	766	3.99	0.99	1	5
Powerful leader	683	1.94	0.80	1	3
Experts	633	1.93	0.68	1	3
Military government	646	1.55	0.72	1	3
Democratic political system	651	1.85	0.68	1	3
Bribe	777	8.12	2.51	1	10
(F) Satisfaction with rights					
Right to vote	752	2.83	0.85	1	4
Right to participate in any organizations	651	2.74	0.75	1	4
Right to gather and demonstrate	686	2.41	0.93	1	4
Right to be informed about government	693	2.29	0.86	1	4
Freedom of speech	750	2.39	0.98	1	4
Right to criticize the government	699	1.93	0.88	1	4
(H) Demographics					
Female	800	0.53	0.50	0	1
Age	800	38.9	13.2	20	69
Level of education	796	2.27	0.73	1	3
Married	799	0.72	0.45	0	1
Unemployed	800	0.11	0.31	0	1
Income	708	17.98	3.22	1	20
No religion	797	0.02	0.12	0	1
(I) Region (Base = Dushanbe)					
Mountain-Badakhshan Autonomic	800	0.03	0.17	0	1
Sogd Region	800	0.30	0.46	0	1
Khatlon Region	800	0.35	0.48	0	1
Republican Subordination	800	0.23	0.42	0	1
(K) Rural					
Rural	800	0.73	0.44	0	1

Frequency Distribution of 7 Responses and Partially Aggregated 4 Responses
Tajikistan

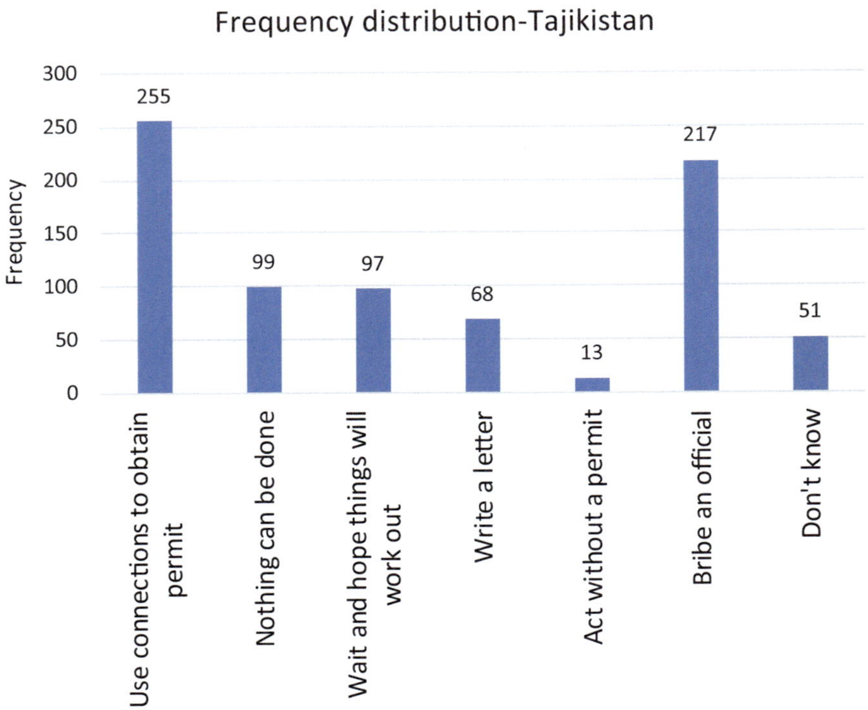

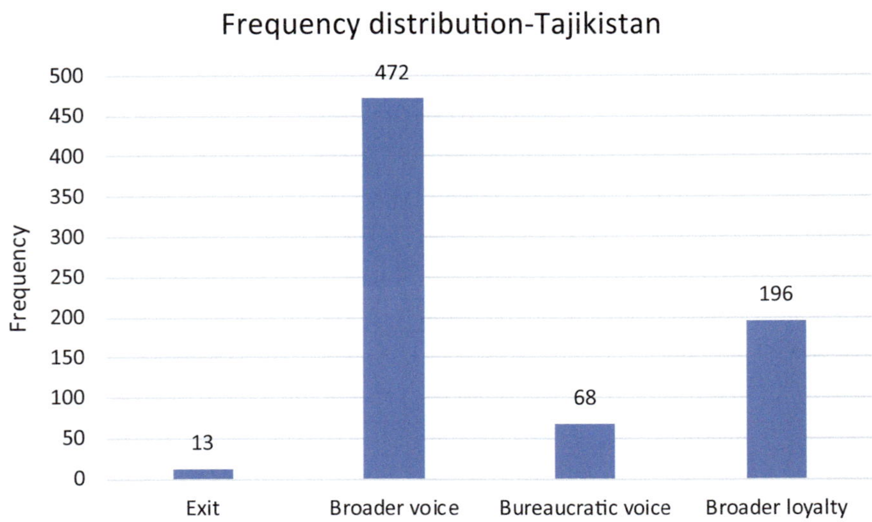

Logit regression analysis results by country Tajikistan								
Dependent variable	Exit		Broader voice		Bureaucratic voice		Broader loyalty	
Independent variables	Coeff.	z-stat.	Coeff.	z-stat.	Coeff.	z-stat.	Coeff.	z-stat.
(A) Lifestyles								
Homeownership	–	–	−1.08	−1.02	–	–	1.31	1.30
Number of family members	–	–	−0.04	−0.48	–	–	0.13	1.28
Pray	–	–	0.21	1.49	–	–	−0.08	−0.49
National elections	–	–	−0.35	−1.17	–	–	−0.26	−0.88
Proud	–	–	0.95	2.99[b]	–	–	−0.97	(−2.69)[b]
Relative Standard of Living	–	–	0.97	2.97[b]	–	–	−1.04	(−2.69)[b]
(B) Exposure to globalization								
Internet	–	–	−0.75	(−2.56)[a]	–	–	0.48	1.29
Living internationally	–	–	0.46	1.59	–	–	−0.01	−0.02
English ability	–	–	−0.50	−1.08	–	–	0.57	1.07
(C) Satisfaction with aspects of life								
Housing	–	–	0.30	1.16	–	–	−0.78	(−2.60)[b]
Friendships	–	–	0.58	1.83	–	–	−0.46	−1.28
Household income	–	–	−0.84	(−3.10)[b]	–	–	0.54	1.75
Health	–	–	−0.43	−1.77	–	–	0.08	0.30
Education	–	–	0.21	0.73	–	–	0.19	0.57
Job	–	–	−0.07	−0.23	–	–	0.38	1.10
Neighbors	–	–	0.04	0.12	–	–	0.10	0.27
Public safety	–	–	0.54	1.98[a]	–	–	−0.29	−0.90
The condition of the environment	–	–	0.03	0.11	–	–	0.19	0.60
Social welfare system	–	–	−0.48	−1.77	–	–	0.94	3.10[b]
The democratic system	–	–	−0.35	−1.37	–	–	−0.27	−0.92
Family life	–	–	−0.04	−0.12	–	–	−0.51	−1.50
Leisure	–	–	−0.14	−0.47	–	–	0.40	1.16
Spiritual life	–	–	0.14	0.44	–	–	−0.33	−0.95
Happiness	–	–	0.35	1.39	–	–	−0.54	−1.91
(D) Trust in social institution								
Trust generally	–	–	0.34	0.64	–	–	−0.17	−0.29
Trust the central government	–	–	0.04	0.09	–	–	0.15	0.36
Trust local governments	–	–	−0.12	−0.33	–	–	−0.34	−0.74
Trust the army	–	–	−0.51	−1.47	–	–	0.14	0.34
Trust the legal system	–	–	0.54	1.53	–	–	0.26	0.63
Trust the police	–	–	−0.65	(−1.98)[a]	–	–	1.13	2.82[b]
(E) Assessment of government performance								
Worry about corruption	–	–	0.09	0.18	–	–	−0.36	−0.66
Worry about Economic inequality	–	–	0.61	1.01	–	–	−0.82	−1.20

(continued)

(continued)

Logit regression analysis results by country Tajikistan								
Dependent variable	Exit		Broader voice		Bureaucratic voice		Broader loyalty	
Independent variables	Coeff.	z-stat.	Coeff.	z-stat.	Coeff.	z-stat.	Coeff.	z-stat.
Political corruption	–	–	−0.57	−1.64	–	–	0.19	0.49
Duty to vote	–	–	−0.05	−0.14	–	–	−0.33	−0.75
Widespread corruption	–	–	−0.17	−0.66	–	–	−0.15	−0.49
No power	–	–	−0.10	−0.37	–	–	0.09	0.29
Complicated	–	–	−0.11	−0.47	–	–	0.03	0.12
No matter whether vote	–	–	0.15	0.66	–	–	−0.51	−1.84
Stop thinking	–	–	−0.35	−1.18	–	–	0.32	0.87
Pay little attention	–	–	−0.07	−0.22	–	–	0.42	1.09
Powerful leader	–	–	−0.26	−0.73	–	–	0.30	0.72
Experts	–	–	−0.25	−0.70	–	–	0.63	1.49
Military government	–	–	−0.40	−1.18	–	–	0.20	0.48
Democratic political system	–	–	0.26	0.65	–	–	0.21	0.48
Bribe	–	–	0.09	0.74	–	–	−0.03	−0.21
(F) Satisfaction with rights								
Right to vote	–	–	−0.94	(−2.28)[a]	–	–	1.15	2.30[a]
Right to participate in any organizations	–	–	−0.54	−1.48	–	–	0.73	1.71
Right to gather and demonstrate	–	–	0.47	1.46	–	–	−0.29	−0.84
Right to be informed about government	–	–	0.63	1.91	–	–	−0.46	−1.20
Freedom of speech	–	–	0.48	1.70	–	–	0.18	0.53
Right to criticize the government	–	–	−0.46	−1.32	–	–	−0.23	−0.59
(H) Demographics								
Female	–	–	0.28	0.57	–	–	−0.31	−0.57
Age	–	–	−0.02	−1.15	–	–	0.02	0.89
Level of education	–	–	−0.22	−0.55	–	–	0.83	1.78
Married	–	–	0.01	0.01	–	–	0.74	1.19
Unemployed	–	–	−0.45	−0.61	–	–	0.22	0.28
Income	–	–	0.04	0.41	–	–	−0.11	−1.19
No religion	–	–	−1.13	−0.72	–	–	0.13	0.08
(I) Region (Base = Dushanbe)								
Mountain-Badakhshan Autonomic	–	–	−0.18	−0.11	–	–	−0.80	−0.41
Sogd Region	–	–	0.49	0.40	–	–	−2.01	−1.28
Khatlon Region	–	–	1.59	1.40	–	–	−1.67	−1.21
Republican Subordination	–	–	0.74	0.57	–	–	−1.05	−0.65

(continued)

(continued)

Logit regression analysis results by country Tajikistan								
Dependent variable	Exit		Broader voice		Bureaucratic voice		Broader loyalty	
Independent variables	Coeff.	z-stat.	Coeff.	z-stat.	Coeff.	z-stat.	Coeff.	z-stat.
(K) Rural								
Rural	–	–	−0.76	−1.08	–	–	1.28	1.54
Constant	–	–	5.16	1.36	–	–	−5.32	−1.32

Note [a]5% significance level; [b]1% significance level

6.27 Thailand

The Thai frequency distribution of options reveals that the broader loyalty option is predominant, registering 70%. Contributing to those loyalists are those who are proud of Thailand, are satisfied with friendships, are not satisfied with family life, assess widespread corruption with negative nonchalance, assess government performance as complicated, are senior in age, and do not have a high income level. With a geographical breakdown of this group, those who choose the broader loyalty option reside in the northern and northeast regions, which are inhabited by lower income farmers, in the south region, which is inhabited by Malay Muslim minorities, and are in general represented by rural populations. Contributing to the bureaucratic voice option are those who pray, are satisfied with family life, assess government performance with answers that politics is complicated and that it does not matter whether I vote or not, are not satisfied with the right to vote, are young, have a high income level, and reside in the northern region.

Summary statistics of countries Thailand					
	n	Mean	SD	Min	Max
Exit	1795	0.01	0.08	0	1
Broader voice	1795	0.10	0.30	0	1
Bureaucratic voice	1795	0.19	0.39	0	1
Broader loyalty	1795	0.70	0.46	0	1
(A) Lifestyles					
Public water supply	1800	0.90	0.30	0	1
Electricity	1800	0.99	0.08	0	1
Homeownership	1800	0.71	0.45	0	1
Number of family members	1800	3.97	1.93	1	20
Pray	1799	2.81	1.42	1	5

(continued)

(continued)

Summary statistics of countries Thailand					
	n	Mean	SD	Min	Max
National elections	1795	4.67	0.77	1	5
Local elections	1769	4.49	0.97	1	5
Proud	1800	3.95	0.25	1	4
Relative Standard of Living	1800	2.96	0.54	1	5
(B) Exposure to globalization					
Living internationally	1800	0.40	0.78	0	6
English ability	1800	1.76	0.82	1	4
(C) Satisfaction with aspects of life					
Housing	1800	4.19	0.92	1	5
Friendships	1795	4.23	0.70	1	5
Household income	1798	3.53	1.11	1	5
Health	1800	3.92	1.09	1	5
Education	1800	3.64	1.05	1	5
Job	1642	3.78	1.03	1	5
Neighbors	1798	4.09	0.77	1	5
Public safety	1797	3.66	1.10	1	5
The condition of the environment	1798	3.78	1.05	1	5
Social welfare system	1782	3.54	1.08	1	5
The democratic system	1790	3.64	1.11	1	5
Family life	1794	4.32	0.80	1	5
Leisure	1799	4.09	0.84	1	5
Happiness	1800	3.95	0.79	1	5
(D) Trust in social institution					
Trust generally	1795	0.22	0.41	0	1
Trust the central government	1787	2.87	0.75	1	4
Trust local governments	1759	3.02	0.64	1	4
Trust the army	1780	3.21	0.70	1	4
Trust the legal system	1781	3.01	0.71	1	4
Trust the police	1795	2.75	0.77	1	4
(E) Assessment of government performance					
Worry about corruption	1800	0.14	0.34	0	1
Worry about Economic inequality	1800	0.22	0.42	0	1
Political corruption	1760	2.23	0.81	1	4
Duty to vote	1800	4.69	0.51	2	5
Widespread corruption	1782	3.75	1.08	1	5

(continued)

(continued)

Summary statistics of countries Thailand					
	n	Mean	SD	Min	Max
No power	1790	3.51	1.06	1	5
Complicated	1793	3.67	0.97	1	5
No matter whether vote	1792	2.13	1.08	1	5
Stop thinking	1794	3.61	1.02	1	5
Pay little attention	1792	3.67	0.97	1	5
Powerful leader	1777	1.33	0.58	1	3
Experts	1761	1.78	0.70	1	3
Military government	1765	1.66	0.70	1	3
Democratic political system	1793	2.74	0.49	1	3
Bribe	1797	9.14	1.84	1	10
(F) Satisfaction with rights					
Right to vote	1799	3.58	0.59	1	4
Right to participate in any organizations	1740	3.11	0.61	1	4
Right to criticize the government	1751	2.82	0.78	1	4
(H) Demographics					
Female	1800	0.56	0.50	0	1
Age	1800	39.1	12.2	20	69
Level of education	1800	1.66	0.86	1	3
Married	1800	0.7	0.5	0	1
Unemployed	1800	0.05	0.22	0	1
Income	1799	6.22	4.47	1	17
(I) Region (Base = Bangkok)					
Central	1800	0.19	0.39	0	1
North	1800	0.14	0.34	0	1
North-east	1800	0.26	0.44	0	1
South	1800	0.11	0.32	0	1
(K) Urban/Rural					
Rural	1800	0.36	0.48	0	1
(L) Yearly dummy variable (Base = 2004)					
2007	1800	0.56	0.50	0	1

Frequency Distribution of 7 Responses and Partially Aggregated 4 Responses

Thailand

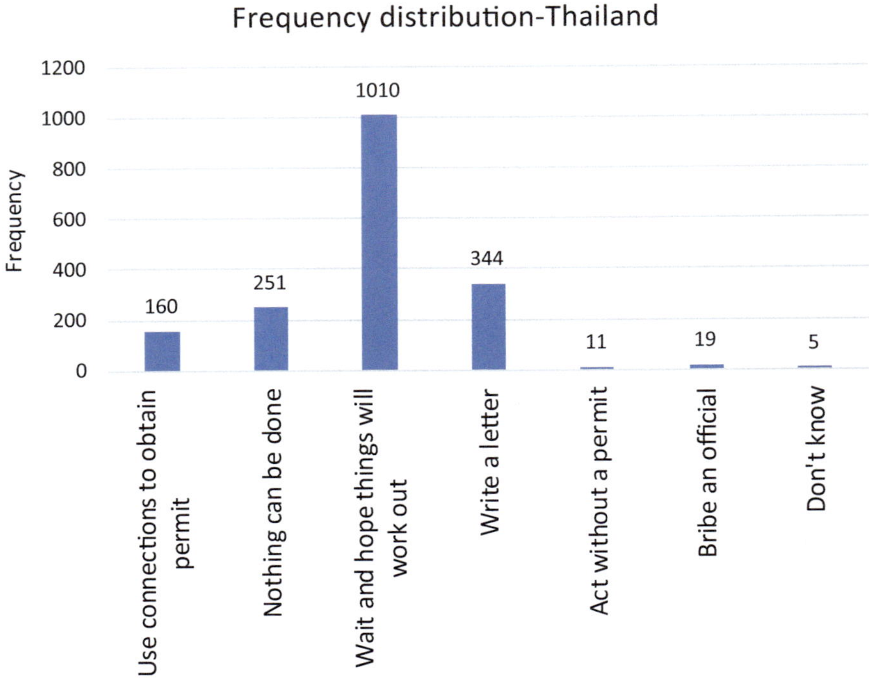

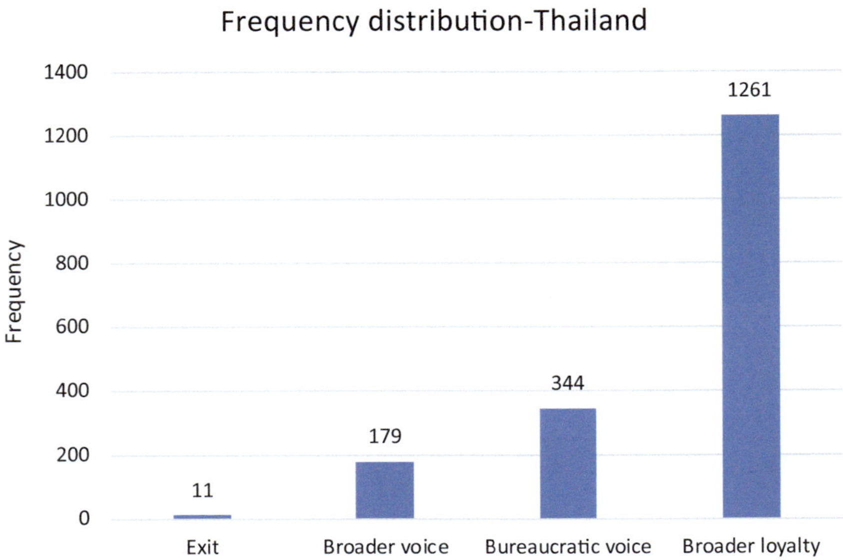

Logit regression analysis results by country Thailand								
Dependent variables	Exit		Broader voice		Bureaucratic voice		Broader loyalty	
Independent variables	Coeff.	z-stat.	Coeff.	z-stat.	Coeff.	z-stat.	Coeff.	z-stat.
(A) Lifestyles								
Public water supply	–	–	−0.42	−1.26	0.61	1.79	−0.09	−0.38
Electricity	–	–	–	–	0.71	0.62	−1.38	−1.24
Homeownership	–	–	−0.31	−1.29	0.12	0.65	0.02	0.15
Number of family members	–	–	−0.07	−1.21	0.02	0.47	0.01	0.37
Pray	–	–	−0.06	−0.83	0.12	2.12[a]	−0.06	−1.20
National elections	–	–	0.16	0.81	0.03	0.20	−0.08	−0.62
Local elections	–	–	−0.09	−0.66	−0.07	−0.63	0.07	0.72
Proud	–	–	−0.60	−1.96	−0.40	−1.41	0.70	2.72[b]
Relative Standard of Living	–	–	0.64	2.94[b]	0.05	0.31	−0.23	−1.62
(B) Exposure to globalization								
Living internationally	–	–	0.01	0.11	−0.04	−0.41	−0.04	−0.45
English ability	–	–	0.12	0.72	0.08	0.60	−0.06	−0.51
(C) Satisfaction with aspects of life								
Housing	–	–	0.06	0.45	−0.13	−1.35	0.05	0.63
Friendships	–	–	−0.27	−1.75	−0.09	−0.73	0.24	2.30[a]
Household income	–	–	−0.15	−1.32	0.11	1.19	0.03	0.34
Health	–	–	0.08	0.69	−0.08	−0.89	0.001	0.01
Education	–	–	0.08	0.67	−0.05	−0.52	−0.03	−0.38
Job	–	–	−0.01	−0.10	0.07	0.72	−0.07	−0.81
Neighbors	–	–	−0.12	−0.76	−0.21	−1.77	0.18	1.73
Public safety	–	–	0.11	0.88	0.03	0.28	−0.06	−0.82
The condition of the environment	–	–	0.01	0.10	0.04	0.38	−0.07	−0.79
Social welfare system	–	–	0.01	0.12	0.07	0.78	−0.04	−0.55
The democratic system	–	–	−0.12	−1.02	0.05	0.57	0.01	0.16
Family life	–	–	0.32	1.82	0.26	2.15[a]	−0.30	(−2.81)[b]
Leisure	–	–	−0.12	−0.81	−0.21	−1.93	0.22	2.30[a]
Happiness	–	–	0.15	0.96	−0.02	−0.18	−0.07	−0.78
(D)Trust in social institution								
Trust generally	–	–	−0.45	−1.61	0.15	0.76	0.11	0.64
Trust the central government	–	–	−0.14	−0.78	−0.04	−0.31	0.06	0.52

(continued)

(continued)

Logit regression analysis results by country Thailand								
Dependent variables	Exit		Broader voice		Bureaucratic voice		Broader loyalty	
Independent variables	Coeff.	z-stat.	Coeff.	z-stat.	Coeff.	z-stat.	Coeff.	z-stat.
Trust local governments	–	–	0.27	1.37	0.05	0.37	−0.17	−1.36
Trust the army	–	–	0.16	0.95	0.20	1.43	−0.17	−1.51
Trust the legal system	–	–	−0.01	−0.04	−0.10	−0.73	0.05	0.43
Trust the police	–	–	−0.34	(−2.23)[a]	−0.04	−0.31	0.20	1.94
(E) Assessment of government performance								
Worry about corruption	–	–	−0.43	−1.39	0.02	0.11	0.14	0.71
Worry about Economic inequality	–	–	−0.03	−0.13	−0.05	−0.27	0.05	0.32
Political corruption	–	–	0.18	1.30	−0.35	(−3.26)[b]	0.21	2.29[a]
Duty to vote	–	–	−0.11	−0.52	0.02	0.15	−0.04	−0.26
Widespread corruption	–	–	0.04	0.34	0.26	3.07[b]	−0.21	(−2.84)[b]
No power	–	–	−0.06	−0.56	−0.03	−0.32	0.08	1.02
Complicated	–	–	−0.18	−1.51	−0.19	(−2.11)[a]	0.22	2.76[b]
No matter whether vote	–	–	0.18	1.76	−0.32	(−3.82)[b]	0.16	2.31[a]
Stop thinking	–	–	0.13	1.08	−0.01	−0.15	−0.05	−0.61
Pay little attention	–	–	0.13	1.05	0.04	0.47	−0.09	−1.14
Powerful leader	–	–	−0.60	(−2.53)[a]	0.22	1.45	0.03	0.20
Experts	–	–	0.26	1.78	−0.08	−0.65	−0.07	−0.69
Military government	–	–	−0.16	−0.93	0.07	0.54	0.02	0.15
Democratic political system	–	–	0.10	0.44	0.23	1.35	−0.14	−1.00
Bribe	–	–	−0.03	−0.65	−0.01	−0.22	0.04	1.04
(F) Satisfaction with rights								
Right to vote	–	–	0.12	0.56	−0.33	(−2.27)[a]	0.23	1.82
Right to participate in any organizations	–	–	−0.10	−0.51	0.14	0.94	−0.11	−0.86
Right to criticize the government	–	–	0.03	0.20	0.07	0.69	−0.05	−0.55
(H) Demographics								
Female	–	–	−0.17	−0.84	0.09	0.54	0.04	0.28
Age	–	–	0.005	0.46	−0.03	(−3.92)[b]	0.02	3.19[b]

(continued)

(continued)

Logit regression analysis results by country Thailand								
Dependent variables	Exit		Broader voice		Bureaucratic voice		Broader loyalty	
Independent variables	Coeff.	z-stat.	Coeff.	z-stat.	Coeff.	z-stat.	Coeff.	z-stat.
Level of education	–	–	0.05	0.29	−0.07	−0.57	0.07	0.61
Married	–	–	−0.14	−0.60	0.09	0.46	0.04	0.25
Unemployed	–	–	0.72	1.62	0.07	0.16	−0.41	−1.25
Income	–	–	0.05	1.61	0.05	2.17[a]	−0.06	(−3.20)[b]
(I) Region (Base = Bangkok)								
Central	–	–	0.33	0.99	−0.27	−1.03	0.08	0.36
North	–	–	0.28	0.72	0.59	2.16[a]	−0.52	(−2.15)[a]
North-east	–	–	0.25	0.70	0.02	0.08	−0.14	−0.60
South	–	–	0.84	2.20[a]	−0.08	−0.23	−0.38	−1.42
(K) Urban/Rural								
Rural	–	–	−0.24	−1.00	−0.29	−1.51	0.36	2.24[a]
(L) Yearly dummy variable (Base = 2004)								
2007	–	–	−0.58	(−2.33)[a]	−0.04	−0.23	0.27	1.69
Constant	–	–	−1.89	−0.89	0.26	0.12	−0.93	−0.49
n	–		1412		1412		1412	
Pseudo R squared	–		0.1145		0.1111		0.0980	

Note [a]5% significance level; [b]1% significance level

6.28 Turkmenistan

A glance at the frequency distribution of options, for Turkmenistan, reveals that the broader voice option registers 49.9% and the broader loyalty option registers 33.1%. Contributing to the broader voice option are those who use Internet, assess government performance negatively with the answer that politics is complicated and that politicians do not pay attention to citizens, and reside in the northern Dashoguz region that borders Uzbekistan. Those who choose the broader loyalty option assess government performance by answering that politicians have stopped thinking about citizens

Those who favor the broader voice option use Internet and assess government performance negatively focusing on corruption and complexity of politics and on the little attention they receive from politicians. Although it is not statistically significant, those regions bordering the Caspian Sea and Iran register high for the broader voice option.

Summary statistics of countries Turkmenistan					
	n	Mean	SD	Min	Max
Exit	513	0.09	0.29	0	1
Broader voice	513	0.50	0.50	0	1
Bureaucratic voice	513	0.08	0.27	0	1
Broader loyalty	513	0.33	0.47	0	1
(A) Lifestyles					
Homeownership	792	0.96	0.20	0	1
Number of family members	800	3.75	1.19	1	8
(B) Exposure to globalization					
Internet	794	1.17	0.59	1	5
Living internationally	800	0.40	0.69	0	4
English ability	800	1.23	0.48	1	4
(C) Satisfaction with aspects of life					
Friendships	741	4.07	1.11	1	5
Health	706	3.07	1.56	1	5
Education	734	3.46	1.34	1	5
Neighbors	771	4.28	1.10	1	5
Public safety	710	3.78	1.50	1	5
Spiritual life	721	3.98	1.29	1	5
Happiness	729	3.45	1.04	1	5
(E) Assessment of government performance					
Worry about corruption	800	0.16	0.37	0	1
Widespread corruption	759	4.34	0.78	1	5
No power	736	3.33	1.46	1	5
Complicated	702	3.68	1.35	1	5
Stop thinking	719	3.37	0.95	1	5
Pay little attention	703	3.86	1.10	1	5
Powerful leader	763	2.91	0.36	1	3
Bribe	777	8.84	2.29	1	10
(H) Demographics					
Female	800	0.51	0.50	0	1
Age	800	37.06	12.69	20	69
Level of education	800	2.27	0.56	1	3
Married	800	0.84	0.37	0	1
Unemployed	800	0.11	0.32	0	1
Income	786	4.76	2.99	1	20
No religion	774	0.01	0.11	0	1
(I) Region (Base = Ashgabat)					
Balkan	800	0.08	0.28	0	1
Dashoguz	800	0.21	0.41	0	1
Mary	800	0.23	0.42	0	1
Lebap	800	0.21	0.41	0	1
Ahal	800	0.14	0.35	0	1
(K) Rural					
Rural	800	0.55	0.50	0	1

Frequency Distribution of 7 Responses and Partially Aggregated 4 Responses Turkmenistan

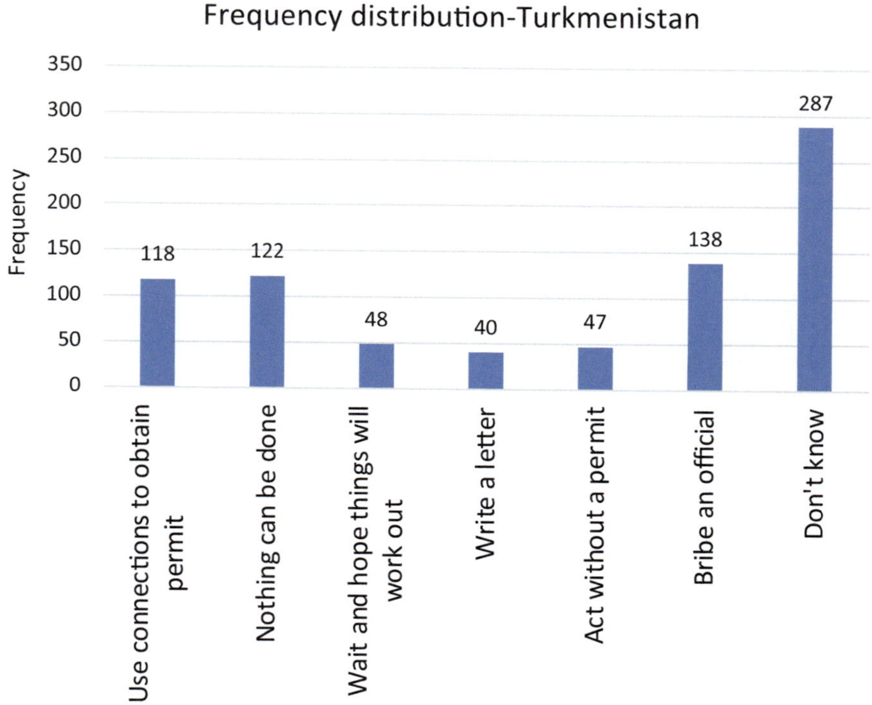

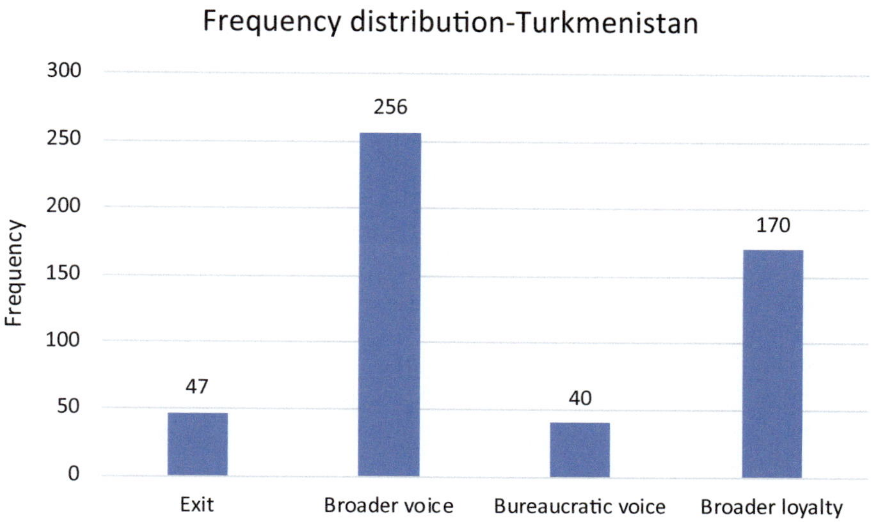

Logit regression analysis results by country Turkmenistan								
Dependent variable	Exit		Broader voice		Bureaucratic voice		Broader loyalty	
Independent variables	Coeff.	z-stat.	Coeff.	z-stat.	Coeff.	z-stat.	Coeff.	z-stat.
(A) Lifestyles								
Homeownership	–	–	−1.72	−1.33	–	–	−0.04	−0.03
Number of family members	–	–	−0.08	−0.29	−0.58	−1.08	−0.18	−0.71
(B) Exposure to globalization								
Internet	–	–	1.79	2.55[a]	−0.31	−0.29	−0.90	−1.52
Living internationally	–	–	−0.36	−1.00	−0.55	−0.89	0.46	1.42
English ability	–	–	−0.93	−1.68	0.74	1.09	0.14	0.33
(C) Satisfaction with aspects of life								
Friendships	–	–	−0.35	−1.57	−0.42	−0.93	0.23	1.03
Health	–	–	−0.03	−0.19	−0.46	−1.52	0.21	1.19
Education	–	–	0.13	0.66	0.25	0.66	−0.10	−0.51
Neighbors	–	–	−0.23	−0.98	0.53	1.10	−0.06	−0.30
Public safety	–	–	0.01	0.04	−0.16	−0.58	0.13	0.76
Spiritual life	–	–	−0.005	−0.03	0.23	0.72	−0.02	−0.10
Happiness	–	–	−0.10	−0.46	−0.30	−0.74	0.09	0.42
(E) Assessment of government performance								
Worry about corruption	–	–	2.46	2.89[b]	−1.28	−0.82	−0.91	−1.18
Widespread corruption	–	–	−0.65	(−2.23)[a]	1.38	1.49	0.31	1.20
No power	–	–	0.34	1.77	−1.27	(−2.06)[a]	0.10	0.52
Complicated	–	–	−0.63	(−2.78)[b]	1.85	2.15[a]	0.29	1.33
Stop thinking	–	–	1.32	4.19[b]	−0.81	−1.47	−0.86	(−3.13)[b]
Pay little attention	–	–	−1.36	(−3.34)[b]	0.77	1.20	0.68	1.95
Powerful leader	–	–	−1.92	−1.83	–	–	1.28	1.29
Bribe	–	–	0.02	0.19	0.56	1.51	0.14	1.17
(H) Demographics								
Female	–	–	0.27	0.53	1.61	1.68	−0.71	−1.44
Age	–	–	0.01	0.30	0.01	0.20	0.01	0.29
Level of education	–	–	−0.61	−1.30	−0.52	−0.60	0.52	1.22
Married	–	–	−0.07	−0.10	1.55	1.22	0.17	0.24
Unemployed	–	–	−0.43	−0.53	0.39	0.31	0.77	0.97
Income	–	–	0.00	−0.01	−0.28	−1.17	0.02	0.16
No religion	–	–	−0.28	−0.11	–	–	–	–

(continued)

(continued)

Logit regression analysis results by country Turkmenistan								
Dependent variable	Exit		Broader voice		Bureaucratic voice		Broader loyalty	
Independent variables	Coeff.	z-stat.	Coeff.	z-stat.	Coeff.	z-stat.	Coeff.	z-stat.
(I) Region (Base = Ashgabat)								
Balkan	–	–	1.57	1.14	−1.35	−0.69	−1.66	−1.33
Dashoguz	–	–	−0.14	−0.10	−0.84	−0.42	0.65	0.55
Mary	–	–	1.50	1.12	−2.35	−1.07	−0.39	−0.32
Lebap	–	–	0.10	0.08	−1.70	−0.86	0.15	0.13
Ahal	–	–	0.87	0.70	−4.13	−1.69	−0.97	−0.85
(K) Rural								
Rural	–	–	0.85	1.41	−0.18	−0.16	0.58	0.96
Constant	–	–	13.8	2.70[b]	−13.8	−1.82	−10.2	(−2.13)’
n	–		151		167		156	
Pseudo R squared	–		0.2909		0.2998		0.2057	

Note [a]5% significance level; [b]1% significance level

6.29 United States

A glance at the frequency distribution reveals that, in the United States, the voice options are favorite. The option of “writing a letter” and “using connections” stand out with the former being a bureaucratic voice option and the latter being a broader voice option. The exit option registers 3%, whereas one of the broader voice options, “bribing an official” registers 0.5%. The average American profile of being positive and active is supported here as well.

Those contributing to a broader voice option have a relatively good standard of living and worry about corruption and inequality. Those negatively contributing to the broader voice option register a poor English ability and bad health. Geographically, those residing along the South Atlantic coast are prone to the broader voice option.

Those contributing to the bureaucratic voice suffer from poor public utilities, are satisfied with family life, negatively assess government performance on issues of inequality, bemoan the lack of a powerful leader, and yearn for good government performance led by experts. Geographically, they do not reside along the South Atlantic coast.

Those contributing to the broader loyalty option have access to a number of public utilities, do not use Internet, do not care about the condition of the environment, and yearn for a powerful leader. Who resembles this profile? Donald Trump.

Summary statistics of countries United States					
	n	Mean	SD	Min	Max
Exit	879	0.04	0.18	0	1
Broader voice	879	0.34	0.47	0	1
Bureaucratic voice	879	0.35	0.48	0	1
Broader loyalty	879	0.28	0.45	0	1
(A) Lifestyles					
Number of public utilities	1002	5.32	1.16	2	7
Homeownership	997	0.73	0.45	0	1
Number of family members	1002	2.98	1.63	1	12
Pray	974	3.72	1.49	1	5
National elections	960	4.06	1.27	1	5
Local elections	959	3.79	1.28	1	5
Proud	960	3.67	0.60	1	4
Relative Standard of Living	985	3.27	0.78	1	5
(B) Exposure to globalization					
Internet	996	3.76	1.54	1	5
Living internationally	1002	1.36	1.55	0	6
English ability	1000	3.95	0.26	1	4
(C) Satisfaction with aspects of life					
Housing	991	4.18	0.94	1	5
Friendships	989	4.43	0.76	1	5
Household income	982	3.67	1.15	1	5
Health	991	4.12	1.00	1	5
Education	987	4.10	0.93	1	5
Job	950	3.87	1.11	1	5
Neighbors	968	4.03	0.90	1	5
Public safety	953	3.81	0.91	2	5
The condition of the environment	978	3.01	1.16	1	5
Family life	984	4.28	0.89	1	5
Leisure	982	4.07	0.96	1	5
Spiritual life	964	4.14	0.90	1	5
(D) Trust in social institution					
Trust generally	957	0.49	0.50	0	1
Trust the central government	935	2.57	0.79	1	4
Trust local governments	942	2.66	0.77	1	4
Trust the army	919	3.03	0.81	1	4
Trust the legal system	947	2.56	0.80	1	4
Trust the police	954	2.84	0.84	1	4
(E) Assessment of government performance					
Worry about corruption	1002	0.35	0.48	0	1
Worry about Economic inequality	1002	0.36	0.48	0	1

(continued)

(continued)

Summary statistics of countries United States					
	n	Mean	SD	Min	Max
Political corruption	936	1.92	0.81	1	4
Duty to vote	987	4.33	0.81	1	5
Widespread corruption	967	3.49	1.08	1	5
No power	984	3.20	1.16	1	5
Complicated	982	3.18	1.17	1	5
No matter whether vote	982	2.23	1.06	1	5
Stop thinking	977	3.32	1.03	1	5
Pay little attention	968	3.32	1.04	1	5
Powerful leader	894	1.20	0.49	1	3
Experts	866	1.49	0.64	1	3
Democratic political system	911	2.48	0.62	1	3
Bribe	967	9.35	1.43	1	10
(F) Satisfaction with rights					
Right to vote	980	3.71	0.58	1	4
Right to participate in any organizations	972	3.63	0.60	1	4
Right to gather and demonstrate	959	3.50	0.69	1	4
Right to be informed about government	965	3.28	0.82	1	4
Freedom of speech	988	3.52	0.68	1	4
Right to criticize the government	957	3.41	0.78	1	4
(G) Political spectrum					
Political spectrum	812	5.09	2.22	1	10
(H) Demographics					
Female	1002	0.51	0.50	0	1
Age	1002	43.8	14.2	20	69
Level of education	1000	2.53	0.59	1	3
Married	1002	0.57	0.50	0	1
Unemployed	997	0.07	0.25	0	1
Income	835	4.17	2.58	1	10
No religion	994	0.13	0.34	0	1
(I) Region (Base = New England)					
Middle Atlantic	1002	0.13	0.34	0	1
East North Central	1002	0.17	0.38	0	1
West North Central	1002	0.07	0.26	0	1
South Atlantic	1002	0.19	0.39	0	1
East South Central	1002	0.06	0.24	0	1
West South Central	1002	0.11	0.31	0	1
Mountain	1002	0.06	0.24	0	1
Pacific	1002	0.16	0.37	0	1
(K) Rural					
Rural	1002	0.14	0.35	0	1

Frequency Distribution of 7 Responses and Partially Aggregated 4 Responses
United States

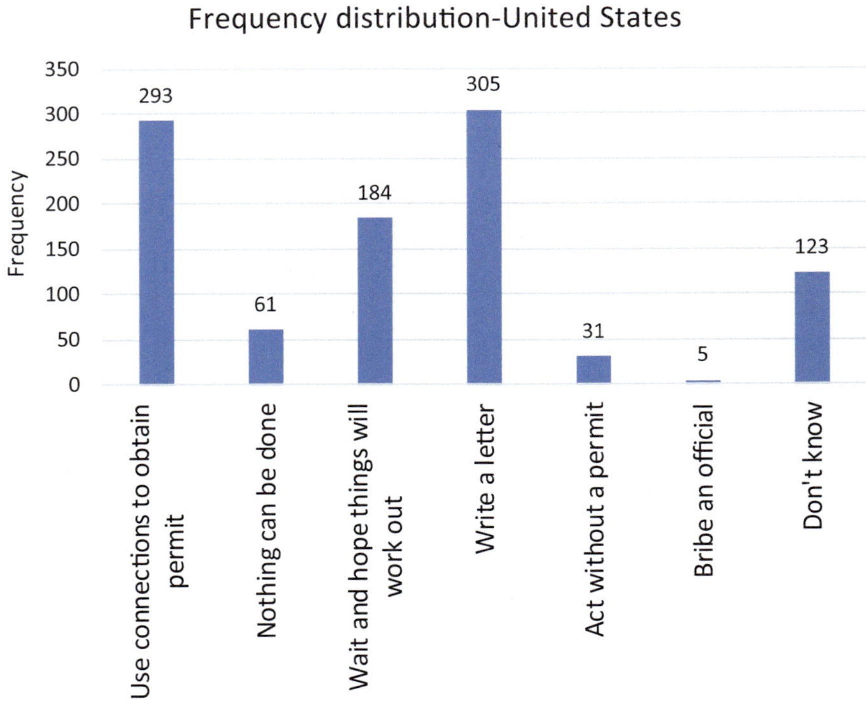

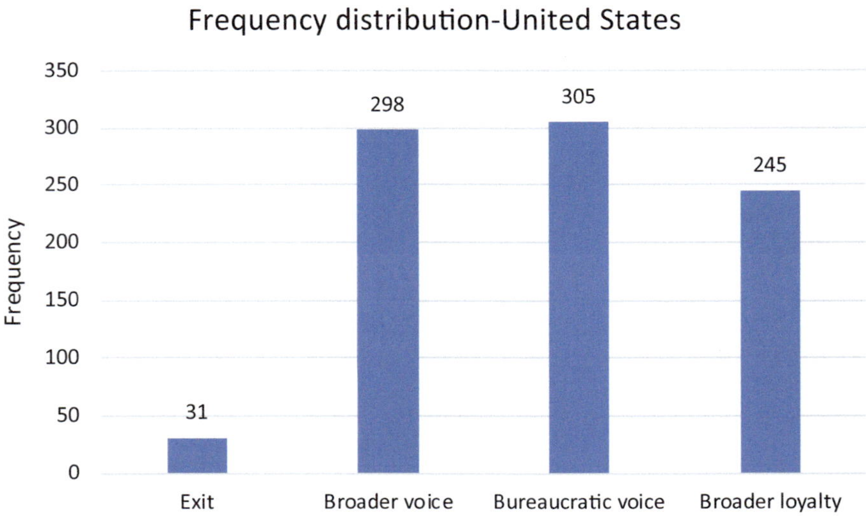

Logit regression analysis results by country United States								
Dependent variable	Exit		Broader voice		Bureaucratic voice		Bureaucratic loyalty	
Independent variables	Coeff.	z-stat.	Coeff.	z-stat.	Coeff.	z-stat.	Coeff.	z-stat.
(A) Lifestyles								
Number of public utilities	–	–	0.01	0.09	−0.45	(−3.08)[b]	0.47	2.90[b]
Homeownership	–	–	−0.59	−1.32	0.83	1.93	−0.33	−0.70
Number of family members	–	–	0.13	1.14	−0.15	−1.32	−0.02	−0.16
Pray	–	–	−0.07	−0.54	0.03	0.25	−0.07	−0.53
National elections	–	–	0.13	0.53	−0.38	−1.66	0.04	0.16
Local elections	–	–	−0.15	−0.75	0.33	1.61	−0.15	−0.72
Proud	–	–	−0.35	−1.20	−0.17	−0.60	0.30	0.84
Relative Standard of Living	–	–	0.55	2.21[a]	−0.23	−1.00	−0.39	−1.50
(B) Exposure to globalization								
Internet	–	–	0.21	1.54	0.15	1.25	−0.30	(−2.41)[a]
Living internationally	–	–	0.02	0.15	0.03	0.31	0.02	0.17
English ability	–	–	−1.38	(−2.27)[a]	1.68	1.72	0.41	0.60
(C) Satisfaction with aspects of life								
Housing	–	–	−0.13	−0.55	0.05	0.23	0.04	0.16
Friendships	–	–	0.26	0.98	−0.09	−0.38	−0.10	−0.35
Household income	–	–	−0.02	−0.08	0.01	0.05	0.16	0.83
Health	–	–	−0.47	(−2.24)[a]	0.08	0.44	0.37	1.86
Education	–	–	0.21	0.95	−0.10	−0.54	−0.15	−0.70
Job	–	–	0.27	1.49	−0.22	−1.37	−0.01	−0.08
Neighbors	–	–	0.18	0.90	−0.21	−1.09	0.23	1.10
Public safety	–	–	−0.07	−0.36	0.22	1.19	−0.15	−0.71
The condition of the environment	–	–	−0.01	−0.06	−0.09	−0.60	−0.10	−0.53
Family life	–	–	−0.07	−0.29	0.60	2.66[b]	−0.57	(−2.48)[a]
Leisure	–	–	−0.27	−1.26	−0.18	−0.91	0.39	1.69
Spiritual life	–	–	−0.01	−0.03	0.05	0.20	−0.02	−0.08
(D) Trust in social institution								
Trust generally	–	–	0.44	1.39	−0.13	−0.46	−0.24	−0.72
Trust the central government	–	–	0.21	0.67	0.15	0.54	0.10	0.30
Trust local governments	–	–	0.04	0.12	−0.05	−0.18	−0.31	−0.91
Trust the army	–	–	0.04	0.17	−0.18	−0.80	0.18	0.69
Trust the legal system	–	–	−0.08	−0.31	−0.01	−0.03	0.09	0.38
Trust the police	–	–	−0.11	−0.43	0.05	0.19	0.28	1.06

(continued)

(continued)

Logit regression analysis results by country United States								
Dependent variable	Exit		Broader voice		Bureaucratic voice		Bureaucratic loyalty	
Independent variables	Coeff.	z-stat.	Coeff.	z-stat.	Coeff.	z-stat.	Coeff.	z-stat.
(E) Assessment of government performance								
Worry about corruption	–	–	0.24	0.68	−0.14	−0.44	0.16	0.46
Worry about Economic inequality	–	–	0.85	2.73[b]	−0.25	−0.82	−0.48	−1.39
Political corruption	–	–	0.65	2.87[b]	−0.51	(−2.36)[a]	0.13	0.57
Duty to vote	–	–	−0.01	−0.06	0.30	1.31	−0.14	−0.55
Widespread corruption	–	–	−0.15	−0.80	0.28	1.50	−0.17	−0.88
No power	–	–	0.14	0.84	−0.28	−1.84	0.14	0.83
Complicated	–	–	0.07	0.46	−0.10	−0.73	0.03	0.21
No matter whether vote	–	–	−0.04	−0.24	−0.07	−0.41	0.03	0.13
Stop thinking	–	–	0.15	0.68	−0.22	−1.15	0.22	1.08
Pay little attention	–	–	−0.37	−1.75	0.28	1.47	0.15	0.74
Powerful leader	–	–	0.02	0.03	−1.41	(−2.33)[a]	1.16	2.34[a]
Experts	–	–	−0.33	−1.30	0.54	2.22[a]	−0.39	−1.40
Democratic political system	–	–	0.31	1.19	−0.37	−1.50	−0.13	−0.52
Bribe	–	–	0.01	0.07	0.08	0.66	0.09	0.68
(F) Satisfaction with rights								
Right to vote	–	–	0.32	0.75	0.30	0.74	−0.58	−1.16
Right to participate in any organizations	–	–	−0.36	−0.82	0.07	0.17	0.48	1.05
Right to gather and demonstrate	–	–	0.46	1.27	−0.004	−0.01	−0.48	−1.34
Right to be informed about government	–	–	−0.37	−1.45	0.42	1.59	0.15	0.48
Freedom of speech	–	–	−0.03	−0.08	−0.33	−1.10	0.10	0.28
Right to criticize the government	–	–	−0.13	−0.46	−0.07	−0.26	0.23	0.71
(H) Demographics								
Female	–	–	−0.22	−0.73	0.42	1.46	−0.25	−0.76
Age	–	–	0.004	0.29	0.001	0.10	0.01	0.47
Level of education	–	–	−0.22	−0.66	−0.48	−1.48	0.33	0.96
Married	–	–	−0.40	−1.09	0.54	1.52	0.00	0
Unemployed	–	–	−0.76	−0.95	0.67	0.88	−0.38	−0.48
Income	–	–	0.11	1.46	0.02	0.29	−0.13	−1.53
No religion	–	–	0.26	0.49	−0.08	−0.17	0.06	0.10

(continued)

(continued)

Logit regression analysis results by country United States								
Dependent variable	Exit		Broader voice		Bureaucratic voice		Bureaucratic loyalty	
Independent variables	Coeff.	z-stat.	Coeff.	z-stat.	Coeff.	z-stat.	Coeff.	z-stat.
(I) Region (Base = New England)								
Middle Atlantic	–	–	0.69	0.53	−0.05	−0.06	−1.14	−1.12
East North Central	–	–	0.46	0.34	−1.22	−1.45	0.29	0.30
West North Central	–	–	1.20	0.91	−1.37	−1.58	−0.12	−0.12
South Atlantic	–	–	2.61	2.03[a]	−1.97	(−2.25)[a]	−1.42	−1.41
East South Central	–	–	1.62	1.05	−0.51	−0.45	−0.72	−0.56
West South Central	–	–	2.01	1.49	−1.45	−1.56	−0.27	−0.26
Mountain	–	–	1.87	1.39	−1.62	−1.77	−0.10	−0.10
Pacific	–	–	0.60	0.46	−0.03	−0.04	−0.34	−0.35
(K) Rural								
Rural	–	–	−0.70	−1.33	−0.18	−0.38	0.50	1.01
Constant	–	–	1.62	0.43	−3.56	−0.79	−6.58	−1.66
n	–		378		378		378	
Pseudo R squared	–		0.2427		0.2224		0.2259	

Note [a]5% significance level; [b]1% significance level

6.30 Uzbekistan

A quick look at the frequency distribution of seven options, for Uzbekistan, reveals that broader voice options, "using connections" and "bribing an official," are dominant. Next to these two are "waiting patiently and hoping" and "writing a letter."

Those contributing to choosing a broader voice option are not proud of their lifestyles, are satisfied with the condition of the environment, are not satisfied with the democratic system, are satisfied with the right to vote, have a high level of education, and a high level of income.

Those contributing to the bureaucratic voice option are not satisfied with public safety and trust the army.

Those contributing to choosing the broader loyalty option have a poor English ability, have a high education, are satisfied with public safety, are satisfied with the democratic system. Those contributing negatively to choosing the broader loyalty options have a low level of education and a low income. Geographically, those who reside outside of the capital, Samarkand, negatively contribute to the bureaucratic loyalty.

Summary statistics of countries Uzbekistan					
	n	Mean	SD	Min	Max
Exit	1554	0.028	0.17	0	1
Broader voice	1554	0.597	0.49	0	1
Bureaucratic voice	1554	0.093	0.29	0	1
Broader loyalty	1554	0.282	0.45	0	1
(A) Lifestyles					
Public water supply	1600	0.99	0.09	0	1
Homeownership	1600	0.96	0.19	0	1
Number of family members	1600	4.56	2.17	1	18
National elections	1583	3.71	1.47	1	5
Proud	1515	2.99	1.08	1	4
Relative Standard of Living	1598	2.75	0.78	1	5
(B) Exposure to globalization					
Living internationally	1600	1.79	1.27	0	6
English ability	1596	1.48	0.72	1	4
(C) Satisfaction with aspects of life					
Housing	1598	3.48	1.20	1	5
Friendships	1592	4.03	0.94	1	5
Household income	1599	2.85	1.19	1	5
Health	1597	3.43	1.15	1	5
Education	1588	3.51	1.12	1	5
Job	1422	3.40	1.25	1	5
Neighbors	1588	3.76	1.02	1	5
Public safety	1523	3.07	1.15	1	5
The condition of the environment	1584	2.55	1.10	1	5
Social welfare system	1505	2.31	1.14	1	5
The democratic system	1440	2.44	1.16	1	5
Family life	1550	3.96	1.02	1	5
Leisure	1584	3.20	1.27	1	5
Happiness	1589	3.44	1.05	1	5
(D) Trust in social institution					
Trust generally	1593	0.21	0.40	0	1
Trust the central government	1509	2.54	0.89	1	4
Trust local governments	1551	2.35	0.87	1	4
Trust the army	1527	2.74	0.92	1	4
Trust the legal system	1493	2.37	0.89	1	4
Trust the police	1572	2.14	0.95	1	4

(continued)

(continued)

Summary statistics of countries Uzbekistan					
	n	Mean	SD	Min	Max
(E) Assessment of government performance					
Worry about corruption	1600	0.37	0.48	0	1
Worry about Economic inequality	1600	0.38	0.48	0	1
Political corruption	1317	1.93	0.82	1	4
Duty to vote	1589	4.16	0.90	1	5
Widespread corruption	1408	3.97	0.87	1	5
No power	1538	3.96	0.97	1	5
Complicated	1545	3.69	1.06	1	5
No matter whether vote	1564	3.29	1.23	1	5
Stop thinking	1497	3.96	1.03	1	5
Pay little attention	1509	4.03	0.95	1	5
Powerful leader	1374	1.43	0.68	1	3
Experts	1340	1.63	0.65	1	3
Military government	1451	1.17	0.45	1	3
Democratic political system	1434	2.16	0.74	1	3
(F) Satisfaction with rights					
Right to vote	1533	2.94	0.86	1	4
Right to participate in any organizations	1313	2.71	0.83	1	4
Right to be informed about government	1360	2.11	0.95	1	4
Freedom of speech	1521	2.03	1.00	1	4
(H) Demographics					
Female	1600	0.52	0.50	0	1
Age	1600	36.8	11.9	20	69
Level of education	1600	2.59	0.60	1	3
Married	1600	0.65	0.48	0	1
Unemployed	1600	0.08	0.28	0	1
Income	1459	8.53	3.41	1	17
No religion	1585	0.11	0.31	0	1
(I) Region (Base = Tashkent)					
Samarkand	1600	0.13	0.33	0	1
Bukhara	1600	0.13	0.33	0	1
Urgench	1600	0.13	0.33	0	1
Fergana	1600	0.13	0.33	0	1
Andijan	1600	0.13	0.33	0	1
Namangan	1600	0.13	0.33	0	1
(L) Yearly dummy variable (Base = 2003)					
2005	1600	0.50	0.50	0	1

Frequency Distribution of 7 Responses and Partially Aggregated 4 Responses
Uzbekistan

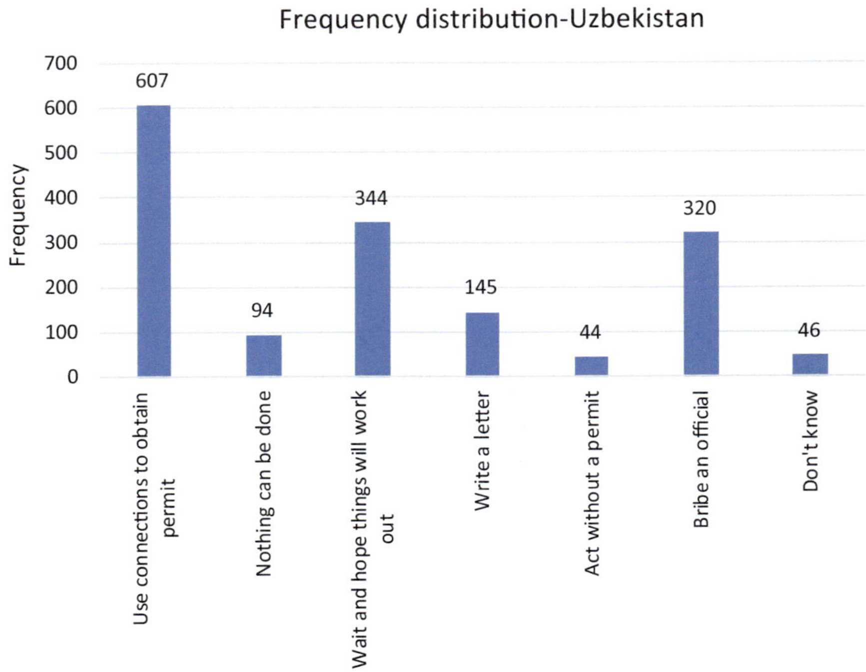

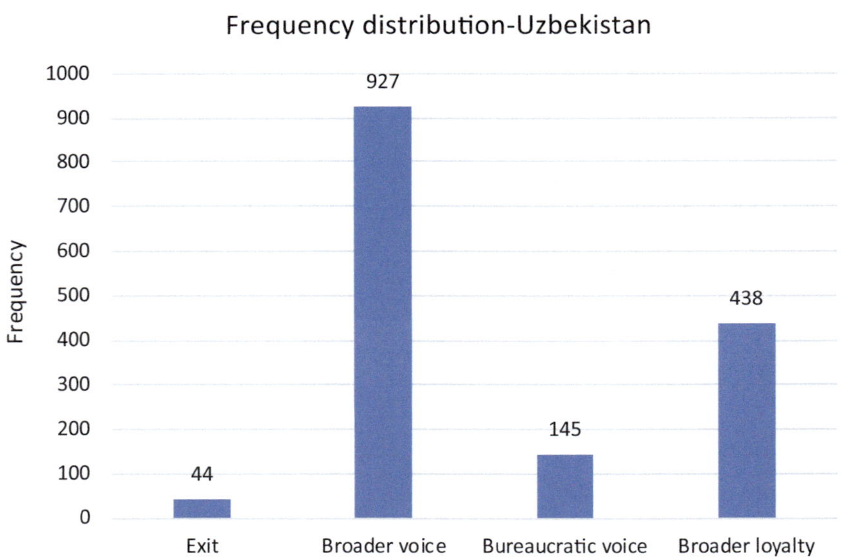

Logit regression analysis results by country Uzbekistan								
Dependent variables	Exit		Broader voice		Bureaucratic voice		Broader loyalty	
Independent variables	Coeff.	z-stat.	Coeff.	z-stat.	Coeff.	z-stat.	Coeff.	z-stat.
(A) Lifestyles								
Public water supply	–	–	−0.76	−0.7	−1.90	−1.48	1.49	1.07
Homeownership	–	–	−0.09	−0.13	−0.15	−0.16	0.75	0.84
Number of family members	–	–	0.003	0.04	−0.08	−0.81	0.04	0.61
National elections	–	–	−0.11	−1.36	0.002	0.02	0.17	1.76
Proud	–	–	−0.30	(−2.37)[a]	0.24	1.18	0.18	1.23
Relative Standard of Living	–	–	0.27	1.51	−0.25	−0.92	0.06	0.27
(B) Exposure to globalization								
Living internationally	–	–	−0.03	−0.36	0.04	0.30	0.04	0.40
English ability	–	–	0.36	2.20[a]	−0.07	−0.29	−0.58	(−2.67)[b]
(C) Satisfaction with aspects of life								
Housing	–	–	0.05	0.44	−0.01	−0.08	0.03	0.23
Friendships	–	–	0.03	0.21	0.31	1.48	−0.22	−1.51
Household income	–	–	−0.10	−0.85	−0.10	−0.50	0.18	1.25
Health	–	–	−0.001	−0.01	0.03	0.16	−0.10	−0.73
Education	–	–	−0.13	−1.22	−0.11	−0.69	0.28	2.15[a]
Job	–	–	0.005	0.05	−0.05	−0.28	−0.03	−0.22
Neighbors	–	–	−0.20	−1.77	0.50	2.48[a]	0.03	0.22
Public safety	–	–	0.04	0.36	−0.55	(−3.08)[b]	0.34	2.44[a]
The condition of the environment	–	–	0.33	2.75[b]	−0.11	−0.61	−0.34	(−2.47)[a]
Social welfare system	–	–	−0.06	−0.48	0.16	0.88	−0.02	−0.17
The democratic system	–	–	−0.32	(−2.75)[b]	−0.03	−0.15	0.34	2.48[a]
Family life	–	–	−0.05	−0.4	−0.08	−0.39	0.04	0.25
Leisure	–	–	0.08	0.79	−0.24	−1.50	−0.07	−0.59
Happiness	–	–	0.09	0.71	0.09	0.44	−0.17	−1.14
(D) Trust in social institution								
Trust generally	–	–	−0.19	−0.74	0.26	0.65	0.30	1.02
Trust the central government	–	–	0.03	0.16	0.06	0.22	−0.12	−0.58
Trust local governments	–	–	0.01	0.06	−0.08	−0.26	0.11	0.51
Trust the army	–	–	−0.16	−1.19	0.48	2.04[a]	−0.09	−0.55
Trust the legal system	–	–	0.21	1.25	−0.27	−0.97	−0.07	−0.35
Trust the police	–	–	−0.10	−0.68	0.48	1.78	−0.04	−0.23
(E) Assessment of government performance								
Worry about corruption	–	–	0.22	0.92	0.43	1.12	−0.49	−1.75
Worry about Economic inequality	–	–	−0.10	−0.44	0.15	0.43	0.06	0.24
Political corruption	–	–	−0.23	−1.38	0.28	1.11	−0.05	−0.26

(continued)

(continued)

Logit regression analysis results by country Uzbekistan								
Dependent variables	Exit		Broader voice		Bureaucratic voice		Broader loyalty	
Independent variables	Coeff.	z-stat.	Coeff.	z-stat.	Coeff.	z-stat.	Coeff.	z-stat.
Duty to vote	–	–	−0.07	−0.56	−0.12	−0.60	0.17	1.08
Widespread corruption	–	–	0.26	1.84	−0.28	−1.24	−0.22	−1.44
No power	–	–	−0.16	−1.2	0.10	0.50	0.13	0.86
Complicated	–	–	0.04	0.37	−0.14	−0.80	0.14	1.02
No matter whether vote	–	–	−0.02	−0.19	−0.10	−0.62	−0.01	−0.06
Stop thinking	–	–	0.04	0.28	−0.18	−0.77	0.08	0.44
Pay little attention	–	–	0.10	0.6	−0.10	−0.38	−0.10	−0.55
Powerful leader	–	–	−0.29	−1.82	0.10	0.37	0.33	1.82
Experts	–	–	0.23	1.25	−0.07	−0.24	−0.28	−1.30
Military government	–	–	−0.16	−0.68	−0.24	−0.58	0.07	0.28
Democratic political system	–	–	0.06	0.38	−0.01	−0.04	−0.10	−0.57
(F) Satisfaction with rights								
Right to vote	–	–	0.32	2.12[a]	−0.04	−0.16	−0.32	−1.80
Right to participate in any organizations	–	–	0.25	1.68	−0.17	−0.72	−0.08	−0.47
Right to be informed about government	–	–	−0.21	−1.5	0.20	0.95	0.17	1.05
Freedom of speech	–	–	0.06	0.45	−0.29	−1.34	0.04	0.28
(H) Demographics								
Female	–	–	−0.13	−0.58	0.08	0.21	0.02	0.09
Age	–	–	−0.01	−0.74	0.01	0.64	−0.002	−0.13
Level of education	–	–	0.42	2.15[a]	0.06	0.21	−0.55	(−2.56)[a]
Married	–	–	0.06	0.22	−0.56	−1.44	0.11	0.37
Unemployed	–	–	−0.63	−1.55	0.88	1.49	0.52	1.13
Income	–	–	0.09	2.20[a]	0.01	0.17	−0.13	(−2.63)[a]
No religion	–	–	−0.32	−0.93	1.00	1.94	−0.12	−0.27
(I) Region (Base = Tashkent)								
Samarkand	–	–	0.18	0.39	0.77	1.09	−1.79	(−2.48)[a]
Bukhara	–	–	−0.47	−1.36	0.69	1.29	0.17	0.42
Urgench	–	–	0.02	0.06	−0.13	−0.20	−0.13	−0.29
Fergana	–	–	0.25	0.66	−0.19	−0.30	−0.26	−0.60
Andijan	–	–	−0.13	−0.32	0.52	0.83	−0.01	−0.03
Namangan	–	–	0.20	0.47	0.86	1.37	−0.37	−0.76
(L) Yearly dummy variable (Base = 2003)								
2005	–	–	−0.93	(−3.36)[b]	0.51	1.18	0.89	2.74[b]
Constant	–	–	−0.06	−0.03	0.37	0.13	−2.05	−0.84
n	–		568		568		568	
Pseudo R squared	–		0.1647		0.1849		0.1960	

Note [a]5% significance level; [b]1% significance level

6.31 Vietnam

For Vietnam, the frequency distribution of seven options reveals that the broader loyalty option is dominant. At the same time, the sizable percentage for "using connections" (16.1%), "bribing an official" (4.1%), and "writing a letter" (3.3%) are not insignificant.

Those contributing to choosing the exit option negatively assess government performance and profess no religion. Geographically, no one in Ho Chi Minh City and Hue chose the exit option. Danang (Central Vietnam), Vung Tau (Southern Vietnam), Can Tho (Southern Vietnam) register strong contributions to the exit option.

Those contributing to the broader voice option are not satisfied with housing, have a high level of education, are not satisfied with public safety, are not satisfied with the social welfare system, and are satisfied with leisure. Geographically, those who reside in Hue are significant in this option.

Those contributing to the bureaucratic voice option pray, do not live internationally, are not satisfied with education, bemoan the lack of power in government performance, and bemoan the fact that whether they vote or not does not matter. Demographically, those female contribution to the bureaucratic voice option is negative as those who profess no religion contribute to the bureaucratic voice option. Geographically, respondents reside in Thai Nguyen (northern Vietnam).

Those contributing to the broader loyalty option are satisfied with housing, are not satisfied with neighbors, are satisfied with public safety, are satisfied with the social welfare system, and negatively assess government performance. Demographically, respondents are female. Geographically, those who contribute to this option reside in Thai Nguyen, Da Nang, Can Tho, Vung Tau, and My Tho.

Summary statistics of countries Vietnam

	n	Mean	SD	Min	Max
Exit	979	0.01	0.11	0	1
Broader voice	979	0.21	0.40	0	1
Bureaucratic voice	979	0.03	0.18	0	1
Broader loyalty	979	0.75	0.43	0	1
(A) Lifestyles					
Number of public utilities	1000	4.43	1.12	0	7
Homeownership	1000	0.95	0.23	0	1
Number of family members	1000	4.55	1.89	1	15
Pray	1000	2.18	1.01	1	5
National elections	995	4.67	0.91	1	5
Proud	1000	3.89	0.36	2	4
Relative Standard of Living	1000	2.94	0.63	1	5
(B) Exposure to globalization					
Internet	977	1.72	1.25	1	5
Living internationally	1000	0.89	0.92	0	6

(continued)

(continued)

Summary statistics of countries Vietnam					
	n	Mean	SD	Min	Max
English ability	926	1.76	0.80	1	4
(C) Satisfaction with aspects of life					
Housing	1000	3.72	1.15	1	5
Friendships	1000	3.73	0.91	1	5
Household income	997	3.16	0.84	1	5
Health	1000	3.64	0.97	1	5
Education	998	3.62	0.90	1	5
Job	993	3.46	0.94	1	5
Neighbors	1000	3.62	0.87	1	5
Public safety	1000	3.62	1.00	1	5
The condition of the environment	1000	3.35	1.01	1	5
Social welfare system	986	3.30	0.87	1	5
Family life	999	3.95	0.87	1	5
Leisure	996	3.48	0.79	1	5
Happiness	1000	4.02	0.89	1	5
(D) Trust in social institution					
Trust generally	989	0.19	0.39	0	1
(E) Assessment of government performance					
Worry about Economic inequality	1000	0.25	0.44	0	1
Duty to vote	1000	4.57	0.58	1	5
No power	975	2.97	1.05	1	5
Complicated	958	3.04	0.98	1	5
No matter whether vote	994	2.35	0.96	1	5
(H) Demographics					
Female	1000	0.52	0.50	0	1
Age	1000	37.2	12.6	20	69
Level of education	1000	1.93	0.82	1	3
Married	1000	0.65	0.48	0	1
Unemployed	1000	0.06	0.24	0	1
Income	1000	3.76	2.53	1	16
No religion	1000	0.32	0.46	0	1
(I) City (Base = Ha Noi)					
Thai Nguyen	1000	0.13	0.33	0	1
Da Nang	1000	0.13	0.33	0	1
Hue	1000	0.13	0.33	0	1
HCMC	1000	0.13	0.33	0	1
Vung Tau	1000	0.13	0.33	0	1
Can Tho	1000	0.13	0.33	0	1
My Tho	1000	0.13	0.33	0	1

Frequency Distribution of 7 Responses and Partially Aggregated 4 Responses Viet Nam

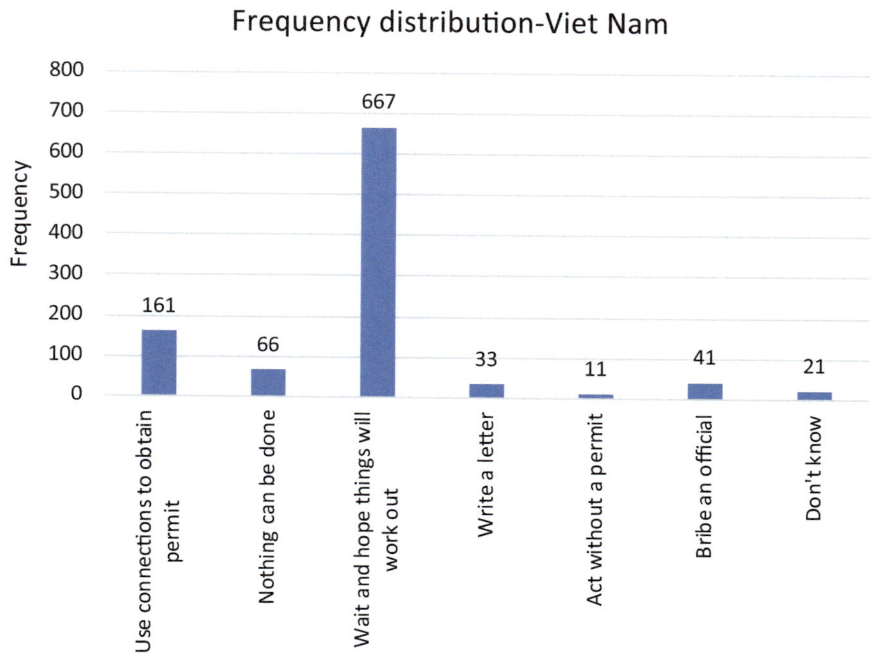

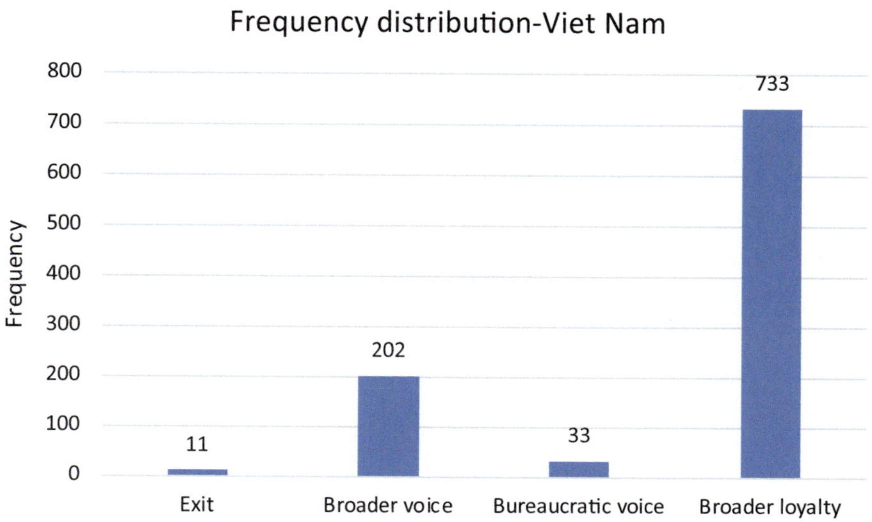

Logit regression analysis results by country Vietnam								
Dependent variable	Exit		Broader voice		Bureaucratic voice		Broader loyalty	
Independent variables	Coeff.	z-stat.	Coeff.	z-stat.	Coeff.	z-stat.	Coeff.	z-stat.
(A) Lifestyles								
Number of public utilities	1.00	1.24	0.09	0.86	−0.05	−0.18	−0.09	−0.87
Homeownership	–	–	0.85	1.41	0.47	0.38	−0.89	−1.61
Number of family members	−0.04	−0.11	−0.03	−0.53	0.14	1.00	0.03	0.51
Pray	−1.03	−1.44	0.004	0.04	0.76	2.68[b]	−0.08	−0.76
National elections	−0.72	−1.10	−0.07	−0.64	0.21	0.50	0.05	0.52
Proud	–	–	−0.18	−0.74	0.49	0.58	−0.02	−0.07
Relative Standard of Living	0.22	0.26	−0.02	−0.13	0.36	0.82	0.01	0.04
(B) Exposure to globalization								
Internet	0.47	1.04	0.01	0.09	0.31	1.28	−0.09	−0.97
Living internationally	0.70	1.24	0.19	1.60	−0.80	(−2.18)[a]	−0.12	−1.08
English ability	2.31	1.91	−0.12	−0.74	0.18	0.44	−0.003	−0.02
(C) Satisfaction with aspects of life								
Housing	0.86	1.44	−0.33	(−3.37)[b]	0.13	0.52	0.25	2.69[b]
Friendships	0.51	0.82	0.08	0.64	−0.005	−0.02	−0.08	−0.73
Household income	−0.01	−0.02	−0.10	−0.70	−0.15	−0.45	0.07	0.54
Health	−0.94	−1.30	0.10	0.86	0.22	0.77	−0.08	−0.72
Education	0.23	0.34	0.28	2.14[a]	−0.79	(−2.35)[a]	−0.12	−0.95
Job	−0.94	−1.26	0.02	0.14	−0.23	−0.81	0.07	0.58
Neighbors	0.53	0.81	0.22	1.66	0.39	1.24	−0.34	(−2.71)[b]
Public safety	0.35	0.63	−0.37	(−3.05)[b]	−0.39	−1.30	0.39	3.50[b]
The condition of the environment	−0.20	−0.36	0.21	1.68	−0.05	−0.18	−0.15	−1.31
Social welfare system	−1.29	−1.45	−0.30	(−2.13)[a]	0.07	0.24	0.28	2.11[a]
Family life	−0.35	−0.47	−0.27	−1.87	0.50	1.44	0.17	1.33
Leisure	−0.13	−0.18	0.29	2.12[a]	0.07	0.20	−0.24	−1.84
Happiness	−1.15	−1.35	−0.13	−1.01	−0.11	−0.36	0.16	1.34

(continued)

(continued)

Logit regression analysis results by country Vietnam								
Dependent variable	Exit		Broader voice		Bureaucratic voice		Broader loyalty	
Independent variables	Coeff.	z-stat.	Coeff.	z-stat.	Coeff.	z-stat.	Coeff.	z-stat.
(D) Trust in social institution								
Trust generally	−1.50	−1.07	−0.04	−0.14	0.16	0.28	−0.04	−0.16
(E) Assessment of government performance								
Worry about Economic inequality	1.35	1.17	0.01	0.06	0.57	1.11	−0.20	−0.99
Duty to vote	−1.02	−0.84	−0.01	−0.06	0.38	0.83	−0.06	−0.36
No power	−0.73	−1.38	0.07	0.67	−0.58	(−2.12)[a]	0.03	0.37
Complicated	−0.07	−0.13	0.02	0.22	0.25	0.93	−0.06	−0.63
No matter whether vote	−2.19	(−2.00)[a]	0.16	1.47	0.68	2.51[a]	−0.22	(−2.16)[a]
(H) Demographics								
Female	0.89	0.85	−0.33	−1.67	−1.34	(−2.43)[a]	0.45	2.42[a]
Age	0.03	0.64	−0.01	−1.30	−0.01	−0.46	0.01	1.33
Level of education	−1.33	−1.21	0.23	1.44	−0.28	−0.71	−0.11	−0.76
Married	0.18	0.14	0.04	0.19	0.66	1.05	−0.11	−0.48
Unemployed	1.15	0.63	0.10	0.25	−0.98	−0.80	0.002	0.01
Income	−0.13	−0.62	0.07	1.87	−0.04	−0.40	−0.06	−1.63
No religion	−4.39	(−2.18)[a]	0.17	0.75	1.70	2.74[b]	−0.25	−1.14
(I) City (Base = Ha Noi)								
Thai Nguyen	−3.66	−1.67	−0.17	−0.44	−2.82	(−2.28)[a]	0.83	2.29[a]
Da Nang	−4.22	(−2.03)[a]	−0.56	−1.42	−1.27	−1.50	1.00	2.77[b]
Hue	–	–	0.76	2.06[a]	–	–	−0.09	−0.25
HCMC	–	–	−0.52	−1.26	−0.75	−0.86	0.92	2.40[a]
Vung Tau	−4.59	(−2.03)[a]	−0.87	(−2.00)[a]	−0.43	−0.47	1.10	2.80[b]
Can Tho	−4.04	(−2.01)[a]	−0.21	−0.60	−0.39	−0.47	0.60	1.80
My Tho	−3.24	−1.52	−0.50	−1.20	−1.52	−1.52	0.96	2.50[a]
Constant	13.2	1.34	−0.96	−0.54	−10.8	(−2.18)[a]	1.42	0.85
n	645		819		725		819	
Pseudo R squared	0.4620		0.128		0.2723		0.1236	

Note [a]5% significance level; [b]1% significance level

Chapter 7
Comparisons with Asian and Non-Asian Societies: The United States, Australia, Japan, Russia, China, and India

7.1 Exit, Voice, and Loyalty

Hirschmann (1970) posits the three choices one faces in organizations when one feels an organization is deteriorating in making profits or getting documents efficiently processed or maintaining harmonious social relations in the workplace, or what not. His model is applied to the situation when a citizen applies for a government permit and is met with a callous response from the government official. The question: What should a person who needs a government permit do if the response of the official handling the application is: "just be patient and wait?" (SA) The question was asked to 50,0000-plus respondents in randomly sampled nationwide surveys in 29 Asian societies, plus three adjacent societies—the United States, Russia and Australia. In 2008, the following six countries were surveyed: the United States, Australia, Japan, India, Russia, and China. These surveys were part of the *AsiaBarometer Survey Project*, conducted throughout the 2000s. In analyzing and interpreting the survey results, we must note at the outset that we are keenly aware of the difficulties in using cross-national surveys with the master questionnaire in English, which is then translated into 35 languages and conducted with face-to-face interviews (Inoguchi 2012). We must be content to refer to Dept (2013) and Inoguchi (2012).

Six options are listed and the respondents are asked to choose one:

(1) Use connections to obtain the permit
(2) Nothing can be done
(3) Wait and hope that things will work out
(4) Write a letter
(5) Act without a permit
(6) Bribe an official
(7) Don't know.

T. Inoguchi, *Exit, Voice and Loyalty in Asia*,
Quality of Life in Asia 10, DOI 10.1007/978-981-10-4724-4_7

If we follow a Hirschmannesque formula, option 5 is an exit option that steps outside the legal framework even if the market is a legitimate arena of activity. Option 1 is a voice option in a weak sense in that it is debatable whether it is inside the legal framework or not. Option 1 is normally called corruption. Yet the difference between giving a bribe and using connections is sometimes blurred and, more importantly, using connections does not necessarily entail giving a bribe. Option 4 is a normal orthodox voice option, although it is a bureaucratic option. Option 6 is a voice option often considered to be outside the legal framework. Option 2 is a passive option. Option 2 is a loyalty option verging on apathy or disenchantment. Option 3 is a loyalty option literally understood.

We posed this question in six societies in Asia or adjacent to Asia: the United States, Australia, Japan, India, Russia and China. They include democratic and authoritarian regimes, Asian and Western societies, developed and developing economies. The frequency distribution of responses is presented, country by country, in Table 7.1.

Adding options 1 and 6 creates a broader voice option. The broader voice option seeks to get things done one way or another (Rose and Peiffer 2012). Option 4 is a bureaucratic voice option. Adding 2 and 3 creates a broader loyalty option (Table 7.2).

Some of the more interesting observations include:

(1) Exit: Of the six societies, Russia and Japan rank the highest in terms of percentage. Russian respondents who choose the exit option represent a tiny fragment of those surveyed, yet the fact that Russia has the highest percentage among this group of countries means that a sizable portion of Russian citizens are more alienated by the "system" or "regime" representing their society. The rate of suicide among those seeking a presidential petition is well documented (Nakamura 2005a, b, p. 233). The documentation reveals that not only does presidential petitioning exist but quite a large number of people use it and a fairly high number commit suicide thereafter. Japan's high exit figure is of little

Table 7.1 Frequency distribution of six options, country by country (%)

	Use connections to obtain the permit	Nothing can be done	Wait and hope that things will work out	Write a letter	Act without a permit	Bribe an official	Don't know	N
United States	29.2	6.1	18.4	30.4	3.1	0.5	12.3	1002
Australia	12.5	6.8	28.7	45.8	2.1	1.2	2.9	1000
Japan	5.3	28.1	34.2	18.2	4.3	0.3	9.6	1012
India	31.8	10.4	28.6	19.1	2.9	5.1	2.1	1052
Russia	35.6	10.2	13.5	18.3	4.8	4.4	13.2	1055
China	21.3	21.8	28.9	21.8	2.5	2.2	1.5	1000
Total	22.8	13.9	25.3	25.5	3.3	2.3	6.9	6121

Table 7.2 Frequency distribution of exit, broader voice and broader loyalty options, country by country (%)

	Exit (5)	Broader voice (1 + 6)	Bureaucratic voice (4)	Broader loyalty (2 + 3)	Don't know	N
United States	3.1	29.7	30.4	24.5	12.3	1002
Australia	2.1	13.7	45.8	35.5	2.9	1000
Japan	4.3	5.6	18.2	62.3	9.6	1012
India	2.9	36.9	19.1	39.0	2.1	1052
Russia	4.8	40.0	18.3	23.7	13.2	1055
China	2.5	23.5	21.8	50.7	1.5	1000
Total	3.3	25.1	25.5	39.2	6.9	6121

surprise. In East and Southeast Asia, Japan's figure is second to that of the Philippines. Our explanation is that given the high level of freedom of speech, choosing the exit option in an interview will not lead to an arrest in Japan. This is in sharp contrast to the unlucky Tunisian fruit vendor who worked outside the legal framework and was caught by police, igniting a series of Arab Springs in North Africa and the Middle East. In the Philippines, the general observation is that the police are not considered effective. Also, of little surprise is the exit propensity of Americans, which Hirschmann seems to stress, seems a little exaggerated. Adding broader loyalty and bureaucratic voice for Americans gives the impression that they are far more conformist and loyalist to organizations, a picture close to what David Riesman (*The Lonely Crowd*) and Paul Lazarsfeld (two-step communication) portrayed. Americans appear to be happy working within the "system." This picture appears more magnified among Australians who register higher figures of bureaucratic voice and broader loyalty than Americans. Lipset (1990) compares the United States and Canada, which are both new settler societies, with the latter retaining the tail end of colonialism, more or less. India and China provide a similar picture. First, there are sizable loyalists. Second, they register a sizable number for the broader voice option, that is, giving bribes and using connections or what is usually termed corruption. Third, there is a fairly strong tendency to write a letter (bureaucratic voice) rather than resorting to exit.

(2) Corruption: In descending order, the ranking among the six countries in terms of corruptibility is: China, Russia, India, the United States, Australia, and Japan. China represents the world's oldest bureaucratic tradition. China's socialism with Chinese characteristics means that to get things done one needs to give incentives to bureaucrats. To live under Russian capitalism with Russian characteristics one needs to give incentives to bureaucrats or small tyrants to get things done (Rose et al. 2011). India's socialist bureaucratism, accentuated by British colonial heritage, enables "small kings" everywhere to be recipients of monetary kickbacks (Roy 1997). Of the three industrial democracies, the United States appears to be the most corruptible. As Etzioni (1988) argues, the amount of

capital corruption is arguably the world's largest, albeit depending on the definition of corruption. Australia's high figure for the bureaucratic voice category may reflect the tail end of its colonial heritage, accentuated by early democratizing forces (Keane 2009). The picture that emerges for Japan is astounding: responses show huge numbers for loyalists, the fewest for corruption, and measurably large numbers for exit. Hirschmann may be correct in saying that loyalty to organizations deteriorating in performance ability is a strength. Loyalty and solidarity from within can convert those docile into those working.

(3) Bureaucratic Voice: Australia, the United States, China, India, Russia, and Japan are ranked in descending order in terms of the response for the bureaucratic voice option. It is not surprising to find that Australia and the United States retain a solid way to governing a stable and yet dynamic society in an industrial democracy. Of little surprise is Japan. Its size is smallish and yet it is on par with the rest on many other terms. Bureaucratic voice is not considered as being sufficiently effective among the Japanese populace. In Japan, action in a written form is limited in frequency. Face-to-face and telephone interactions are regarded as being more polite, more appropriate, and often more effective. In Russia, instead of presenting a written request to bureaucracy, it is more common to engage in direct talks regarding claims and complaints with the president. Also Nakamura (2013) reports that instead of a bureaucratic voice, "direct petition to bribe" does exist. When Vladimir Putin visited a certain place in 2011 and in 2012, one of those who participated in the event twice came up to President Putin and asked him to give him something. Putin, without hesitation, gave an expensive designer watch from his wrist to the participant. In China, not only bureaucratic voice but also anonymous voice is far more frequently deployed through Internet. As freedom of press and speech is suppressed highly in China, Internet has become a formidable instrument for the populace to voice complaints and claims. Yet the regime in enforcing its suppressive standards, reduces or sometimes terminates Internet transactions on a massive scale in a very systematic and tenacious way (The Economist 2013).

(4) Broader Loyalty: Loyalty is a complex matter. Option 1, nothing can be done, is passive. Option 2, wait and hope that things will work out, is a forward-looking option. Options 1 and 2 combined makes up broader loyalty, and is the highest in Japan and the second highest in China. Two former British colonies, India and Australia, both rank third in this area. Two former leaders of a once bipolar world, the United States and Russia, register the lowest in this category.

Japan and China are often traditionally contrasted as being collectivist versus individualist. Yet as the response pattern shows clearly, the majority appears to be loyal, docile, and compliant. If one reflects on the meaning of the loyal voice options, one needs to think about what those who choose these responses will do after exit and voice proliferate in organizations and in society. As Hirschmann's explanation between exit and loyalty, as exit increases in number, the value and weight of loyalty increase. Therefore, one cannot presume that large numbers of loyalists mean high stability and governability. In Japan, for the period between

2006 and 2012, six prime ministers' popularity ratings decreased 3–5% per month after inauguration and within a year or so each rating shrank to 10–15%, queuing the entrance of the next prime minister. This means that voters switch their positions from loyalty to exit steadily and in a short time span (Inoguchi 2013). In China, in a suppressed environment, Internet users have increased rapidly and massively in the 2000s. Although suppression has deepened and further consolidated, social unrest has proliferated.

7.2 Country Analysis

We now turn to the analysis, country by country, of which factors contribute to whatever option a respondent chooses in answering the question. There are six options besides DK (don't know). We name them as Voice 1, Voice 2, Voice 6, Exit 5, Loyalty 2, and Loyalty 3. Explanatory variables consist of the following sets of responses: (A) possession of public utilities, (B) exposure to globalization, (C) satisfaction with aspects of life, (D) trust in social institutions, (E) assessment of government performance, and (F) demographics.

7.2.1 The United States

Use of connections is treated as a type of voice. Contributing to the salience of Voice 1 are: use of Internet, satisfaction with life as a whole, and positive assessment of government performance. American respondents are very firm in their use of Voice 1 as compared to Australian respondents (which equal less than one-half of American respondents in this category) and Japanese respondents (which equal one-sixth of American respondents in this category). American respondents are as affirmative about use of connections as Indian respondents and Chinese respondents. This pattern captures the feature that Amitai Etzioni calls capital corruption in American society.

Writing a letter, voice 4, is the most orthodox and most frequently used voice option in American society. Contributing to this option are: number of public utilities, satisfaction with life, especially public safety and family life, and negative assessment of individuals vis-à-vis government policy or action. The profile for respondents of voice 4 shows a belief in small government, especially public safety, and a satisfaction with family life. Even if household income is not sufficiently satisfactory, the respondent is more or less happy with life and chooses what he or she considers the right option.

Bribe an official, or Voice 6, was not chosen by a statistically sufficiently large number of American respondents. Hence, the exercise of assessing contributing factors has not been done here.

Exit 5 is the option to leave when conditions of an organization or a society declines. Hirschmann (1970) argues that Americans are prone to choosing the exit option. However, this survey demonstrates that this is not the case. Ironically, American respondents are not more prone to resorting to an exit option than Japanese respondents! None of the contributing factors are statistically significant, positive or negative. The profile of those who choose this option include not owning a home, not being satisfied with family life, and neither trusting people nor government.

Loyalty 2, that is, the "nothing can be done" option, registers the smallest number among American respondents, smaller than respondents in the other five societies. The profile of those respondents is: they are not satisfied with household income, they are not satisfied with family life, and they neither trust people not government.

Loyalty 3, that is, wait and hope that things will work out, registers second to the lowest number (after Russian respondents) among the six societies. Does this indicate that Americans are on the whole second in pessimism to the Russians? The antidotes to Russians and Americans in this analysis are Japanese and Indians, in this order. Does this mean that Japanese respondents are the most optimistic in this regard?

7.2.2 Russia

Voice 1, use of connections, is the most popular and overwhelming response among Russian respondents. If Voice 2 (write a letter), Voice 6 (bribe an official), and Voice 1 (use connections) are combined, Russian respondents are the most voice-prone citizens among the six countries. Rose (2013) entitles one of his papers on corruption "By Hook or by Crook." Russia is one of the illustrious societies where by hook or by crook is rampant. Those contributing to the choice of Voice 1 share these traits: satisfaction with friendship, pride in being Russian, and distrust of persons and government. Voice 2, write a letter, is the second popular choice among Russian respondents. Those contributing to this choice also are female, distrust government, and are moderately satisfied with household income. Voice 6, bribe an official, for Russian respondents registers the highest figure among the six countries along with Indian respondents. Those contributing to Voice 6 also share satisfaction with health, trust in people and government, and dissatisfaction with spiritual life.

Exit 5, act without a permit, registers the comparatively highest number for choice among Russian respondents along with Japanese respondents. While Russian respondents apparently choose the exit 5 option after a heavy dose of voice options, Japanese respondents choose the exit 5 option after a heavy dose of loyalty options. Contributing factors are: homeownership, satisfaction with the democratic system, and low level of education. The profile of respondents that choose exit 5 is a broadly self-made person with a dislike for rule and regulations.

Loyalty 2, the nothing can be done option, is an important choice among Russian respondents. Loyalty 3, the wait and hope that things will work out option, is no less an important option. Authoritarian qualities of the Russian political system inculcate and pre-occupy those citizens who choose loyalty options 2 or 3. Contributing factors for those who choose loyalty 2 are: satisfaction with household income, satisfaction with spiritual life, and trust in people and government. In a similar vein, contributing factors for those who select loyalty 3 are: trust in government and positive assessment of the social welfare system. The profile of respondents that choose loyalty 2 is a religious person of frugal income and belief in government. The profile of respondents who choose loyalty 3 is a man or woman of mid-level education who is satisfied with life as a whole and who trust people and government.

7.2.3 Australia

Australian respondents feature what may be called the legacy of British colonial political culture. Voice 4 (write a letter option) is the most popular option, followed by loyalty 3 (wait and hope that things will work out) and by voice 1 (use connections to obtain the permit). Exit 5 (act without a permit) registers a small number. Voice 6 (bribe an official) registers a very small number.

Voice 1, the use connections option, is the third popular choice. Contributing factors for those who select Voice 1 are: heavy Internet users, satisfaction with housing, positive assessment of government performance, and preference for government by experts. The profile of Australian respondents who choose this option looks like a technocrat or businessperson who is satisfied with housing but only moderately satisfied with household income. Voice 4, the write a letter option, is a model response of Australian respondents. Contributing factors for those who choose this option are: dissatisfaction with housing, satisfaction with education, anti-militarism, and strict about not bribing. The profile of Australian respondents for this option is a moderate-income, highly educated, and satisfied with friendship. Voice 6, the bribe an official option, registers such a small number of respondents that further analysis cannot be conducted.

Exit 5, the act without a permit option, is not a large enough sample size to say that statistical significance can be indicated to possibly explanatory variables. Nevertheless, contributing factors for Exit 5 appear to be: dissatisfaction with friendships, distrust in government, and belief in technocrats. The profile of Australian respondents who choose this option is someone who is a loner and who is also frugal due to household income.

Loyalty 2, the nothing can be done option, is a pessimistic version of voice and registers a small number among Australian respondents. Contributing factors for those who choose this option are: dissatisfaction with friendships and dissatisfaction with government performance. The profile of those respondents who choose this option is a passive citizen who is moderately dissatisfied with friends and government performance. Loyalty 3, the wait and hope that things will work out option, is a positive version of the loyalty option. Contributing factors are: satisfaction with household income, satisfaction with health, satisfaction with family life, and satisfaction with the democratic system. The profile of those respondents who choose this option seems to be a happy citizen in harmony with the system.

7.2.4 Japan

Voice 2, the use connections option, does not register a large number among Japanese respondents. Contributing factors to this choice are: non-English speaking, satisfaction with public safety, and male. The profile of those respondents who register this choice seems to be a male citizen who does not speak English and is satisfied with public safety. Voice 4, the write a letter option, is a positive version of voice options. Contributing factors for this choice are: Internet users, English speaking, satisfaction with family life, satisfaction with spiritual life, belief in technocracy, and female. The profile for this category is of a female citizen who is happy with family life and comfortable with technocracy. Voice 6, bribe an official, registers only a small number and, therefore, does not allow us to carry out further analysis.

Exit 5, the act without a permit option, registers a small number among Japanese respondents. But compared among the six societies, Japan is pronounced by the high figure of this option next to Russia. This is a small surprise because Japanese respondents tend to be portrayed in Western literature as predominantly loyal and conformist. This figure reveals another aspect of Japanese respondents. Just like in the traditional play of Noh, actors maintain unchanging facial and physical expressions for a time, but at a certain moment, suddenly not only facial and physical but also phonetical expressions change and the whole tempo of expressions quickens.

Loyalty 2, the nothing can be done option, is a passive version of loyalty. Loyalty 3 (wait and hope that things will work out) is a positive version of voice options. Both register the largest and second largest numbers among Japanese respondents. Hirschmann (1970) perceptively observes that out of those who choose loyalty a strong voice emerges during the really difficult moments of organizations or societies because of their long loyal solidarity. They would say that solidarity is strength. Contributing factors for loyalty 2 option are: frequent participation in national elections, belief in citizen's impotence, and lower level of education. The profile of those respondents who register this choice is a lower income citizen with belief in his or her impotence in society. Contributing factors for loyalty 3 are: perceived inability of comprehending politics, satisfaction with friendships, and moderate assessment of government performance. The profile of those respondents of this choice seems to be a citizen with a medium level of education and wealth and little exposure to globalization in life.

7.2.5 China

A glance at the frequency table of exit, voice, and loyalty for Chinese respondents enables us to see the nearly equal frequency of voice 2, voice 4, loyalty 2, and loyalty 3. Against this nearly equal frequency of these choices, two figures stand out: First, voice 5 registers a very small figure amid all the government's slogans on curtailing bribery; and second, exit 5 registers a very small figure amid all the government's slogans on rule of law. One conjecture is that, in a very authoritarian system, even the mere mention of giving a bribe or breaking the law might well induce the police or taxation officer to act against the person uttering such taboo words, even if only responding to a survey. In other words, who knows if an interviewer may convey to a police or taxation officer the responses of surveyed individuals who favor bribery or breaking the law? Therefore, we suspect that voice 6 and exit 5 are, more than likely, instinctually suppressed by respondents in a very authoritarian society.

Voice 1, the use connections option, and voice 4, the write a letter option, register an equally large number of responses, whereas voice 6, the bribe an official option, registers a very small figure. What is important to note here, is how much voice 2 is understood to be part of corruption or something else. Reviewing the comparative figures of voice 1 across the six nations enables us to present the following proposition: voice 1 (use connections to obtain a permit) is interpreted and understood very differently by respondents in the six societies. The difference stems from how the phrase, use connections, is understood. Ranking the six societies by the size of voice 1 gives us the following ranking: Russia, India, the United States, China, Australia, and Japan. China is placed in the middle, sandwiched by two sets of qualitatively different free societies: on the one side are Russia, India, and the United States, and on the other side are Australia and Japan. The former three countries are broadly free societies where to "use connections" does not necessarily imply corruption as prohibited by law. In contrast, in the latter two countries, to "use connections" is more consciously associated with corruption. Australia, aside from practice, is deeply influenced by the political culture inherited from the British colonial elite culture of strict moral conduct. Japan, again aside somewhat from practice, is deeply penetrated by a political culture inherited from Tokugawa samurai ethos of enduring moral rectitude, even under difficult circumstances.

Exit 5, the act without a permit option, registers a small number when practice is to the contrary.

Loyalty 1, the nothing can be done option, elicits a fairly large number, suggesting a pervasive feeling that nothing can be done when government says no. Loyalty 2, the wait and hope that things will work out option, registers a large number, suggesting that conformism to the system is an important element of political culture under communism.

In answering the question, we might as well consider the meaning of the high or low frequency of "don't know" (DK) among Chinese and Indian respondents. Contrasting figures are found among American, Russian, and Japanese respondents, which might indicate a wavering in decision between which option they should choose. Those DK respondents may well have been thinking about choosing non-DK options, be they exit, voice, or loyalty. Yet at the last moment, they chose the DK response to alleviate the psychological dissonance that might otherwise have arisen.

7.2.6 India

A glance at the frequency table of Indian choices enables us to observe the following: Whatever their choice, Indian citizens choose more positive and optimistic versions of exit, voice, and loyalty. Hence, exit 5 is the largest in size among the six countries. Hence, loyalty 3, the wait and hope that things will work out option, registers a larger figure than loyalty 2 (nothing can be done). Hence, voice 1, the use connections option, is larger than voice 4, the write a letter option. Rose's phrase, by hook or by crook, finds a most pro-active version among Indian respondents.

Voice 1, the use connections option, registers the highest figure. How to differentiate between voice 1 and voice 6 when responding to the question might not be easy for Indian citizens. Even voice 4 (write a letter) might be possibly a first step in moving toward voice 1 (use connections) and voice 6 (bribe an official).

Loyalty 2 (nothing can be done) is a passive version of the loyalty option, whereas loyalty 3 (wait and hope that things will work out) is a positive and optimistic version.

7.3 Concluding Remarks

We used the *AsiaBarometer Survey* data to analyze patterns of citizen responses to a situation where a citizen's request for a government permit is an official's callous response, "Just be patient and wait." In 2008, the *AsiaBarometer Survey* executed surveys in the Asian countries of Japan, China, and India and, in three adjacent countries of Asia, the United States, Russia, and Australia. First, country by country and cross-nationally, a number of evidence-based findings may require revisions to some of the folklore narratives about corruption and related political practice.

(1) Folklore theory says that Americans prefer voice to loyalty. However, the survey data tell us that American appear more conformist than they want to portray themselves.
(2) Folklore theory says that Americans prefer exit to voice. However, the survey data tell us that they look as if they voice more vociferously than they want to portray themselves.
(3) Folklore theory says that Americans portray themselves as being free from bribery. However, the survey data tell us that Americans appear to "use connections" to distinguish themselves from putatively more bribery-prone peoples. The fact that the response choice, don't know, registers very highly may suggest a possible cognitive dissonance when they chose "use connection."
(4) Folklore theory says that Russians carry out whatever they want to do, by hook or by crook, whether it is exit, voice, or loyalty. However, the survey data tell us that there are a sizable number of loyalists.
(5) Folklore theory says that under "imperial democracy," loyalty is a strong current among Russians. Some of them, however, smoothly change their

position to voice or exit when conditions are suitable. For example, a petitioner directly demanding President Vladimir Putin give him a luxurious watch from his wrist or a petitioner setting himself on fire at the Kremlin gates after unsuccessfully petitioning the President.

(6) Folklore theory says that Australians portray themselves as robust democrats who do not resort to duplicitous practices. However, the survey data tell us that there appear to be more voices that verge on the act of bribery.

(7) Folklore theory says that Japanese portray themselves as loyalists in the system. However, the survey data tell us that there are a small but cross-nationally comparatively large number of responses that choose the exit option.

(8) Folklore theory says that Japanese are like sticky rice, meaning that they are tenacious loyalist. However, the survey data tell us that respondents register a massive and swift shift in their position at the last moment.

(9) Folklore theory says that Chinese portray themselves as vociferously choosing voice. However, the survey data tell us that a sizable number are loyalists.

(10) Folklore theory says that Chinese portray themselves as assertive individualists. However, the survey data tell us that there is a strong sense of self-restraint when they hesitate to choose "bribe an official" and "act without a permit."

(11) Folklore theory says that Indians portray themselves as assertive individualists. However, the survey data tell us that there are a very large number of loyalists who believe their predicament to be their destiny.

(12) Folklore theory says that Indians are vociferous in choosing voice. However, the survey data tell us that there is a strong sense of self-restraint when they hesitate to choose "bribe an official" and "act without a permit."

Second, given the dynamic diversity observed in the survey data of the six societies, the comparative study of individual choices in organizational decline or economic austerity needs to move in the direction of sub-national and supra-national directions of polling and analysis. We want to emphasize polling as well, in that if global analysis has to be conducted, global polling (Gilani 2013) is a must. Cross-national comparisons reveal many things. But as long as they are based on national polling, they have limits. What we are interested in is a global analysis of how people respond to the predicament of being callously told by an official to "just be patient and wait." Cross-national comparisons based on a set of national polling tend to exaggerate what is called national characters. Global polling is a method of polling in an era of deep globalization. It is not an era of a sovereign nation state for which national polling is most appropriate. Merits and demerits of national and global (regional) polling still remain to be examined, preferably empirically as well.

Third, given the enormous linguistic diversity and culture complicity in 29 Asian societies, we must be sensitive to the local language versions in 35 non-English languages.

Fourth, Richard Rose kindly commented on our draft paper to say that the Almond/Verba framework of civic culture is no less applicable to our data than the framework of Hirschmann (Rose 2013). We are working on how the Almond/Verba framework can be rendered to our kind of analysis with our data across the six societies.

Fifth, Taiki Takahashi, Hokkaido University (biophysics), brought our attention to Scott Gehlbach's formal model of exit and voice, whereby he formulated "loyalty as exit tax" and "loyalty as voice subsidy" in formulating loyalty's dual functions on citizen welfare (Gehlbach 2006). We are working on whether these two kinds of loyalty (exit tax and voice subsidy) can be observed in our empirical data and how his model can be tested on our data.

Appendix 1: Coding of Dependent Variables and Independent Variables

List of dependent variables

Voice1 = 1 if the respondent chooses (1) for the following question; *Voice1* = 0 otherwise
Voice4 = 1 if the respondent chooses (4) for the following question; *Voice4* = 0 otherwise
Voice6 = 1 if the respondent chooses (6) for the following question; *Voice6* = 0 otherwise
Exit5 = 1 if the respondent chooses (5) for the following question; *Exit5* = 0 otherwise
Loyalty2 = 1 if the respondent chooses (2) for the following question; *Royalty2* = 0 otherwise
Loyalty3 = 1 if the respondent chooses 3 for the following question; *Royalty3* = 0 otherwise

Question: What should a person who needs a government permit do if the response of the official handling the application is: "just be patient and wait?"

(1) Use connections to obtain the permit
(2) Nothing can be done
(3) Wait and hope that things will work out
(4) Write a letter
(5) Act without a permit
(6) Bribe an official
(7) Don't know.

List of independent variables

*Independent variables consist of six groups:

(A) Lifestyles
(B) Exposure to globalization
(C) Satisfaction with aspects of life
(D) Trust in social institution
(E) Assessment of government performance
(F) Demographics.

(A) Lifestyles

Number of public utilities counts the number of public utilities the household of the respondents have of the following public utilities: public water supply; electricity; liquefied petroleum gas (LPG), piped gas; fixed-line phone; mobile phone; facsimile; cable TV.

Homeownership = 1 if the respondent lives in own house, not rented house.

Pray takes on the values from 1 to 5 for question: How often do you pray or meditate? The coding is as follows: Daily = 5; Weekly = 4; Monthly = 3; On special occasions = 2; Never = 1.

National elections takes on the values from 1 to 5 for question: How often do you vote in national election? The coding is as follows: Every time = 5; Most of the time = 4; Sometimes = 3; Rarely = 2; Never voted = 1.

Proud takes on the values from 1 to 5 as follows for question: How proud are you of being [YOUR COUNTRY'S PEOPLE]?: Very proud = 4; Somewhat proud = 3; Not really proud = 2; Not proud at all = 1.

(B) Exposure to globalization

Internet takes the values from 1 to 5 for question: How often do you view Internet web pages by computers? The coding is as follows: Almost every day = 5; Several times a week = 4; Several times a month = 3; Seldom = 2; Never = 1.

Living internationally counts the number of items that apply to the respondent in question: Which, if any, of the following statements apply to you?

The six items are the following: (1) A member of my family or a relative lives in another country; (2) I have traveled abroad at least three times in the past three years, on holiday or for business purposes; (3) I have friends from other country who are in [YOUR COUNTRY]; (4) I often watch foreign-produced programs on TV; (5) I often communicate with people in other countries via the Internet or email; (6) My job involves contact with organizations or people in other countries.

In Russia, the translations of the words "another country," "abroad," "other counties," and "foreign" in the question specifically excluded countries of former Soviet Union to clarify the definition.

English ability takes the values from 1 to 4 for question: How well do you speak English? The coding is as follows: I can speak English fluently = 4; I can speak it well enough to get by in daily life = 3; Very little = 2; Not at all = 1.

(C) Satisfaction with aspects of life

Housing takes on the values from 1 to 5 for question: Please tell me how satisfied or dissatisfied you are with your housing. The coding is as follows: Very satisfied = 5; Somewhat satisfied = 4; Neither satisfied nor dissatisfied = 3; Somewhat dissatisfied = 2; Very dissatisfied = 1.

Friendships take on the values from 1 to 5 for question: Please tell me how satisfied or dissatisfied you are with your friendships. The coding is as follows: Very satisfied = 5; Somewhat satisfied = 4; Neither satisfied nor dissatisfied = 3; Somewhat dissatisfied = 2; Very dissatisfied = 1.

Marriage takes on the values from 1 to 5 for question: Please tell me how satisfied or dissatisfied you are with your marriage. The coding is as follows: Very satisfied = 5; Somewhat satisfied = 4; Neither satisfied nor dissatisfied = 3; Somewhat dissatisfied = 2; Very dissatisfied = 1.

Standard of living takes on the values from 1 to 5 for question: Please tell me how satisfied or dissatisfied you are with the standard of living. The coding is as follows: Very satisfied = 5; Somewhat satisfied = 4; Neither satisfied nor dissatisfied = 3; Somewhat dissatisfied = 2; Very dissatisfied = 1.

Household income takes on the values from 1 to 5 for question: Please tell me how satisfied or dissatisfied you are with household income. The coding is as follows: Very satisfied = 5; Somewhat satisfied = 4; Neither satisfied nor dissatisfied = 3; Somewhat dissatisfied = 2; Very dissatisfied = 1.

Health takes on the values from 1 to 5 for question: Please tell me how satisfied or dissatisfied you are with your health. The coding is as follows: Very satisfied = 5; Somewhat satisfied = 4; Neither satisfied nor dissatisfied = 3; Somewhat dissatisfied = 2; Very dissatisfied = 1.

Education takes on the values from 1 to 5 for Q8: Please tell me how satisfied or dissatisfied you are with education. The coding is as follows: Very satisfied = 5; Somewhat satisfied = 4; Neither satisfied nor dissatisfied = 3; Somewhat dissatisfied = 2; Very dissatisfied = 1.

Neighbors takes on the values from 1 to 5 for question: Please tell me how satisfied or dissatisfied you are with neighbors. The coding is as follows: Very satisfied = 5; Somewhat satisfied = 4; Neither satisfied nor dissatisfied = 3; Somewhat dissatisfied = 2; Very dissatisfied = 1.

Public safety takes on the values from 1 to 5 for question: Please tell me how satisfied or dissatisfied you are with public safety. The coding is as follows: Very satisfied = 5; Somewhat satisfied = 4; Neither satisfied nor dissatisfied = 3; Somewhat dissatisfied = 2; Very dissatisfied = 1.

The condition of the environment takes on the values from 1 to 5 for question: Please tell me how satisfied or dissatisfied you are with the condition of the environment. The coding is as follows: Very satisfied = 5; Somewhat satisfied = 4; Neither satisfied nor dissatisfied = 3; Somewhat dissatisfied = 2; Very dissatisfied = 1.

Social welfare system takes on the values from 1 to 5 for question: Please tell me how satisfied or dissatisfied you are with the social welfare system. The coding is as follows: Very satisfied = 5; Somewhat satisfied = 4; Neither satisfied nor dissatisfied = 3; Somewhat dissatisfied = 2; Very dissatisfied = 1.

The democratic system takes on the values from 1 to 5 for Q8: Please tell me how satisfied or dissatisfied you are with the democratic system. The coding is as follows: Very satisfied = 5; Somewhat satisfied = 4; Neither satisfied nor dissatisfied = 3; Somewhat dissatisfied = 2; Very dissatisfied = 1.

Family life takes on the values from 1 to 5 for question: Please tell me how satisfied or dissatisfied you are with family life. The coding is as follows: Very satisfied = 5; Somewhat satisfied = 4; Neither satisfied nor dissatisfied = 3; Somewhat dissatisfied = 2; Very dissatisfied = 1.

Leisure takes on the values from 1 to 5 for question: Please tell me how satisfied or dissatisfied you are with leisure. The coding is as follows: Very satisfied = 5; Somewhat satisfied = 4; Neither satisfied nor dissatisfied = 3; Somewhat dissatisfied = 2; Very dissatisfied = 1.

Spiritual life takes on the values from 1 to 5 for question: Please tell me how satisfied or dissatisfied you are with spiritual life. The coding is as follows: Very satisfied = 5; Somewhat satisfied = 4; Neither satisfied nor dissatisfied = 3; Somewhat dissatisfied = 2; Very dissatisfied = 1.

Your life as a whole takes on the values from 1 to 5 for question: Please tell me how satisfied or dissatisfied you are with your life as a whole. The coding is as follows: Very satisfied = 5; Somewhat satisfied = 4; Neither satisfied nor dissatisfied = 3; Somewhat dissatisfied = 2; Very dissatisfied = 1.

Happiness takes on the values from 1 to 5 for question: All things considered, would you say that you are happy these days? The coding is as follows: Very happy = 5; Quite happy = 4; Neither happy nor unhappy = 3; Not too happy = 2; Very unhappy = 1.

(D) Trust in social institution

Trust generally = 1 if the respondent thinks that most people can be trusted for question: Generally, do you think people can be trusted or do you think that you can't be too careful in dealing with people (that it pays to be wary of people)?; 0 otherwise.

Trust the central government takes on the values from 1 to 4 for question: "Please indicate to what extent you trust the central government to operate in the best interests of society. If you don't know what to reply or have no particular opinion, please say so." The coding is as follows: Trust a lot = 4; Trust to a degree = 3; Don't really trust = 2; Don't trust at all = 1.

Trust the army takes on the values from 1 to 4 for question: "Please indicate to what extent you trust the army to operate in the best interests of society. If you don't know what to reply or have no particular opinion, please say so." The coding is as follows: Trust a lot = 4; Trust to a degree = 3; Don't really trust = 2; Don't trust at all = 1.

Trust the legal system takes on the values from 1 to 4 for question: "Please indicate to what extent you trust the legal system to operate in the best interests of society. If you don't know what to reply or have no particular opinion, please say so." The coding is as follows: Trust a lot = 4; Trust to a degree = 3; Don't really trust = 2; Don't trust at all = 1.

Trust the police takes on the values from 1 to 4 for question: "Please indicate to what extent you trust the police to operate in the best interests of society. If you don't know what to reply or have no particular opinion, please say so." The coding is as follows: Trust a lot = 4; Trust to a degree = 3; Don't really trust = 2; Don't trust at all = 1.

(E) Assessment of government performance

Worry about corruption = 1 if the respondent worries about corruption in question: "Which, if any, of the following issues cause you great worry? Please choose all issues that cause you serious worry."

Political corruption takes on the values from 1 to 4 for question: How well do you think the [YOUR COUNTRY'S] government is dealing with political corruption. The coding is as follows: Very well = 4; Fairly well = 3; Not so well = 2; Not well at all = 1.

Duty to vote takes on the values from 1 to 5 for question: "I am going to read out some statements about society and politics. Please indicate how much you agree or disagree with the statement: Citizens have a duty to vote in elections." The coding is as follows: Strongly agree = 5; Agree = 4; Neither agree nor disagree = 3; Disagree = 2; Strongly disagree = 1.

Widespread corruption takes on the values from 1 to 5 for question: "I am going to read out some statements about society and politics. Please indicate how much you agree or disagree with the statement: There is widespread corruption among those who govern the country." The coding is as follows: Strongly agree = 5; Agree = 4; Neither agree nor disagree = 3; Disagree = 2; Strongly disagree = 1.

No power takes on the values from 1 to 5 for question: "I am going to read out some statements about society and politics. Please indicate how much you agree or disagree with the statement Generally speaking, people like me don't have the power to influence government policy or actions." The coding is as follows: Strongly agree = 5; Agree = 4; Neither agree nor disagree = 3; Disagree = 2; Strongly disagree = 1.

Complicated takes on the values from 1 to 5 for question: "I am going to read out some statements about society and politics. Please indicate how much you agree or disagree with the statement: Politics and government are so complicated that sometimes I don't understand what's happening." The coding is as follows: Strongly agree = 5; Agree = 4; Neither agree nor disagree = 3; Disagree = 2; Strongly disagree = 1.

No matter whether I vote takes on the values from 1 to 5 for question: "I am going to read out some statements about society and politics. Please indicate how much you agree or disagree with the statement: Since so many people vote in elections, it really doesn't matter whether I vote or not." The coding is as follows: Strongly agree = 5; Agree = 4; Neither agree nor disagree = 3; Disagree = 2; Strongly disagree = 1.

Stop thinking takes on the values from 1 to 5 for question: "I am going to read out some statements about society and politics. Please indicate how much you agree or disagree with the statement: Generally speaking, the people who are elected to the [NATIONAL PARLIAMENT] stop thinking about the public once they're elected." The coding is as follows: Strongly agree = 5; Agree = 4; Neither agree nor disagree = 3; Disagree = 2; Strongly disagree = 1.

Pay little attention takes on the values from 1 to 5 for question: I am going to read out some statements about society and politics. Please indicate how much you agree or disagree with the statement: Government officials pay little attention to what citizens like me think." The coding is as follows: Strongly agree = 5; Agree = 4; Neither agree nor disagree = 3; Disagree = 2; Strongly disagree = 1.

Experts takes on the values from 1 to 3 for question: "I'm going to describe various types of political systems. Please indicate whether you think it would be very good, fairly good or bad for this country for a system whereby decisions affecting the country are made by experts (such as bureaucrats with expertise in a particular field) according to what they think is best for the country." The coding is as follows: Very good = 3; Fairly good = 2; Bad = 1.

Bribe takes on the values from 1 to 10 for question: Please tell me whether you think it can always be justified, never be justified, or something in between for the statement: Someone accepting a bribe in the course of their duties. This variable takes on the values from 1 to 10. 1 corresponds to "Never justifiable" and 10 corresponds to "Always justifiable."

(F) Demographics

Female = 1 if the respondent is female; 0 if male.

Age is the age of the respondent.

Level of education is the highest level of education the respondent completed. This variable takes on the values from 1 to 5 from low to high. 1 corresponds to either no formal education or illiterate.

Married = 1 if the marital status of the respondent is married; 0 otherwise.

Income is the level of household income of the respondent. The variable takes on the values from 1(low) to 3(high).

Appendix 2: Estimation Results (Logit Regression)

US

Dependent variable	Voice 1		Voice 4		Voice 6		Exit 5		Loyalty 2		Loyalty 3	
Independent variables	Coeff.	z-stat.	Coeff.	z-stat.	Coeff.	z-stat.	Coeff.	z-stat.	Coeff.	z-stat.	Coeff.	z-stat.
(A) Lifestyles												
Number of public utilities	0.07	0.6	−0.27	(−2.35)[a]	–	–	0.04	0.14	0.53	(2.25)[a]	0.14	0.96
Homeownership	−0.01	−0.02	0.29	0.88	–	–	−0.59	−0.67	−0.80	−1.27	−0.16	−0.39
Pray	−0.13	−1.3	0.03	0.28	–	–	−0.13	−0.49	−0.12	−0.62	0.15	1.28
National elections	0.19	1.31	−0.16	−1.22	–	–	0.59	1.38	0.52	1.69	−0.14	−0.89
Proud	0.01	0.03	−0.06	−0.28	–	–	0.56	0.8	−0.26	−0.52	0.24	0.73
(B) Exposure to globalization												
Internet	0.24	(2.35)[a]	0.09	0.95	–	–	0.50	1.5	−0.36	−1.87	−0.29	(−2.75)[b]
Living internationally	0.10	1.28	0.02	0.27	–	–	−0.33	−1.16	−0.14	−0.77	−0.06	−0.57
English ability	0.16	0.29	0.88	1.27	–	–	−1.82	−1.73	−0.50	−0.67	−0.17	−0.28
(C) Satisfaction with aspects of life												
Housing	−0.16	−0.83	0.17	0.91	–	–	0.11	0.2	−0.45	−1.14	−0.03	−0.13
Friendships	0.10	0.48	−0.11	−0.53	–	–	0.06	0.09	0.01	0.04	−0.17	−0.67
Standard of living	−0.41	−1.94	0.04	0.23	–	–	−0.50	−0.84	0.44	1.02	0.50	(1.97)[a]
Household income	0.26	1.45	−0.14	−0.82	–	–	0.06	0.12	1.39	(3.12)[b]	−0.38	−1.93
Health	−0.30	−1.85	−0.05	−0.31	–	–	0.44	0.81	0.10	0.31	0.17	0.91
Education	0.21	1.1	−0.21	−1.3	–	–	0.51	0.82	0.55	1.31	−0.23	−1.16
Job	0.08	0.55	−0.19	−1.43	–	–	0.44	0.95	−0.20	−0.68	0.35	1.88
Neighbors	0.10	0.64	−0.02	−0.16	–	–	−0.31	−0.75	0.01	0.03	0.05	0.27
Public safety	−0.13	−0.9	0.29	(2.00)[a]	–	–	−0.76	−1.7	−0.03	−0.08	−0.09	−0.46

(continued)

(continued)

Dependent variable	Voice 1		Voice 4		Voice 6		Exit 5		Loyalty 2		Loyalty 3	
Independent variables	Coeff.	z-stat.	Coeff.	z-stat.	Coeff.	z-stat.	Coeff.	z-stat.	Coeff.	z-stat.	Coeff.	z-stat.
The condition of the environment	−0.19	−1.31	−0.11	−0.85	–	–	0.40	0.95	0.15	0.5	0.24	1.47
Social welfare system	0.14	0.9	−0.12	−0.87	–	–	−0.49	−1.04	−0.23	−0.8	0.02	0.11
The democratic system	−0.08	−0.6	0.09	0.71	–	–	0.35	0.91	0.41	1.44	−0.07	−0.42
Family life	−0.22	−1.21	0.44	(2.50)[a]	–	–	−0.59	−1.25	−1.46	(−3.72)[b]	0.11	0.53
Leisure	−0.11	−0.62	−0.07	−0.44	–	–	−0.55	−1.11	0.14	0.33	0.27	1.23
Spiritual life	0.07	0.38	−0.12	−0.7	–	–	−0.13	−0.3	0.76	1.86	−0.21	−0.97
Your life as a whole	0.67	(2.45)[a]	−0.14	−0.57	–	–	1.14	1.42	−0.85	−1.63	−0.35	−1.21
Happiness	0.10	0.52	0.05	0.27	–	–	0.01	0.03	−0.03	−0.09	−0.32	−1.41
(D) Trust in social institution												
Trust generally	−0.03	−0.1	−0.01	−0.06	–	–	−0.77	−1.09	−0.71	−1.4	0.31	1
Trust the central government	−0.002	−0.01	0.15	0.77	–	–	−0.41	−0.72	−0.21	−0.46	−0.02	−0.09
Trust the army	0.04	0.19	−0.04	−0.19	–	–	0.31	0.6	0.07	0.17	−0.05	−0.23
Trust the legal system	0.03	0.15	0.01	0.06	–	–	−0.13	−0.24	0.45	1.13	−−0.33	−1.42
Trust the police	−0.32	−1.58	0.01	0.04	–	–	−0.59	−0.98	0.44	1.13	0.42	1.77
(E) Assessment of government performance												
Worry about corruption	0.11	0.39	−0.17	−0.67	–	–	−0.75	−0.84	0.50	1.02	−0.06	−0.19
Political corruption	0.39	(2.26)[a]	−0.29	−1.72	–	–	−0.38	−0.83	−0.18	−0.59	0.18	0.92
Duty to vote	−0.19	−1.02	0.34	1.84	–	–	−0.61	−1.18	−0.04	−0.11	−0.35	−1.66
Widespread corruption	−0.02	−0.12	0.20	1.4	–	–	−0.76	−1.82	−0.87	(−2.83)[b]	0.07	0.4
No power	0.19	1.36	−0.26	(−2.02)[a]	–	–	0.45	1.26	−0.10	−0.35	0.12	0.76
Complicated	0.10	0.8	−0.06	−0.58	–	–	−0.11	−0.37	0.07	0.29	−0.06	−0.42
No matter whether vote	0.07	0.5	−0.20	−1.43	–	–	0.59	1.51	0.70	(2.74)[b]	−0.25	−1.43
Stop thinking	−0.01	−0.07	−0.12	−0.75	–	–	−0.36	−0.63	1.11	(2.85)[b]	−0.07	−0.36

(continued)

(continued)

Dependent variable	Voice 1		Voice 4		Voice 6		Exit 5		Loyalty 2		Loyalty 3	
Independent variables	Coeff.	z-stat.	Coeff.	z-stat.	Coeff.	z-stat.	Coeff.	z-stat.	Coeff.	z-stat.	Coeff.	z-stat.
Pay little attention	−0.36	(−2.02)[a]	0.22	1.34	–	–	0.48	0.88	0.25	0.67	−0.03	−0.14
Experts	−0.18	−0.89	0.26	1.38	–	–	−0.86	−1.2	0.50	1.47	−0.19	−0.78
Bribe	−0.05	−0.53	−0.07	−0.74	–	–	0.33	1.53	−0.23	−1.28	−0.01	−0.12
(F) Demographics												
Female	−0.25	−1.03	0.37	1.61	–	–	0.29	0.42	0.18	0.4	−0.07	−0.26
Age	−0.01	0.82	0.01	0.71	–	–	0.01	0.34	−0.08	(−3.28)[b]	0.01	0.66
Level of education	−0.13	−0.84	−0.09	−0.59	–	–	0.68	1.6	−0.02	−0.05	0.09	0.5
Married	−0.34	−1.16	0.13	0.48	–	–	0.05	0.06	0.51	0.88	0.11	0.32
Income	0.12	1.79	0.003	0.04	–	–	−0.14	−0.77	−0.29	(−2.06)[a]	−0.08	−0.98
Constant	−2.80	−1.01	−3.29	−1.04	–	–	−0.12	−0.02	−5.50	−1.3	0.76	0.24
n	441		441		–		441		441		441	
Pseudo R squared	0.1381		0.1126		–		0.3543		0.3698		0.1281	

Note [a]5% significance level; [b]1% significance levels

Russia

Dependent variable	Voice 1		Voice 4		Voice 6		Exit 5		Loyalty 2		Loyalty 3	
Independent variables	Coeff.	z-stat.	Coeff.	z-stat.	Coeff.	z-stat.	Coeff.	z-stat.	Coeff.	z-stat.	Coeff.	z-stat.
(A) Lifestyles												
Number of public utilities	0.11	0.77	−0.32	−1.69	1.44	1.96	0.10	0.19	−0.48	−1.61	0.33	1.57
Homeownership	−0.07	−0.21	−0.32	−0.7	−0.75	−0.65	2.28	1.54	0.61	0.79	−0.04	−0.08
Pray	−0.21	−1.92	0.23	1.74	−0.72	−1.43	0.54	1.5	−0.16	−0.77	0.01	0.08
National elections	0.02	0.14	−0.29	−1.41	−1.12	−1.8	−0.02	−0.03	0.38	1.1	0.25	1.08
Proud	0.40	(2.16)[a]	−0.39	−1.56	−2.35	(−2.76)[b]	0.20	0.35	−0.38	−1.01	0.26	0.87

(continued)

(continued)

Dependent variable	Voice 1		Voice 4		Voice 6		Exit 5		Loyalty 2		Loyalty 3	
Independent variables	Coeff.	z-stat.	Coeff.	z-stat.	Coeff.	z-stat.	Coeff.	z-stat.	Coeff.	z-stat.	Coeff.	z-stat.
(B) Exposure to globalization												
Internet	0.03	0.28	0.09	0.6	0.41	0.91	−3.26	(−2.64)[b]	0.32	1.26	−0.05	−0.27
Living internationally	−0.10	−0.58	−0.12	−0.52	0.14	0.26	1.86	1.81	−0.35	−0.87	0.32	1.14
English ability	0.19	0.82	−0.39	−1.31	0.39	0.47	0.30	0.31	−0.60	−1.29	0.18	0.48
(C) Satisfaction with aspects of life												
Housing	−0.13	−0.84	−0.11	−0.56	−0.17	−0.28	1.21	(2.09)[a]	−0.17	−0.55	0.13	0.55
Friendships	0.44	(2.08)[a]	0.25	0.85	−1.33	−1.81	−0.53	−0.6	−0.27	−0.68	−0.46	−1.57
Standard of living	0.39	1.84	−0.11	−0.38	−0.55	−0.73	−1.08	−1.57	−0.54	−1.15	−0.01	−0.02
Household income	−0.32	−1.76	0.30	1.33	0.10	0.16	1.18	1.76	0.93	(2.25)[a]	−0.02	−0.08
Health	−0.03	−0.16	−0.24	−1.12	2.14	(2.42)[a]	0.72	1.15	0.19	0.58	−0.23	−0.96
Education	−0.12	−0.66	0.17	0.73	−1.14	−1.51	0.78	1.07	0.06	0.2	0.14	0.54
Job	−0.04	−0.23	−0.09	−0.38	1.01	1.52	−0.61	−0.87	0.12	0.34	−0.04	−0.15
Neighbors	−0.30	−1.19	0.52	1.63	2.31	1.91	−0.73	−0.82	−1.92	(−3.35)[b]	0.45	1.19
Public safety	0.20	1.19	0.20	0.85	0.05	0.09	−0.38	−0.7	0.004	0.01	−0.32	−1.27
The condition of the environment	−0.01	−0.06	0.14	0.63	−1.21	−1.74	0.57	1	−0.65	−1.77	−0.33	−1.39
Social welfare system	−0.27	−1.53	−0.38	−1.66	0.62	1.05	−1.23	−1.56	0.65	1.84	0.64	(2.46)[a]
The democratic system	0.29	1.73	0.09	0.4	−0.32	−0.56	1.89	(2.23)[a]	−0.33	−0.96	−0.25	−0.96
Family life	−0.26	−1.33	−0.37	−1.49	0.37	0.6	0.61	0.75	0.56	1.37	0.49	1.55
Leisure	0.05	0.27	0.08	0.32	−0.14	−0.2	0.07	0.1	0.37	0.89	−0.17	−0.63
Spiritual life	0.27	1.15	−0.14	−0.5	−2.00	(−2.39)[a]	−1.31	−1.59	1.50	(2.63)[b]	−0.54	−1.7
Your life as a whole	0.06	0.22	−0.41	−1.14	0.78	0.91	1.81	1.71	−1.11	−1.72	0.54	1.28
Happiness	−0.24	−1.07	0.46	1.58	−0.92	−1.14	−1.47	−1.61	0.50	1.09	−0.03	−0.08

(continued)

(continued)

Dependent variable	Voice 1		Voice 4		Voice 6		Exit 5		Loyalty 2		Loyalty 3	
Independent variables	Coeff.	z-stat.	Coeff.	z-stat.	Coeff.	z-stat.	Coeff.	z-stat.	Coeff.	z-stat.	Coeff.	z-stat.
(D) Trust in social institution												
Trust generally	−0.59	(−2.09)[a]	0.68	1.88	3.00	(2.18)[a]	−1.36	−1.26	0.83	1.47	0.10	0.24
Trust the central government	−0.30	−1.4	−0.27	−0.97	1.70	(2.02)[a]	−0.46	−0.67	1.21	(2.58)[a]	0.14	0.43
Trust the army	−0.07	−0.35	0.10	0.4	−0.22	−0.33	0.68	0.75	0.66	1.58	0.08	0.28
Trust the legal system	−0.45	−1.85	−0.21	−0.65	−1.36	−1.46	−0.30	−0.37	0.56	1	0.70	1.96
Trust the police	0.48	1.9	0.01	0.04	0.14	0.13	−1.03	−1.11	−1.04	−1.94	−0.41	−1.14
(E) Assessment of government performance												
Worry about corruption	0.34	1.18	−0.18	−0.46	0.01	0.01	−2.21	−1.81	−1.60	(−2.42)[a]	0.23	0.51
Political corruption	−0.41	−1.96	0.40	1.43	0.17	0.23	0.77	1.15	−0.33	−0.8	−0.10	−0.36
Duty to vote	0.06	0.31	0.40	1.66	0.12	0.24	−0.78	−1.22	0.34	0.85	−0.31	−1.16
Widespread corruption	−0.38	(−2.06)[a]	0.20	0.82	1.77	(2.37)[a]	1.47	1.83	0.02	0.06	−0.18	−0.7
No power	0.31	(2.10)[a]	−0.19	−1.13	−1.31	(−2.21)[a]	−1.05	−1.75	0.29	0.93	−0.16	−0.72
Complicated	−0.08	0.63	−0.02	−0.13	0.63	1.08	−1.42	(−2.36)[a]	0.11	0.35	0.39	1.75
No matter whether vote	−0.06	0.41	−0.17	−0.97	0.34	0.61	1.11	1.81	−0.11	−0.39	0.11	0.5
Stop thinking	0.22	1.02	0.48	1.67	−1.31	−1.7	−0.63	−0.8	−0.03	−0.08	−0.49	−1.63
Pay little attention	−0.31	1.3	−0.70	(−2.26)[a]	1.52	1.67	1.68	1.64	0.44	0.86	0.64	1.8
Experts	0.18	0.83	−0.19	−0.68	0.46	0.6	−0.25	−0.39	0.42	0.88	0.14	0.42
Bribe	−0.07	0.96	−0.20	−1.94	0.04	0.17	0.19	0.97	0.40	(2.53)[a]	0.03	0.26
(F) Demographics												
Female	−0.23	−0.83	1.00	(2.62)[b]	−2.07	−1.86	−0.81	−0.92	0.25	0.41	−0.25	−0.58
Age	−0.02	−1.24	0.02	1.24	0.03	0.54	−0.04	−0.84	0.03	1.23	−0.01	−0.39
Level of education	0.14	0.96	0.26	1.35	−0.36	−0.64	−2.08	(−2.46)[a]	0.13	0.43	−0.32	−1.35
Married	0.33	1.11	0.38	0.9	−2.57	(−2.06)[a]	0.03	0.03	−0.15	−0.27	−0.41	−0.93
Income	0.10	1.11	0.20	1.61	−0.06	−0.18	0.59	1.65	−0.52	(−2.34)[a]	−0.42	(−2.73)[a]
Constant	0.16	0.09	−1.79	−0.73	−7.44	−1.04	−3.74	−0.58	−9.20	(−2.35)[a]	−3.87	−1.34

(continued)

(continued)

Dependent variable	Voice 1		Voice 4		Voice 6		Exit 5		Loyalty 2		Loyalty 3	
Independent variables	Coeff.	z-stat.	Coeff.	z-stat.	Coeff.	z-stat.	Coeff.	z-stat.	Coeff.	z-stat.	Coeff.	z-stat.
n	335		335		335		335		335		335	
Pseudo R squared	0.1443		0.2151		0.514		0.4825		0.3297		0.2148	

Note [a]5% significance level; [b]1% significance level

Australia

Dependent variable	Voice 1		Voice 4		Voice 1		Exit 5		Loyalty 2		Loyalty 3	
Independent variables	Coeff.	z-stat.	Coeff.	z-stat.	Coeff.	z-stat	Coeff.	z-stat.	Coeff.	z-stat.	Coeff.	z-stat.
(A) Lifestyles												
Number of public utilities	0.22	1.05	0.07	0.55	–	–	−0.66	−0.53	−0.47	−1.64	−0.03	−0.2
Homeownership	−0.43	−1.02	0.20	0.74	–	–	−0.96	−0.45	0.12	0.21	−0.18	−0.61
Pray	0.18	1.42	0.02	0.31	–	–	1.46	1.54	−0.19	−1.15	−0.04	−0.52
National elections	0.33	1.13	−0.25	−1.69	–	–	–	–	0.64	1.4	0.02	0.1
Proud	0.12	0.29	0.13	0.56	–	–	−5.72	−1.62	0.48	1	−0.12	−0.47
(B) Exposure to globalization												
Internet	0.51	(3.32)[b]	−0.10	−1.18	–	–	−0.70	−0.93	0.08	0.4	−0.14	−1.57
Living internationally	−0.14	−1.1	0.06	0.8	–	–	−0.34	−0.5	0.13	0.77	−0.01	−0.16
English ability	0.59	0.49	0.56	1.28	–	–	–	–	−0.76	−1.34	0.01	0.03
(C) Satisfaction with aspects of life												
Housing	0.50	(1.99)[a]	−0.32	(−2.26)[a]	–	–	1.75	1.26	0.04	0.12	0.15	1.02
Friendships	−0.49	−1.6	0.46	(2.25)[a]	–	–	−2.24	−1.13	−0.83	(−2.52)[a]	0.03	0.16
Standard of living	−0.15	−0.51	0.06	0.35	–	–	−1.03	−0.59	−0.16	−0.47	−0.04	−0.2
Household income	−0.17	−0.72	−0.24	−1.6	–	–	−1.21	−0.93	0.18	0.63	0.32	(2.01)[a]

(continued)

(continued)

Dependent variable	Voice 1		Voice 4		Voice 1		Exit 5		Loyalty 2		Loyalty 3	
Independent variables	Coeff.	z-stat.	Coeff.	z-stat.	Coeff.	z-stat	Coeff.	z-stat.	Coeff.	z-stat.	Coeff.	z-stat.
Health	−0.19	−0.8	−0.34	(−2.32)[a]	–	–	0.60	0.55	0.14	0.5	0.36	(2.24)[a]
Education	−0.15	−0.55	0.40	(2.24)[a]	–	–	2.73	1.13	−0.24	−0.68	−0.37	−1.9
Job	0.10	0.5	0.05	0.4	–	–	0.91	0.85	0.16	0.62	−0.16	−1.22
Neighbors	0.30	1.36	−0.01	−0.06	–	–	0.52	0.44	−0.18	−0.79	−0.13	−1.02
Public safety	−0.20	−0.9	0.06	0.41	–	–	−2.41	−1.27	0.12	0.42	0.02	0.16
The condition of the environment	0.22	1.1	0.06	0.44	–	–	0.28	0.33	−0.42	−1.44	−0.04	−0.26
Social welfare system	0.05	0.25	−0.05	−0.41	–	–	−1.68	−1.33	0.14	0.49	0.11	0.74
The democratic system	−0.05	−0.21	0.12	0.81	–	–	3.14	1.78	−0.19	−0.65	−0.20	−1.3
Family life	−0.14	−0.48	−0.22	−1.3	–	–	0.51	0.46	−0.27	−0.77	0.41	(2.04)[a]
Leisure	0.23	0.64	−0.16	−0.8	–	–	1.96	1	0.22	0.49	0.16	0.75
Spiritual life	−0.09	−0.35	−0.14	−0.91	–	–	−1.21	−0.84	0.10	0.31	0.20	1.25
Your life as a whole	0.32	0.76	0.34	1.42	–	–	1.70	0.84	−0.08	−0.17	−0.58	(−2.28)[a]
Happiness	0.15	0.52	−0.30	−1.6	–	–	−0.34	−0.19	0.47	1.15	0.16	0.79
(D) Trust in social institution												
Trust generally	−0.06	−0.16	0.09	0.36	–	–	2.21	0.99	−1.01	−1.89	0.04	0.15
Trust the central government	0.04	0.15	0.09	0.58	–	–	−1.97	−1.37	−0.11	−0.38	0.11	0.67
Trust the army	0.39	1.25	−0.46	(−2.64)[b]	–	–	2.01	1.05	0.001	0	0.33	1.74
Trust the legal system	−0.26	−0.96	0.26	1.54	–	–	−1.54	−1.07	−0.15	−0.48	−0.08	−0.45
Trust the police	−0.07	−0.28	−0.01	−0.08	–	–	2.85	1.47	0.27	0.84	0.01	0.03
(E) Assessment of government performance												
Worry about corruption	0.39	1.02	−0.21	−0.84	–	–	0.56	0.3	−0.32	−0.59	0.03	0.1
Political corruption	0.65	(2.35)[a]	−0.10	−0.57	–	–	−1.08	−0.58	−0.14	−0.4	−0.18	−0.97
Duty to vote	−0.17	−0.7	−0.03	−0.22	–	–	−0.46	−0.29	0.32	0.91	0.10	0.6
Widespread corruption	−0.06	−0.29	0.17	1.24	–	–	−0.54	−0.34	−0.36	−1.32	−0.11	−0.72

(continued)

(continued)

Dependent variable	Voice 1		Voice 4		Voice 1		Exit 5		Loyalty 2		Loyalty 3	
Independent variables	Coeff.	z-stat.	Coeff.	z-stat.	Coeff.	z-stat	Coeff.	z-stat.	Coeff.	z-stat.	Coeff.	z-stat.
No power	−0.07	−0.35	−0.09	−0.72	–	–	−2.23	−1.39	0.56	1.95	0.07	0.51
Complicated	0.27	1.49	0.001	0.01	–	–	−1.51	−1.09	0.11	0.45	−0.07	−0.59
No matter whether vote	0.13	0.69	−0.07	−0.58	–	–	1.62	1.3	0.22	0.98	−0.04	−0.33
Stop thinking	0.39	1.66	−0.24	−1.67	–	–	−0.33	−0.31	0.45	1.6	−0.06	−0.39
Pay little attention	−0.19	−0.77	0.18	1.17	–	–	1.05	0.75	−0.16	−0.47	−0.10	−0.62
Experts	0.65	(2.27)[a]	−0.17	−0.92	–	–	2.37	1.28	−0.67	−1.64	0.03	0.15
Bribe	0.24	1.91	−0.27	(−2.69)[b]	–	–	−0.49	−0.56	−0.24	−1.06	0.13	1.48
(F) Demographics												
Female	−0.0001	0	0.30	1.24	–	–	−0.66	−0.32	−0.44	−0.9	−0.09	−0.36
Age	0.02	1.44	0.02	1.88	–	–	−0.14	−1.02	−0.03	−1.56	−0.02	(−2.00)[a]
Level of education	0.10	0.47	0.06	0.46	–	–	−4.15	−1.76	0.05	0.19	−0.07	−0.51
Married	0.05	0.11	0.12	0.49	–	–	−1.68	−0.86	−0.33	−0.65	0.07	0.28
Income	0.03	0.33	0.19	(3.07)[b]	–	–	0.06	0.1	−0.08	−0.62	−0.16	(−2.47)[a]
Constant	−16.48	(−2.79)[b]	−1.39	−0.55	–	–	19.64	0.96	0.44	0.1	0.09	0.03
n	430		430		–		379		430		430	
Pseudo R squared	0.1788		0.1374		–		0.4939		0.2512		0.1083	

Note [a]5% significance level; [b]1% significance level

Japan

Dependent variable	Voice 1		Voice 4		Voice 6		Exit 5		Loyalty 2		Loyalty 3	
Independent variables	Coeff.	z-stat.	Coeff.	z-stat.	Coeff.	z-stat.	Coeff.	z-stat.	Coeff.	z-stat.	Coeff.	z-stat.
(A) Lifestyles												
Number of public utilities	0.79	(2.76)[b]	0.05	0.37	–	–	0.62	(2.14)[a]	−0.16	−1.4	−0.09	−0.9
Homeownership	−0.90	−1.4	−0.70	−1.96	–	–	−1.25	(−1.97)[a]	0.35	1.16	0.45	1.63
Pray	0.01	0.08	0.01	0.16	–	–	0.11	0.66	−0.01	−0.16	−0.04	−0.56
National elections	−0.44	−1.73	0.09	0.53	–	–	−0.06	−0.19	0.25	(2.01)[a]	−0.15	−1.24
Proud	−0.10	−0.27	0.004	0.02	–	–	−0.17	−0.47	−0.12	−0.74	0.09	0.62
(B) Exposure to globalization												
Internet	0.06	0.43	0.18	(2.13)[a]	–	–	−0.43	(−2.40)[a]	−0.10	−1.43	0.03	0.47
Living internationally	0.14	0.76	0.05	0.44	–	–	0.56	(2.53)[a]	−0.06	−0.6	−0.17	−1.74
English ability	−0.93	(−2.33)[a]	0.45	(2.02)[a]	–	–	−0.72	−1.59	0.28	1.52	−0.22	−1.36
(C) Satisfaction with aspects of life												
Housing	0.42	1.13	0.33	1.86	–	–	0.13	0.42	−0.26	−1.88	−0.09	−0.74
Friendships	0.14	0.33	−0.38	−1.86	–	–	−0.18	−0.41	0.11	0.62	0.13	0.79
Standard of living	−0.23	−0.53	0.02	0.08	–	–	−0.41	−0.91	0.03	0.17	0.05	0.26
Household income	0.23	0.67	−0.34	−1.72	–	–	0.28	0.74	0.02	0.15	0.08	0.56
Health	−0.19	−0.63	0.09	0.52	–	–	−0.55	−1.68	0.18	1.34	−0.06	−0.46
Education	0.05	0.14	−0.45	(−2.30)[a]	–	–	0.77	1.94	0.06	0.36	0.14	0.89
Job	0.62	1.62	0.16	0.86	–	–	0.35	0.99	−0.07	−0.41	−0.21	−1.41
Neighbors	−0.13	−0.35	−0.07	−0.36	–	–	0.07	0.19	−0.18	−1.13	0.25	1.67
Public safety	0.84	(2.11)[a]	0.02	0.09	–	–	−0.06	−0.17	−0.12	−0.76	−0.04	−0.32
The condition of the environment	−0.38	−0.87	−0.21	−1.06	–	–	0.33	0.93	0.20	1.22	−0.10	−0.65
Social welfare system	0.15	0.38	0.25	1.32	–	–	−0.44	−1.17	−0.15	−0.86	0.06	0.36

(continued)

(continued)

Dependent variable	Voice 1		Voice 4		Voice 6		Exit 5		Loyalty 2		Loyalty 3	
Independent variables	Coeff.	z-stat.	Coeff.	z-stat.	Coeff.	z-stat.	Coeff.	z-stat.	Coeff.	z-stat.	Coeff.	z-stat.
The democratic system	−0.38	−0.99	−0.26	−1.32	–	–	0.001	0	0.12	0.66	0.11	0.7
Family life	−0.23	−0.5	0.54	(2.20)[a]	–	–	−0.27	−0.68	−0.29	−1.42	0.08	0.43
Leisure	−0.17	−0.48	−0.24	−1.29	–	–	−0.25	−0.66	0.33	1.94	−0.09	−0.61
Spiritual life	−0.07	−0.13	0.67	(2.73)[b]	–	–	0.70	1.47	−0.35	−1.76	−0.18	−0.99
Your life as a whole	−0.44	−0.75	0.06	0.19	–	–	−0.60	−0.98	0.09	0.35	0.07	0.3
Happiness	−0.43	−1.07	−0.31	−1.5	–	–	−0.21	−0.54	0.22	1.31	0.14	0.93
(D) Trust in social institution												
Trust generally	−0.17	−0.37	−0.01	−0.05	–	–	−0.54	−1.03	−0.21	−0.99	0.29	1.47
Trust the central government	0.55	1.17	0.02	0.1	–	–	0.21	0.43	−0.27	−1.32	0.05	0.27
Trust the army	−0.08	−0.19	−0.05	−0.25	–	–	−0.37	−1.01	−0.11	−0.69	0.19	1.26
Trust the legal system	0.54	1.14	0.05	0.22	–	–	−0.07	−0.16	−0.14	−0.69	−0.08	−0.41
Trust the police	−0.54	−1.22	0.09	0.38	–	–	−0.38	−0.85	0.00	0	0.20	1.1
(E) Assessment of government performance												
Worry about corruption	0.33	0.57	−0.17	−0.56	–	–	−0.84	−1.26	0.15	0.6	0.03	0.12
Political corruption	0.35	0.93	−0.05	−0.21	–	–	−0.28	−0.67	0.12	0.66	0.01	0.08
Duty to vote	0.40	0.97	0.10	0.46	–	–	−0.20	−0.48	−0.002	−0.01	−0.19	−1.16
Widespread corruption	0.32	1.09	0.11	0.83	–	–	−0.30	−1.34	0.06	0.54	−0.09	−0.83
No power	0.39	1.38	−0.37	(−2.62)[b]	–	–	−0.08	−0.31	0.25	(2.08)[a]	−0.04	−0.37
Complicated	−0.57	−2	−0.09	−0.57	–	–	−0.36	−1.24	−0.01	−0.1	0.27	(2.26)
No matter whether vote	0.45	1.81	−0.15	−1.04	–	–	−0.24	−0.86	0.30	(2.76)[b]	−0.18	−1.71
Stop thinking	−0.03	−0.11	−0.21	−1.34	–	–	0.35	1.09	−0.12	−0.86	0.11	0.87
Pay little attention	0.54	1.64	−0.12	−0.77	–	–	0.50	1.35	−0.09	−0.71	−0.02	−0.2
Experts	−0.02	−0.05	0.52	(2.42)[a]	–	–	−0.14	−0.34	−0.23	−1.28	−0.14	−0.88

(continued)

(continued)

Dependent variable	Voice 1		Voice 4		Voice 6		Exit 5		Loyalty 2		Loyalty 3	
Independent variables	Coeff.	z-stat.	Coeff.	z-stat.	Coeff.	z-stat.	Coeff.	z-stat.	Coeff.	z-stat.	Coeff.	z-stat.
Bribe	0.08	0.7	−0.06	−0.76	–	–	0.01	0.11	−0.05	−0.84	0.03	0.57
(F) Demographics												
Female	−1.43	(−2.52)[a]	0.71	(2.56)[a]	–	–	−0.50	−0.93	0.27	1.23	−0.31	−1.53
Age	−0.02	−0.72	0.01	0.45	–	–	−0.0003	−0.01	−0.01	−1.35	0.02	1.71
Level of education	0.20	0.74	0.20	1.34	–	–	0.17	0.55	−0.35	(−2.63)[b]	0.11	0.91
Married	0.37	0.54	0.09	0.26	–	–	−0.71	−1.14	−0.12	−0.42	0.20	0.74
Income	0.04	0.55	−0.01	−0.22	–	–	−0.02	−0.3	0.07	(2.33)[a]	−0.04	−1.58
Constant	−9.60	(−2.50)[a]	−3.29	−1.64	–	–	1.48	0.38	1.08	0.66	−1.96	−1.31
n	565		565		–		565		565		565	
Pseudo R squared	0.2867		0.1784		–		0.2664		0.1032		0.0697	

Note [a]5% significance level; [b]1% significance level

China

Dependent variable	Voice 1		Voice 4		Voice 6		Exit 5		Loyalty 2		Loyalty 3	
Independent variables	Coeff.	z-stat.	Coeff.	z-stat.	Coeff.	z-stat.	Coeff.	z-stat.	Coeff.	z-stat.	Coeff.	z-stat.
(A) Lifestyles												
Number of public utilities	−0.002	−0.01	−0.003	−0.02	–	–	0.79	1.17	−0.09	−0.6	0.16	1.04
Homeownership	−0.12	−0.51	−0.22	−0.92	–	–	−2.25	(−2.56)[a]	0.66	(2.56)[a]	−0.16	−0.74
Pray	−0.01	−0.09	−0.11	−0.83	–	–	−0.46	−0.75	0.11	0.95	0.02	0.19
National elections	0.12	1.41	−0.04	−0.46	–	–	–	–	0.01	0.12	−0.11	−1.27
Proud	0.05	0.32	0.23	1.25	–	–	0.40	0.68	−0.26	−1.5	−0.08	−0.48

(continued)

(continued)

Dependent variable	Voice 1		Voice 4		Voice 6		Exit 5		Loyalty 2		Loyalty 3	
Independent variables	Coeff.	z-stat.	Coeff.	z-stat.	Coeff.	z-stat.	Coeff.	z-stat.	Coeff.	z-stat.	Coeff.	z-stat.
(B) Exposure to globalization												
Internet	0.09	0.92	0.06	0.59	–	–	−0.06	−0.17	−0.15	−1.5	0.02	0.22
Living internationally	−0.01	−0.06	0.32	(2.09)[a]	–	–	−2.26	−1.9	0.01	0.05	−0.18	−1.18
English ability	−0.28	−1.18	−0.18	−0.73	–	–	0.15	0.18	0.24	0.93	0.18	0.78
(C) Satisfaction with aspects of life												
Housing	−0.05	−0.34	0.10	0.69	–	–	1.25	(2.18)[a]	0.01	0.04	−0.04	−0.27
Friendships	0.17	0.92	−0.27	−1.53	–	–	−0.29	−0.5	−0.03	−0.15	0.09	0.52
Standard of living	0.10	0.47	0.26	1.21	–	–	−0.78	−1.2	−0.57	(−2.64)[b]	0.22	1.09
Household income	−0.10	−0.5	−0.37	−1.82	–	–	0.16	0.23	0.20	0.98	0.19	1.03
Health	−0.02	−0.13	0.06	0.41	–	–	−0.22	−0.44	0.03	0.19	−0.09	−0.67
Education	0.05	0.29	−0.10	−0.58	–	–	0.10	0.19	0.14	0.83	−0.21	−1.34
Job	−0.28	−1.63	0.11	0.63	–	–	−0.36	−0.79	−0.01	−0.06	0.25	1.57
Neighbors	−0.08	−0.48	−0.09	−0.5	–	–	0.61	1.07	0.19	1.07	−0.05	−0.33
Public safety	0.32	1.9	0.05	0.3	–	–	0.36	0.65	−0.16	−0.87	−0.14	−0.87
The condition of the environment	−0.42	(−2.35)[a]	0.21	1.15	–	–	−0.11	−0.17	0.36	1.94	−0.15	−0.9
Social welfare system	0.26	1.57	−0.13	−0.75	–	–	−0.04	−0.07	−0.06	−0.33	0.11	0.68
The democratic system	−0.13	−0.81	−0.09	−0.53	–	–	0.42	0.81	0.29	1.71	−0.10	−0.61
Family life	0.09	0.49	0.08	0.4	–	–	−1.55	(−2.33)[a]	−0.05	−0.27	−0.08	−0.5
Leisure	−0.07	−0.43	0.12	0.65	–	–	−0.22	−0.34	−0.02	−0.13	−0.22	−1.34
Spiritual life	0.38	(2.00)[a]	0.19	0.99	–	–	−0.14	−0.2	−0.35	−1.75	−0.17	−0.99
Your life as a whole	−0.23	−0.98	−0.27	−1.12	–	–	−1.58	−1.92	0.17	0.75	0.29	1.34
Happiness	0.11	0.64	−0.07	−0.4	–	–	1.06	1.62	0.19	1.09	−0.03	−0.19

(continued)

(continued)

Dependent variable	Voice 1		Voice 4		Voice 6		Exit 5		Loyalty 2		Loyalty 3	
Independent variables	Coeff.	z-stat.	Coeff.	z-stat.	Coeff.	z-stat.	Coeff.	z-stat.	Coeff.	z-stat.	Coeff.	z-stat.
(D) Trust in social institution												
Trust generally	−0.15	−0.64	0.22	0.86	–	–	−1.19	−1.56	0.06	0.25	0.05	0.21
Trust the central government	−0.01	−0.07	0.17	0.8	–	–	−0.04	−0.05	−0.23	−1.09	0.03	0.13
Trust the army	−0.33	−1.9	0.27	1.39	–	–	−0.80	−1.36	0.08	0.42	0.10	0.56
Trust the legal system	−0.34	−1.89	−0.09	−0.48	–	–	−0.23	−0.41	0.19	1.03	0.28	1.61
Trust the police	−0.01	−0.05	−0.08	−0.46	–	–	0.46	0.89	0.09	0.49	−0.01	−0.07
(E) Assessment of government performance												
Worry about corruption	−0.15	−0.64	−0.07	−0.3	–	–	0.50	0.68	0.08	0.32	0.11	0.48
Political corruption	−0.24	−1.39	0.37	(2.17)[a]	–	–	−1.57	(−2.26)[a]	−0.10	−0.6	0.14	0.9
Duty to vote	−0.06	−0.28	−0.04	−0.22	–	–	−1.11	−1.46	−0.27	−1.36	0.26	1.4
Widespread corruption	0.09	0.7	−0.04	−0.32	–	–	−0.11	−0.25	−0.0002	0	−0.12	−1.08
No power	0.21	1.46	−0.27	−1.83	–	–	0.35	0.63	−0.02	−0.11	0.06	0.44
Complicated	−0.04	−0.22	0.27	1.49	–	–	−0.32	−0.56	0.04	0.22	−0.17	−1.05
No matter whether vote	0.05	0.36	−0.10	−0.74	–	–	1.18	(2.11)[a]	−0.01	−0.05	0.04	0.36
Stop thinking	−0.01	−0.08	−0.002	−0.02	–	–	0.30	0.58	0.08	0.59	−0.12	−0.93
Pay little attention	−0.18	−1.28	−0.12	−0.81	–	–	−1.02	−1.94	0.09	0.63	0.24	1.75
Experts	−0.04	−0.21	0.08	0.42	–	–	−0.32	−0.49	−0.04	−0.19	0.07	0.38
Bribe	0.16	(2.82)[b]	−0.02	−0.33	–	–	0.15	0.74	−0.09	−1.25	−0.10	−1.58
(F) Demographics												
Female	−0.25	−1.16	0.35	1.58	–	–	−1.82	(−2.36)[a]	0.19	0.84	−0.09	−0.42
Age	−0.005	−0.38	−0.01	−0.57	–	–	0.04	0.99	−0.02	−1.26	0.02	(2.01)[a]
Level of education	0.22	1.31	−0.04	−0.23	–	–	0.91	1.56	−0.23	−1.32	0.02	0.12
Married	0.61	1.75	−0.04	−0.11	–	–	1.81	1.15	−0.04	−0.13	−0.51	−1.65
Income	0.04	1.21	0.01	0.37	–	–	0.08	0.63	−0.02	−0.54	−0.05	−1.38

(continued)

(continued)

Dependent variable	Voice 1		Voice 4		Voice 6		Exit 5		Loyalty 2		Loyalty 3	
Independent variables	Coeff.	z-stat.	Coeff.	z-stat.	Coeff.	z-stat.	Coeff.	z-stat.	Coeff.	z-stat.	Coeff.	z-stat.
Constant	−0.56	−0.31	−1.76	−0.94	–	–	−0.73	−0.12	0.10	0.05	−3.59	(−2.05)[a]
n	564		564		–	–	809		564		564	
Pseudo R squared	0.1047		0.0742		–	–	0.4557		0.0845		0.0706	

Note [a]5% significance level; [b]1% significance level

India

Dependent variable	Voice 1		Voice 4		Voice 6		Exit 5		Loyalty 2		Loyalty 3	
Independent variables	Coeff.	z-stat.	Coeff.	z-stat.	Coeff.	z-stat.	Coeff.	z-stat.	Coeff.	z-stat.	Coeff.	z-stat.
(A) Lifestyles												
Number of public utilities	0.01	0.04	0.01	0.05	−0.25	−0.82	−0.11	−0.28	−0.02	−0.08	0.23	1.39
Homeownership	−0.46	−1.93	0.16	0.53	0.87	1.32	0.17	0.23	0.03	0.08	0.16	0.61
Pray	−0.24	−1.86	−0.11	−0.77	0.11	0.37	0.52	0.88	0.55	1.89	0.25	1.4
National elections	0.04	0.35	−0.33	(−2.23)[a]	0.32	1.02	0.51	1.44	−0.36	−1.63	0.21	1.5
Proud	−0.17	−0.5	0.14	0.37	−0.60	−0.79	–	–	−1.44	(−3.09)[b]	0.55	1.31
(B) Exposure to globalization												
Internet	−0.29	(−2.71)[b]	−0.21	−1.52	−0.27	−0.98	0.29	1.06	0.56	(3.19)[b]	0.23	(2.27)[a]
Living internationally	0.04	0.3	−0.11	−0.57	0.21	0.68	0.30	0.86	−0.003	−0.01	0.02	0.12
English ability	0.25	1.61	0.17	0.88	0.81	1.91	−0.19	−0.39	−0.34	−1.16	−0.36	(−2.13)[a]
(C) Satisfaction with aspects of life												
Housing	−0.13	−0.7	0.09	0.42	0.54	0.95	0.88	1	−0.34	−1.13	0.20	0.92
Friendships	0.23	1.31	0.22	0.98	−0.35	−0.73	−0.54	−0.95	−0.24	−0.91	−0.24	−1.28

(continued)

(continued)

Dependent variable	Voice 1		Voice 4		Voice 6		Exit 5		Loyalty 2		Loyalty 3	
Independent variables	Coeff.	z-stat.	Coeff.	z-stat.	Coeff.	z-stat.	Coeff.	z-stat.	Coeff.	z-stat.	Coeff.	z-stat.
Standard of living	−0.36	−1.87	0.22	0.97	1.14	(2.06)[a]	1.67	(2.54)[a]	0.05	0.18	−0.06	−0.31
Household income	0.16	0.96	−0.07	−0.35	−0.20	−0.47	0.13	0.22	−0.15	−0.58	0.09	0.5
Health	0.39	(2.23)[a]	−0.44	(−2.22)[a]	−0.74	−1.77	−0.05	−0.1	−0.01	−0.05	0.23	1.18
Education	−0.03	−0.18	0.54	(2.68)[b]	−0.05	−0.12	−1.01	−1.88	−0.52	(−2.08)[a]	−0.28	−1.49
Job	0.33	(2.17)[a]	−0.36	−1.95	−0.18	−0.5	1.06	(2.00)[a]	−0.59	(−2.42)[a]	0.12	0.74
Neighbors	−0.22	−1.33	0.23	1.21	0.18	0.42	−0.29	−0.56	0.30	1.1	−0.17	−0.97
Public safety	0.28	(2.00)[a]	−0.24	−1.44	0.10	0.31	0.15	0.35	−0.26	−0.93	0.02	0.16
The condition of the environment	−0.35	(−2.70)[b]	0.07	0.45	0.67	1.91	0.73	1.69	0.23	0.99	0.16	1.15
Social welfare system	0.01	0.05	−0.42	(−2.23)[a]	−0.03	−0.08	−0.68	−1.46	0.48	1.76	0.12	0.71
The democratic system	−0.05	−0.34	0.29	1.71	−0.25	−0.67	−0.56	−1.43	−0.10	−0.42	0.06	0.39
Family life	0.43	(2.35)[a]	−0.47	(−2.28)[a]	−0.45	−0.94	−0.44	−0.91	0.25	0.91	−0.12	−0.66
Leisure	0.08	0.49	−0.11	−0.51	−0.16	−0.36	−0.98	−1.81	0.20	0.66	−0.13	−0.7
Spiritual life	−0.06	−0.37	0.09	0.43	0.004	0.01	−0.35	−0.65	0.10	0.34	0.01	0.05
Your life as a whole	0.10	0.54	−0.02	−0.08	0.80	1.55	−0.16	−0.3	−0.57	−1.95	−0.09	−0.43
Happiness	−0.14	−0.87	0.12	0.66	−0.30	−0.73	0.08	0.14	0.44	1.51	−0.17	−1.04
(D) Trust in social institution												
Trust generally	−0.43	−1.89	−0.16	−0.56	−0.43	−0.7	0.06	0.1	0.06	0.16	0.66	(2.68)[b]
Trust the central government	−0.23	−1.79	0.01	0.09	−0.73	(−2.44)[a]	−0.33	−0.85	0.25	1.03	0.33	(2.21)[a]
Trust the army	0.03	0.22	−0.23	−1.43	0.41	1.05	0.45	1	−0.47	(−2.16)[a]	0.26	1.58
Trust the legal system	−0.18	−1.27	−0.14	−0.77	0.18	0.5	−0.25	−0.54	0.19	0.66	0.12	0.77
Trust the police	0.21	1.61	−0.51	(−3.15)[b]	−0.49	−1.55	0.92	1.93	0.13	0.56	0.10	0.74

(continued)

(continued)

Dependent variable	Voice 1		Voice 4		Voice 6		Exit 5		Loyalty 2		Loyalty 3	
Independent variables	Coeff.	z-stat.	Coeff.	z-stat.	Coeff.	z-stat.	Coeff.	z-stat.	Coeff.	z-stat.	Coeff.	z-stat.
(E) Assessment of government performance												
Worry about corruption	−0.04	−0.17	0.13	0.41	0.47	0.65	0.27	0.37	−0.20	−0.51	0.03	0.11
Political corruption	−0.25	−1.92	−0.16	−1.02	−1.13	(−2.87)[b]	−0.31	−0.86	0.53	(2.44)[a]	0.36	(2.69)[b]
Duty to vote	0.26	1.2	0.41	1.6	−0.16	−0.26	−0.41	−0.76	−0.37	−1.05	−0.30	−1.29
Widespread corruption	−0.61	(−3.40)[b]	0.48	(2.20)[a]	0.69	1.49	1.31	(2.37)[a]	0.02	0.06	0.01	0.04
No power	−0.22	−1.63	0.17	0.99	−0.18	−0.59	−0.45	−1.18	0.55	1.96	0.13	0.87
Complicated	0.17	1.24	−0.18	−1.13	−0.08	−0.26	−0.51	−1.21	0.0005	0	0.03	0.25
No matter whether vote	−0.01	−0.15	0.001	0.01	0.30	1.52	1.20	(3.29)[b]	0.16	1.01	−0.24	(−2.61)[b]
Stop thinking	−0.10	−0.67	0.07	0.39	−0.10	−0.25	−0.42	−0.87	0.25	1	0.08	0.49
Pay little attention	0.22	1.48	−0.25	−1.43	0.32	0.93	−0.24	−0.58	0.02	0.08	−0.03	−0.17
Experts	0.09	0.5	0.17	0.8	−1.07	(−2.34)[a]	−0.43	−0.92	−0.15	−0.49	−0.02	−0.1
Bribe	0.05	0.69	−0.15	−1.32	−0.003	−0.01	0.22	1.05	0.34	(2.57)[a]	−0.16	−1.57
(F) Demographics												
Female	0.18	0.78	−0.05	−0.16	0.22	0.35	0.38	0.6	0.11	0.27	−0.19	−0.74
Age	−0.004	−0.41	−0.003	−0.23	0.03	1.15	0.01	0.43	0.01	0.42	−0.01	−0.48
Level of education	−0.03	−0.24	−0.13	−0.8	−0.35	−1.01	−0.10	−0.25	−0.12	−0.51	0.26	1.88
Married	−0.12	−0.42	0.65	1.6	−0.96	−1.46	−1.25	−1.51	1.05	1.7	−0.41	−1.29
Income	−0.03	−0.36	−0.19	−1.78	−0.45	−1.95	−0.77	(−2.26)[a]	0.20	1.49	0.16	(2.22)[a]
Constant	0.62	0.31	0.34	0.15	−2.60	−0.57	−7.59	−1.16	−0.57	−0.16	−7.92	(−3.26)[b]
n	526		526		526		442		526		526	
Pseudo R squared	0.1690		0.1956		0.2968		0.4189		0.344		0.1624	

Note [a]5% significance level; [b]1% significance level

References

Dept, Steven. 2013. Minimizing sources of language- and culture-induced bias in multilingual surveys. Paper Presented at WAPOR Annual Conference at Boston, Massachusetts, USA, May 16, 2013.

Etzioni, Amitai. 1988. *Capital corruption: the new attack on American democracy*. New Brunswick, New Jersey: Transaction Publishers.

Gehlbach, Scott. 2006. A Formal Model of Exit and Voice. *Rationality and Society* 18(4): 395–418. www.sagepublications.com DOI:10.1177/1043463106070280.

Gilani, Ijaz and Bilal Gilani. 2013. Global and Regional Polls: A Paradigmatic Shift in from 'State-centric' to 'Global-centric'. Paper Presented at WAPOR Annual Conference at Boston Massachusetts, USA, May 14–16, 2013.

Hirschmann, Albert O. 1970. *Exit, Voice, and Loyalty: Responses to Decline in Firms, Organizations, and States*. Cambridge, Massachusetts: Harvard University Press.

Inoguchi, Takashi. 2012. AsiaBarometer's achievements, underutilized areas of the survey materials, and future prospects. *Comparative Democratization Newsletter* 10(3): 2, 13–15, Washington D.C.: The American Political Science Association.

Inoguchi, Takashi. 2013. 2012: Voters Swing, and Swing Away Soon. *Asian Survey* 53 (1): 184–197.

Keane, John. 2009. *The Life and Death of Democracy*. London: Simon and Schuster.

Lipset, Seymore Martin. 1990. *Continental Divide: The Values and Institutions of the United States and Canada*. London: Routledge.

Nakamura, Itsuro. 2005a. *Teisei minshushugi kokka Russia: Putin no jidai (Imperial democratic state: an era of Vladimir Putin)*, 236. Tokyo: Iwanami Shoten.

Nakamura, Itsuro. 2005b. *Teikoku Minshushugi Kokka Russia – Putin no Jidai (Imperial democratic state of Russia – Putin's era)*. Tokyo, Japan: Iwanami Shoten.

Nakamura, Itsuro. 2013. *Rokudenashi no Russia – Putin to Russia Seikyo (Russia as a Scoundrel – Putin and Russian Orthodox)*. Tokyo, Japan: Kodansha.

Rose, Richard. 2013. Bribery and Public Services: A Global Comparison. Working Paper, Centre for the Study of Public Policy, University of Strathclyde Glasgow.

Rose, Richard and Caryn Peiffer. 2012. Paying bribes to get public services: a global guide to concepts and survey measures. Working Paper, Centre for the Study of Public Policy, University of Strathclyde Glasgow.

Rose, Richard, William Mishler, and Neil Munro. 2011. *Popular Support for an Undemocratic Regime: The Changing Views of Russians*. New York: Cambridge University Press.

Roy, Arundhati. 1997. *The God of Small Things*. New York: Random House.

The Economist. 2013. *A Giant Cage, Special Report China and the Internet*, 1–16.

Chapter 8
Discussion and Conclusion

This book has been guided by what may be called the Dharmic orientation as contrasted to what may be called the Abrahamic orientation. By the Dharmic orientation, I mean the orientation that emphasizes seeking and respecting differences and anomalies rather than discovering and analyzing commonalities and regularities. The underlying premise of this book is that quality of life focused research needs to be invigorated to produce more data on many subjects related to quality of life. Thus, this book is filled with descriptive contents. Yet some elementary analyses have been attempted to see what variables help to lead respondents to choose what they have chosen in a statistically significant fashion.

To summarize empirical findings of the entire analyses, I would like to summarize them in relation to what I call the types of Asian societies (Inoguchi 2017a and forthcoming in 2017b). Types of Asian societies are generated by an evidence-based approach to quality of life on the basis of factor analysis of data on satisfaction about daily life aspects, domains, and lifestyles. Factor analysis has yielded three key dimensions: materialism, postmaterialism, and public sector dominance, a result in harmony with the results of the World Values Survey led by Ronald Inglehart (Inglehart 1977; Welzel 2013). According to the order of the first two dimensions, five types of societal types have been identified: Ab, Ac, Ba, Bc, Ca. In other words, Ab means a society that is guided by materialism, followed by postmaterialism. Ac means a society that is guided by materialism, followed by public sector dominance. Ba means a society that is guided by postmaterialism, followed by materialism. Bc means a society that is guided by postmaterialism, followed by public sector dominance. Ca means a society that is guided by public sector dominance, followed by materialism. For societies, most representative of each type, I have come up with Japan for Ab, India for Ac, Thailand for Ba, Pakistan for Bc, and Singapore for Ca. Though a survey was not carried out in North Korea, I suggest that if that had been carried out, North Korea would be

T. Inoguchi, *Exit, Voice and Loyalty in Asia*,
Quality of Life in Asia 10, DOI 10.1007/978-981-10-4724-4_8

typed as Cb, that is, a society that is guided by public sector dominance, followed by postmaterialism (Inoguchi 2017a and forthcoming in 2017b).

Here, I pose the following question: Of these five types of Asian societies, which ones do you think are conducive to exit-prone, voice-prone, and loyalty-prone societies?

Type Ab has two sub-types: Ab1 and Ab2. Type Ab1 societies are Japan and Indonesia. They register the smaller number in choosing using connections and bribing an official. Type Ab2 societies are Afghanistan, Uzbekistan, and Tajikistan. They register an almost unrestrained choice in using connections, bribing an official, and acting without a permit.

Type Ac has two sub-types: Ac1 and Ac2. Type Ac1 societies are China, South Korea, and Taiwan. Ac1 register a relatively even choice among the options: waiting and hoping, nothing can be done, and writing a letter. Type Ac2 societies are Cambodia and Laos. Ac2 register the pattern of even more verified choices of waiting and hoping, using connections, writing a letter, and bribing an official. Type Ac3 societies are South Asians and one of the Central Asian societies, Mongols.

Type Ba societies have two types: Ba and Bc. Type Ba societies are pronounced in registering a high percentage of waiting and hoping and yet the choice of using connections and bribing an official is far less than the Ac type. Type Ba societies are Thailand, Malaysia, Vietnam, Hong Kong, and Kyrgyzstan. Thailand is a representative of this type.

Type Bc societies are represented by Brunei, the Philippines, Pakistan, Bhutan, Sri Lanka, and Kazakhstan. Pakistan is a representative of this type. Bc type societies are noted by the heavy choice of using connections.

Type Ca societies are represented by Singapore and the Maldives. Ca type societies almost extinguish the choice of bribing an official because of pervasive and effective use of micro-monitoring.

In sum, significantly depending on daily life satisfaction and lifestyles, types of Asian societies are profiled. Types of Asian societies moderately determine the proneness of exit, voice, and loyalty.

References

Inglehart, Ronald. 1977. *The Silent Revolution*. Princeton: PrincetonUniversity Press.

Inoguchi, Takashi. 2017a. An evidence-based typology of Asian societies: what do societies look like from the bottom up instead of top down? *Japanese Journal of Political Science* 18(1) pp. 216–234.

Inoguchi, Takashi. 2017b. Asia inquiry: a continental analysis. *Seton Hall Journal of Diplomacy and International Relations* (forthcoming).

Welzel, Christian. 2013. *Freedom Rising: Human Enpowerment and the Quest for Emancipation*. New York: Cambledge University Press.

MIX
Papier aus verantwortungsvollen Quellen
Paper from responsible sources
FSC® C105338

If you have any concerns about our products,
you can contact us on
ProductSafety@springernature.com

In case Publisher is established outside the EU,
the EU authorized representative is:
Springer Nature Customer Service Center GmbH
Europaplatz 3, 69115 Heidelberg, Germany

Printed by Libri Plureos GmbH
in Hamburg, Germany